Ray Dearlove is South African-born and educated. In 1987 he and his family emigrated to Australia where he continued in executive positions in the IT industry. Later, his love of sport led to ten years as general manager of the highly successful Sydney University Rugby Club and then time with Rugby World Cup-winning coach, Jake White, at the ACT Brumbies. He has run his own events management company for many years, organising events for the Australian Rugby Union, the University of Sydney, the ACT Brumbies, the International Rugby Academy of Australia and several not-for-profits including the Australian Rhino Project, Lifestart and the Black Dog Institute.

In parallel with Ray's corporate career, his lifelong love of wildlife led to a number of roles in the environmental and sustainability industry. This love continued when he became a founding director of the Ingwelala Private Game Reserve in South Africa. Although living in Australia, Ray and his wife Margaret have ensured that their three children have been exposed to the wonders of the African wild by regular visits to South Africa, Zambia, Zimbabwe, Botswana, Kenya and Tanzania.

In 2013 Ray founded the Australian Rhino Project which focused on establishing breeding herds of white rhinoceros in Australia as an insurance population for the endangered species. In partnership with international organisations such as Investec and the Business and Veterinary Schools of the University of Sydney, this project gained global attention – a daunting but extremely important and satisfying venture (and adventure).

Ray is the author of two previous books, the *Book of Poems for the Rhino* (2019) and *The Crash of Rhinos* (2020). The title of the latter is a play on words; a 'crash' being the collective noun for rhinos, but it also describes the carnage wrought by poachers who have slaughtered more than 10,000 rhinos – three a day – in the past decade. Dr Jane Goodall DBE described it as 'a story that must be told'.

Tales of Two Countries is Ray's third book. He takes the reader through his childhood in apartheid-era South Africa and the turbulent years before Nelson Mandela assumed the presidency in 1994. Living in Australia for more than thirty years brought its own share of interesting people, events and opportunities. There are many stories about the raw challenges of moving countries. It has some very moving and some very humorous moments, all told in Ray's discerning and direct style.

Tales of Two Countries

RAY DEARLOVE

ISBN 978-0-6487578-2-5 (print)

ISBN 978-0-6487578-3-2 (digital)

The moral right of the author has been asserted.

Edited by Joan Eyles

Cover design by David Henley

Typesetting and project management by Words and Pages

Printed and bound in Australia by Ligare Book Printers

The paper this book is printed on is in accordance with the standards of the Forestry Stewardship Council©. The FSC© promotes environmentally responsible, socially beneficial and economically viable management of the world's forests.

This book is dedicated to my wife Margie – a very special Aussie

And to the late Cyril and Irene, Owen and Anne and Les and Yvonne

And to Jeremy, Hayley, Jonty, Christo, Araminta and Olympia;
Kevin, Rebecca, Isabella, Xavier and Amelia; Paul, Melissa,
Leo, Avery and Grace

And to Buster, Trixie, Pugsley and Banjo – our own little rhinos

And my team of medics, to whom I owe so much, including
Alan Chai, David Duckworth, Les Grujic, Pierre Halpern,
Auriel Jameson, Karen Long, Greg Marks, Charlie McDonald,
Margaret Mitchell, David Massasso, Stu Pavely, Prue Storer,
Gabby Vasica, Evelyn Kwok, Andrew Wines and Jim Sullivan

'If there are no dogs in Heaven, then when I die,
I want to go where they went.'
Will Rogers

CONTENTS

FOREWORDS

'Rugby, wildlife, beer, politics and history, Ray Dearlove's *Tales of Two Countries* is an insightful conversation starter for any barbie or braai. He captures the bittersweet highs and lows of swapping one home for another. It is an excellent read for anyone whose heart is torn between two homes. Ray's insights on modern South Africa and Australia make for thought-provoking reading. Moving, humorous and thoughtful – his is a life very well lived.'

 **Tony Park** is an Australian author who has written twenty-one novels, mostly set in Africa, as well as ten non-fiction biographies. He served thirty-four years in the Australian Army Reserve including six months in Afghanistan. Tony and his wife Nicola divide their time between Sydney and Southern Africa.

'Australia is one of my favourite countries and I have always wanted to make a contribution to assist endangered species. Ray arranged meetings for me with politicians and leaders in conservation in Australia to pave the way for me. His and my stories are so similar; I am Belgian-born and live in the US and Ray is South African-born and lives in Australia. I thoroughly enjoyed reading his book with all its ups and downs.'

Jean-Claude van Damme is a Belgian actor, martial artist, filmmaker and fight choreographer. He is known universally as the 'Muscles from Brussels'.

'After reading Ray's fascinating story, I realise we have lived similar lives. Mine has also revolved around sport, wildlife conservation, business and serving communities and I fully endorsed Ray's Australian Rhino Project; our rhinos need all the help they can get. We are so glad Ray wrote this gripping story which will be such an inspiration to all who read it and I hope that, in both our lifetimes, we see the rhinos arrive safely in Australia and silence all the doomsayers who said it could not be done.'

Adrian Gardiner is an entrepreneur, founder of Shamwari Game Reserve and of the Mantis Group and patron of the Wilderness Foundation. A giant in wildlife conservation and in building bridges between communities.

INTRODUCTION

I have had a good life. I have lived in three countries and love them all. I have travelled widely and been exposed to many diverse cultures. Blessed with a good education by my parents, some of which I squandered, I had a strong foundation to explore life and the world.

My family was certainly not disadvantaged. In South Africa we would have been classified as middle-class, but compared with the millions of indigenous Africans we were very well off.

I went from being a fairly shy young man who had to seek out a blind date for our school leavers' dance to being a bit of a wild child discovering wine and women. No song required; I'd always loved music.

This book chronicles the highs and lows of a life well lived, including being fortunate to live on the favoured side of the ledger in a bitterly divided country. It relates personal experiences, most happy, but some sad. It tells of the challenges of moving countries with a young family to an unknown and uncertain future.

I have met some wonderful people throughout this journey. Some are perceived as famous, others not, but all are just ordinary people who put their shoes on one at a time. Just like you and me.

I have also been blessed with a wonderful wife and extremely supportive children. I could not have had the success and fun that I have had without them.

'When you arise in the morning, think of what a precious privilege it is to be alive – to breathe, to think, to enjoy and to love.'
Marcus Aurelius

CHAPTER 1

TO STAY OR TO GO

One of the biggest decisions I had to make when I arrived in Sydney in 1987 was which beer? After being a Castle Lager man for more than twenty years this was an important decision. I finally decided on Foster's which my South African friends thought was pretty cool but my few Australian friends thought was seriously lame. Foster's was world famous, but derided in Australia. I didn't mind; I really enjoyed it.

While my Australian wife Margie and I had spent fifteen happy years together in South Africa – which included a magical three-year assignment in Paris – it was now time to embark on the next phase of our lives together.

In 1972 my sister Yvonne followed her heart to England, having recently married her British-born husband James. In all the time we lived in South Africa, Margie never once pushed for us to leave the country to return to her native Australia. Having said that, there was an unspoken agreement that once my parents had passed on we would consider such a move. In 1985, six years after my dad died from a stroke, my mum died in hospital from pneumonia after breaking her hip. We then sat down and listed the advantages and disadvantages of remaining in the land of my birth and the decision was taken to emigrate. It was a truly tough decision. My heart said stay, my brain said go.

I then had to go through the rigorous vetting process enforced by the Australian Consulate in Pretoria. Then, like now, there were literally hundreds of South Africans keen, or in some cases desperate, to move to Australia. My wife being an Australian citizen made my application a whole lot easier than so many others. Something I am regularly reminded about!

On 28 July 1986, I wrote an article which was published in the *Johannesburg Star* newspaper. It was titled 'It Could Have Been a Different, Fair Land'.

'I am a white South African. My parents were born in South Africa, as were their parents of British stock. I am proud of the fact that I am a South African. I am proud of my country. I am not proud of my government.

'I was born in September 1947 which makes me thirty-eight. As long as I have been around there has been one party governing my country. That's unhealthy. And what an awful botch-up it has made of things.

'I am proud of my country, of the achievements of thousands of people like my father who recognised evil in 1939 and left his new wife to fight that evil although his country was not directly threatened.

'Many of those in power today opposed South Africa's entry into that war on the side of "good". And yet today these same people expect me and my sons to fight on their side against the "total onslaught". Whatever that means. Naïve I may be, but I am not quite sure what or why I am being asked to fight. To protect apartheid? To fight communism? To fight the "blacks"? To protect the Afrikaner nation? It's so confusing and, therefore, not acceptable.

'I am proud of my country's achievements on the sports

field. For a small nation, we have produced an extraordinary number of world-class sportsmen and women. And yet because of the policies of this government it is twenty-six years since we competed in the Olympic Games. It is sixteen years since we played in a cricket test match.

'One whole generation has missed the excitement of having sporting heroes. There have been sporadic "unofficial" rugby tests, but our players are not welcome anywhere in the world. Our cricketers have not competed overseas as a national side since 1965. More than twenty years! They, because of our government's detested policies, have never competed against the West Indies, India or Pakistan in official tests. South African spectators are the poorer for this.

'We are no longer allowed to compete in the world's great tennis team competitions – the Davis and Federation Cups. We're excluded from the great spectacle of the Football World Cup. One hundred and twenty-four nations took part in the recent tournament. One did not.

'Some of our great sportsmen and sportswomen of the 1970s and 1980s have had to renounce the land of their birth in order to compete on the world stage, where Ugandans, Soviets, Iraqis and Israelis are accepted despite their domestic policies.

'Nowadays South Africans cling to the South Africanism of Johan Kriek, Kevin Curren, Allan Lamb, Kepler Wessels, Ray Mordt, Rob Louw, Zola Budd and Sydney Maree – all displaying their skills in foreign lands. Nobody else does.

'I am proud of my country's technological achievements. However, no technological inventiveness is able to prevent countries from barring television shows from being sold to South Africa.

'South Africa is probably the only reasonably developed country in the world where full, live coverage of the Football World Cup did not take place, where five minutes of highlights from the previous day's Olympic Games are flashed on the evening news.

'Thank God for the technological advances which enable the

jetliners of the 1980s to fly sufficient distances to circumvent the ban preventing us from overflying or landing in any number of African countries. There is now talk of former allies, the US and Australia, withdrawing the landing rights of our national carrier.

'I am proud of my country; I keep telling myself. Why then must I be subjected to special rules because I am a South African?

'Apart from a few, very few countries, I need to obtain a visa to travel. My South African passport is now a burden. This was not always so.

'How can I be proud of my country when a resident of South Africa is not welcome in the capitals of Europe, in the United States, in Australia, in New Zealand?

'Bishop Desmond Tutu is considered to be the official spokesman on South Africa by those overseas because the views of the country's white leaders are unacceptable to the world at large.

'I am proud of the magnificent scenery of my country, of the rich fauna and flora with which we have been blessed. It is something which I wish to share with the outside world. But the outside world no longer wishes to visit our lovely country because of the sickening violence which is projected into their homes every night.

'How long can one keep the faith? The track record of the South African government inspires neither hope nor loyalty.

'I cannot see the current generation of South Africans now going through school looking back and being proud of their parents.'

It was really interesting how the article was received and perceived. Many of my friends agreed with my opinion and said so, indeed many were quietly also looking to emigrate. Quietly, because there was a certain stigma attached to such thoughts or plans and some labelled me as some form of traitor or coward who was preparing to 'run away', to join the 'chicken run' or 'packed for Perth' and had no hesitation in telling me so. Others said nothing to us, but had quite a bit to say behind our backs.

Within a year of publishing that article our little nuclear family left South Africa for Australia and so here we were in Sydney, me about to turn forty with three children under the age of seven, very little money, and the promise of a pretty ordinary job with the global IT company IBM. Sure, we had left South Africa and spent three years in France, but we always knew that we would return to Johannesburg at the end of that assignment. Moving to Australia was entirely different; it was permanent with no looking back. Given that I was a fourth-generation South African there was unquestionably a deep sadness at leaving, but there was also plenty of excitement about exploring a new continent. To the children we were merely embarking on an exciting adventure.

CHAPTER 2

GROWING UP
IN SOUTH AFRICA

I was born in Pietersburg, now Polokwane, a smallish town in the Northern Transvaal province. My parents were solidly middle-class. My dad Cyril was the accountant in Barclays Bank which meant he was second in command. My mother Irene was a housewife and cared for me and my sister Yvonne, a 1944 war baby. Our dad went off to war in 1940 and was demobilised in 1945 after spending those five years serving his country in North Africa and the Middle East as a gunner in the South African Airforce. He was no war hero but he made it home safely and was awarded five medals. Like so many of his colleagues, Dad never ever spoke about the war. How I now regret not asking him about it when he was still alive. Basic questions like how long did it take for letters from home to reach you? Did you get rations of your favourite Springbok cigarettes or the occasional beer? How did you occupy your time or how often did you engage the Italians and then the Germans? He was at the battle of El Alamein; what was that like? And what about Sidi Rezegh, which I had heard him mention, where the 5th South African Brigade was destroyed but apparently inflicted many German tank casualties? I'll never know.

We led a simple life. We could not afford a car, so we walked everywhere. My dad would walk to work in the morning, return for lunch, return to the bank and then walk home again. Sport played an important part in my parents' lives. Both were very good tennis players with Dad representing North-Eastern Transvaal in tennis and cricket.

My mother was always relaxed and affectionate, much more so than my dad. Maybe it was the mother/son thing, but she would always take my side. Spare money was in short supply. Mum would sell peaches, apricots and the like which she cultivated in her beautifully tended garden to raise a few bob for her own use since Dad was pretty frugal unless it was for absolute necessities. I made a minuscule contribution by doing bob-a-job tasks for friends and neighbours. No TV or Xbox in those days.

With very recent memories of war rationing, our parents were careful with money. A special treat for Sunday night dinner for Yvonne and me were slices of bread covered with syrup served in a plate of milk. Try that on the current generation.

There were two schools in Pietersburg, one for English-speaking children and the other for the Afrikaans kids. Afrikaans being the language which had arisen in the Dutch Cape Colony through a gradual divergence from European Dutch dialects during the course of the 18th century. Both schools were for whites only. We did not have a lot to do with each other; the Afrikaans kids largely kept to themselves, as did we. Yvonne and I attended the Pietersburg English Medium School. To get to school we had to walk past the Afrikaans School and we were regularly pelted with stones and yelled at. One needs to understand that in the early 1950s, these children's grandparents would probably have fought the British in the Anglo-Boer War from 1899 to 1902. This war had left deep scars and after the predominantly Afrikaans Nationalist government came to power in 1948, they were clearly emboldened in believing they were the superior race. We played rugby matches against Afrikaans schools and they were fierce contests. There was often more action on the sidelines between the parents than on the field!

In 1957 my dad was promoted to manager of the Messina branch of Barclays Bank. It was an exciting time in that at last, the Dearlove family could afford a car. A brand spanking new two-tone Zephyr. Really cool.

Messina, a coal-mining town now renamed Musina, is about 200 kilometres north of Pietersburg lying on the Limpopo River, the border between South Africa and Rhodesia. We were given a bank house that had mangoes, paw paws, figs and mulberries in the garden – important for kids when returning home for school holidays. Messina was in a drought belt and boasted an outdoor cinema, apparently the only one in the country; unsurprisingly for whites only. Demonstrating how naïve I was, and I'm sure I wasn't alone, there was a siren that pierced the night air across the town every night at 9 pm. I asked my dad what it was and he explained, not particularly well, that it was a curfew and that 'everybody' had to be off the streets. It was some years later that I realised that 'everybody' did not include whites.

There was one major family problem with the move. Messina did not have an English-speaking school and my parents had no interest in sending us to an all-Afrikaans school, so Yvonne and I had to move into the boarding school, known as the hostel, in Pietersburg.

I was eight years old and I hated it. Yvonne did her best to look after me but I missed my parents, I missed my dog, I missed everything. It wasn't exactly Dickensian but it was a tough place. I was tall for my age and was regularly picked on by older boys. We also had a housemaster who was supposed to look after the young boarders but he was an absolute menace. As a late developer I was not in his sphere of interest but he would attend the evening communal showers and if he noticed puberty emerging, he would invite the lad to his study for tea and biscuits after lights-out and then ask questions like, 'Have your balls dropped? Have you got spoof yet? Did you have a wet dream? Do you know what a stiffie is? Are you a roundhead [circumcised] or a cavalier [uncircumcised]?' He encouraged the use of Brylcreem as an ideal lubricant. The boys did not know what they didn't know. These days he would be locked up.

Interestingly, in Prince Harry's book *Spare*, he uses the same terminology of cavaliers and roundheads.

*

In my final year of primary school our parents asked us if we would like to attend private schools in Johannesburg. Yvonne was not interested. She was three years ahead of me and had formed firm friendships and chose to continue to board at what is now known as Capricorn High.

I had never heard of St John's College other than knowing that my dad and one of his two brothers had attended the school, but it certainly sounded exciting. We drove the 500 kilometres to Johannesburg for the interview and when we arrived all I could see was cricket and rugby fields, tennis courts and even a swimming pool with a diving board. A twelve year old's version of heaven.

I jumped at the opportunity, but as the time grew closer to starting boarding school, I became more and more apprehensive. Messina was a helluva long way from Johannesburg and the only means of communication was by writing letters. Only for emergencies were we allowed to phone home. The first few months were hard and there were many nights where I cried myself to sleep, and I was not the only one in the dormitory of twelve boys who did. The boarding staff were very kind but, in many ways, not particularly sympathetic. They knew time would heal the pangs of homesickness.

A few years earlier my cousin Christopher Dearlove, universally known as Kip, had become something of a legendary character at St John's. In his final year of boarding, he and another boy by the name of Le Grange decided to run away from school rather than face disciplinary action for some relatively trivial matter. One afternoon after cadets they took off and hitchhiked to Northern Rhodesia, now Zambia, home to Kip and brother Peter's family on the Copperbelt. A distance of some 1500 kilometres.

Without passports, they had to swim the Limpopo River to Southern Rhodesia, reaching a town called Gwanda before being caught. The story grew to mystical and mythical proportions about encounters with crocodiles when crossing the Limpopo while the reality was that for most of the year the river was bone dry. At St John's I was often asked if I was related to Kip and gladly took the reflected glory of him being my cousin. His younger brother Peter, who was also at St John's, told me that after this great escape, rugby coach and St John's legend Maxie Burger would summon him with these words, 'You there, boy, whose brother swims crocodile-infested rivers, come here!'

Kip went on to enjoy a successful life as a tobacco and citrus farmer in Rhodesia until being dispossessed in the ongoing so-called land reform by the widely despised despot Robert Mugabe.

As with most schools in South Africa, sport was a strong part of the curriculum and all boys were expected to play cricket in summer and rugby in winter. As an indication of how important the national sport of rugby was, at St John's you were actually required to have a medical certificate stating you *weren't* able to play rugby, and only then were you permitted to play hockey.

Unsurprisingly, hockey was not very strong at St John's.

As with many private boys' schools, St John's boys carried the label of being a bunch of poofters. It wasn't a label that sat easily with any of us and it certainly was a motivating factor in inter-school matches. In the British public school tradition, we were known by our surnames, and mine certainly caused some merriment. One afternoon we were playing rugby against our close neighbours and rivals King Edward's School, a state boys' school. I was injured in a tackle and saw stars causing our teacher to run onto the field saying, 'Dearlove, Dearlove, are you okay?' The opposition looked at each other with arms folded and knowing looks which said it all, 'See, we told you so.'

There was a science teacher at St John's who was universally known as 'Rat' MacPhail. At the same time there was a well-known company in Johannesburg by the name MacPhails which delivered coal around the city. Their motto was *Mac won't fail you* which was boldly emblazoned on their delivery trucks. One enterprising St John's boy who did not prepare at all well for his science exam, wrote as a footnote on his papers, 'Mac won't fail me.' To his consternation and his parents' anger and quiet amusement, his report read, 'Mac did fail you.' Epic.

Another teacher was 'Bloater' Marais, a large man by any measure. Because of his size he was the subject of much sniggering and comments behind cupped ears. He was also hard of hearing and used hearing aids. Every day he would enter the classroom and require us all to stand, then say, 'Good morning, class', to which we would respond, 'Good morning, Sir'. One day, one of our more adventurous cohorts hatched a plan. When Bloater greeted us, the whole class mouthed our good mornings. As he turned up his hearing aid another notch, 'Morning, boys', we all mouthed our response. Up went the volume of the hearing aids as he tried again. This time we let him have it with a raucous greeting at which the poor fellow almost fell off his chair. We thought it was hilarious. Boys can certainly be cruel.

Each morning, we would line up in the quadrangle for roll call and there were occasional chortles when the name 'Dearlove' was called, particularly since we had a boy named 'Darling' in the same house. One lad from South West Africa by the name of Rissik had a dreadful stutter. He had enormous difficulty in yelling out the required Latin word 'adsum', meaning present, when his name was called. Roll call was done in alphabetical order and when the head of house got to the letter F, Rissik's mates would nudge him and he would start, hmmm, hmmmmm. If he was lucky, he would respond in time but more often than not he couldn't and the head would just say, 'I can't see you, Rissik, but I can hear you and I'll move on'. Talk about puerile humour.

Being at St John's opened up all sorts of opportunities and I was excited to be chosen to play for the Transvaal Primary Schools cricket team for the annual tour to Natal. We all piled onto the overnight train with the rock-hard green cushions and our family-size bottles of Coca-Cola, six sleeper bunks per compartment, and had a wonderful time, but little sleep. Our coach was all-rounder Peter Walker who had played cricket for England. During the tournament we played against Natal Primary Schools who had two promising young cricketers by the name of Mike Proctor and Barry Richards. Bowling my leg-spin I managed to get Proctor out, but not before he had scored plenty. One cynic suggested the roof of my mouth must be sunburned as I watched open-mouthed as the balls sailed over my head towards the boundary. Many years later there was an unconfirmed story about these two that did the rounds in Johannesburg cricket circles. Proctor's and Richards' genius had caught the eye of the English county cricket scouts and they were awarded scholarships with Sussex and Hampshire respectively.

Allegedly, after their county match against each other they

were having a drink at a local Southampton pub and after several they decided to try their luck with some of the local lasses. Being both naïve and fairly direct one said to the young damsel, 'Hi babe, what would you say to a little fuck?', to which she replied, 'Hello little fuck'. The lads had an early night.

Both having been good at sport, Mum and Dad were proud of my sporting achievements, but there were very few times they would make the 1000-kilometre round trip to watch me play. I was often the only boy whose parents were not enjoying the tea and scones at cricket matches. Nevertheless, I was never neglected since other boys' families were always very kind to me.

I knew money was tight at home and St John's was one of the most expensive schools in the country. I can clearly remember when I was awarded full school colours for rugby, a pretty rare award at that time, and Dad said they couldn't afford to buy me the blazer. That hurt.

St John's was a relatively small school with only about 400 boys and as a result our sport was not strong. We had few Springbok rugby alumni and only a handful of Springbok cricketers but that didn't deter our teachers from organising tours to other regions such as when the First XV rugby team toured Rhodesia in 1965.

Since there was no direct rail link between Johannesburg and Rhodesia, all travel was by train via Botswana through Francistown. What a trip. Being the 'milk run' we stopped at every siding and every station to pick up or drop off locals carrying live chickens, ducks and even a little monkey.

Arriving in Rhodesia, our first match was to be against Plumtree School. This was cancelled because of an outbreak of measles, so on we chugged to Bulawayo. We lost a very close match and that night the hosts, with their sister school, put on a dance for us which was enjoyed by some more than others. We then drew with Prince Edward School in Salisbury and headed

15

off to play our final match of the tour against Peterhouse situated about 80 kilometres away.

Peterhouse was a young school with magnificent facilities and even a golf course. The head boy of Peterhouse was Tim Peach who was also First XV captain. An enormously strong man, Tim anchored their scrum and single-handedly destroyed our front row, in particular our hooker, Erik Bjornsgaard. Erik had a badly bruised breastbone after Tim literally lifted him out of the scrum with his powerful neck and shoulders. We got thrashed, but Tim kindly made a gracious after-match speech about how close the match had been.

Tim later became well known across Rhodesia for his progressive policies in building up trust between black and white in the civil war which led to Rhodesia becoming independent in 1980. He and his family established a school and housing for the families of his employees on his farm. His was considered a model for the rest of a country facing an uncertain future.

One evening Tim set out, alone and unarmed, to meet with nationalist guerrillas or terrorists, depending on whose side you were on, to discuss peace terms. Unfortunately, these men had other ideas and clubbed Tim to death which shocked the nation and made international news. I vividly recall reading about his murder in *Time* magazine in Paris in 1978. Such a tragic and senseless waste of a life.

We were due to stay at Peterhouse for three days before we played them. Soon there were whispers that two of our team had gone AWOL. It transpired John Balderson and Mike Sutherland had fallen in love with the local damsels at the dance in Bulawayo and decided to hitchhike back to make a personal assessment if this was indeed true love. Bear in mind we were eighteen-year-old boys in a foreign country on a school rugby tour and our school had a tough reputation for enforcing discipline. The rest of the team was instructed to say John and Mike were unwell and were staying in the dormitory. For three days?

This unplanned side trip was always going to end badly, and it did. The star-struck lovers never made it to Bulawayo so the potential romances were never consummated. John and Mike were returned to Peterhouse sitting glumly in the back of the teacher's car, more than a little crestfallen. Our teachers were less than impressed, but the rest of the team thought they were heroes. When we got back to Johannesburg the punishment was swift and harsh with expulsion narrowly averted.

In what would be seen today as an archaic practice, caning was part of the disciplinary process at St John's. The headmaster dealt with the most serious offences and 'six of the best' was quite common. Housemasters were the next layer of enforcers then it was the house prefects' turn. Prefects were allowed to cane boys for stepping out of line for relatively minor misdemeanours. The caning was controlled, in a fashion, in that the house prefect had to gain the permission of the housemaster to borrow the cane. Barbaric? Probably. Any lasting damage? Probably not. A deterrent? Absolutely.

I was in Hill House and the prefects' common room was directly above the classroom where we did the evening's study or 'prep'. The word would come down that Jeeves had to report to the prefects between study periods. Jeeves knew he was in for a caning but did not know if it was going to be one, two or six. So, on a clear, hot summer's night with all the windows open, those of us doing prep would hear the prefects practising their strokes on a pillow in the room above, accompanied by much cackling. By the time Jeeves had walked slowly up the stairs to learn his fate he was a nervous wreck, and when he returned everyone would gather around him as he took down his pants displaying the marks from the cane to lots of 'oohs' and 'aahs'. The tribe at work.

Boarding at St John's had its plusses and minuses. One of the latter was the practice of 'fagging' in the British public school tradition whereby younger boys were required to act as 'personal aides or servants' to the senior boys. Fortunately, in my experience, it was seldom malicious and limited to cleaning grubby shoes or muddy rugby boots or being sent on mindless errands such as asking a senior boy in another house what the meaning was of a 'dingleberry'. If you returned with the wrong answer, you would get a hearty kick in the pants and told to return with the correct answer which you may get in exchange for another kick in the bum. The favoured position was for the boy to crouch with his feet between the mattress and the bed to give the assailant a good target. If like me you had no idea, a dingleberry is a term for a small piece of poop clinging to one's butt. Charming.

Another favourite was that I had to get up early on a bitterly cold Johannesburg winter morning and sit on the toilet seat to warm it for my superior, and heaven help you if the natural happened and he entered the toilet to be greeted with the pong of last night's dinner. The same fellow, let's call him Rodney, was particularly well endowed and on one memorable occasion he entered the communal showers naked with his erect penis carrying his towel. Cheers all round.

Many, many years later when son Kevin enrolled at St Paul's residential college in Sydney, one of the initiation challenges for freshers was to have a photograph taken with someone 'famous'. The catch was that the student would need to be in the nude. Kevin and his three mates won the competition hands down by getting the photo with the legendary Jimmy Barnes (with his clothes on), whose daughter was friendly with one of the lads. The quartet each had a guitar strategically covering the dangly bits with a clothed Barnesy singing up front.

Being one of the leading private schools in South Africa, St John's attracted many sons of the rich and famous. As per the apartheid laws, there were no boys 'of colour' at the school but the parents were, by and large, liberal in their words and in their actions. Paul Fischer's father Bram was a South African lawyer of Afrikaner descent, notable for anti-apartheid activism and for the legal defence of anti-apartheid figures, including Nelson Mandela. Following Mandela's trial for treason, sabotage and violent conspiracy, Bram was himself put on trial accused of furthering communism and sentenced to life imprisonment. Paul died of cystic fibrosis at the age of twenty-three while his father was in prison and he was not permitted to attend his funeral. Enforcing apartheid was cruel.

The Kane-Berman family were extremely good to me. There were four brothers at St John's and they came from what would at that time probably be described as a radical family. Their father Louis was staunchly anti-apartheid and considered a radical activist by the government. He was also a leader in the Torch Commando. The Torch Commando was founded in 1951 in protest against the South African government's plan to remove 'coloureds' from the voters' roll in the Cape Province. The Torch Commando principles provided a home to whites in other liberal formations, including those in the opposition United Party, who identified with black grievances.

I recently received a note from good friend and cricket legend, Vince van der Bijl, 'In 1956, my father explained why he was going to join the Torch Commando march of WWII veterans, led by Sailor Malan. The march was organised to protest against the Nationalist government taking away the voting rights of the Coloured people. It was my introduction to our racist world at the age of eight.'

The organisation existed for more than five years and at its height claimed to have 250,000 members. The apartheid government was alarmed by the number of judges, public servants and military officers joining the organisation. A new law was drafted and passed to ban anyone in public service or the military from joining. Subsequently, the National Party government did everything it could to purge the memory of the Torch Commando and men such as their charismatic leader and war hero 'Sailor' Malan, who had great appeal with white Afrikaner youth.

Louis Kane-Berman's late son John, a Rhodes Scholar and one of St John's most popular and successful alumni, later became head of the students representative council at Wits University and was a strident critic of the Nationalist government who had him on their 'watch list' for years.

At the other end of the spectrum was Craig Williamson. He was in the same boarding house as I was and, unusually for one in his teens, was a loner. He was seriously overweight and relentlessly teased about his bulk. Today that 'teasing' would be called bullying. He had no interest in sport which in itself set him apart and made him less than popular as he showed no loyalty to his peers, his house or his school.

In years to come, Craig Williamson would join the small group of famous or infamous Old Johannians. At school the only activity which seemed to capture his attention was cadets. It was probably no surprise that after school he joined the South African Police, the enforcers of apartheid. Years later in 1980, Williamson was exposed as a government spy and was allegedly involved in a series of state-sponsored overseas bombings, burglaries, kidnappings, assassinations and propaganda during the apartheid era.

The Johannesburg *Sunday Times* reported, 'He certainly deserves the title of a spy, somehow managing to infiltrate the likes of the National Union of South African Students [Nusas], the International University Exchange Fund in Geneva, the African National Congress (ANC) in exile and even, according to his handler Johan Coetzee, the KGB.' For many of the anti-apartheid activists he had worked with, Williamson's unveiling was a shocking betrayal. For others it came as less of a surprise.

Within Nusas there had always been those who found something a bit off about the former St John's boy who had been in the police force before he joined the student movement.

In 1995, Williamson applied for amnesty from South Africa's Truth and Reconciliation Commission (TRC) for bombing the London office of the ANC in March 1982. In the British House of Commons in June 1995, MP Peter Hain asked the British police to interview and consider extraditing Williamson to stand trial for the London bombing. The request was turned down and amnesty was eventually granted by the TRC to Williamson.

Williamson was a busy boy. Among his dastardly deeds, he allegedly ordered the assassination of Ruth First, an exiled campaigner for the anti-apartheid movement, a close friend of Swedish Prime Minister Olof Palme and the wife of the South African Communist Party's leader, Joe Slovo. Ruth was killed by a letter bomb in Maputo, Mozambique, in August 1982. Forty years later, in an August 2022 article in the *Daily Maverick*, Mark Heywood wrote, 'Killer and spy Craig Williamson, self-confessed murderer of First (and many others), lives out his life with his wife in peace and plenty – enjoying the very freedoms that he killed first for fighting for. By rights he should be in prison.'

In January 1984, minutes of the apartheid State Security Council chaired by President PW Botha recorded Craig Williamson as plotting the overthrow of the government in Mozambique with which South Africa was engaged in an undeclared war.

In mid-1984, Williamson allegedly mailed a letter bomb killing Jeanette Schoon, wife of Marius Schoon, and their six-year-old daughter Katryn at the family's home in exile in Lubango, Angola. Both Jeanette and Marius Schoon were prominent South African anti-apartheid activists and members of the ANC.

Williamson's hand was allegedly also in several other incidents across the globe. In February 1986, Olof Palme addressed the Swedish parliament against apartheid and effectively granted the ANC a diplomatic presence in Sweden. Palme and close friends were deeply involved in trying to establish, with ANC president Oliver Tambo, a 'third way' anti-apartheid force. This would have made it impossible for the National Party government and its Western allies to continue to portray the ANC as being dominated by the South African Communist Party and therefore, Moscow.

As such, Palme was a high-profile target for Pretoria. At the time, the apartheid state had set up clandestine 'dirty tricks' units, including Operation Longreach, allegedly headed by Williamson. A week after the speech, Palme was shot and killed after attending the cinema with his wife. There were no direct South African leads to the Palme killing until the Truth and Reconciliation Commission began its work in 1996. It was then that Eugene de Kock, the last commander of the notorious Vlakplaas death squad, provided much of the evidence exposing the level of callous brutality carried out on behalf of the apartheid state. He gave evidence to the Supreme Court in Pretoria alleging Palme had been shot and killed because he strongly opposed the apartheid regime and Sweden made substantial contributions to the ANC. De Kock went on to claim he knew the person responsible for Palme's murder, alleging it was former police colleague and South African spy, Craig Williamson. No South Africans were ever charged with the assassination.

When ANC president Oliver Tambo embarked on a world tour in 1987 to drum up support for the liberation movement, Williamson allegedly made sure that wherever Tambo spoke a video was released to the media with footage of 'necklacing'. The footage was accompanied by Winnie Madikizela-Mandela's quote that, 'With our boxes of matches and our necklaces we shall liberate this country.' Necklacing is the practice of execution and torture carried out by forcing a rubber tyre drenched with petrol over the victim's head and around the chest and arms and setting it on fire.

It goes without saying none of Williamson's teachers at St John's have ever claimed any credit for his post-school activities.

*

Mark Gandar was an extremely bright student at St John's. His father Laurence joined the left-leaning *Rand Daily Mail* newspaper as editor in 1957. He would change the editorial style of the newspaper to a liberal tone determined to inform South Africans about the racial and human rights abuses of apartheid and regularly challenge the ruling Afrikaner National Party government. His change in editorial style had a negative effect on circulation, which continued to drop until the paper's demise in 1985, to the delight of the government.

Concerning South Africa's future in a 1963 editorial, Gandar wrote, 'There are two choices and only two. There is racial separation, with massive economic sacrifices, or there is economic integration, with far-reaching political concessions. There is no middle course. At present we are trying to get the best of both worlds, and it is killing us.' Gandar was way ahead of his time.

I am not proud that there is no mention of people other than whites in this part of my growing up. The reality is people of colour were invisible in the day-to-day life at school. Sure, the cleaners, the kitchen and ground staff, mostly men, were black, but by and large the students had no idea where they disappeared to at the end of the working day. The truth was that they caught taxis to their homes an hour or more away in Soweto. These men were known by their first names only and if their names were not known, they were called 'John'. We certainly did not know their full names. It sounds so lame sixty years later but quite literally and this is no excuse, we didn't know what we didn't know. With very few exceptions these men loved St John's College where they were treated with kindness and respect and all served the school for years. In many cases they introduced their sons to the school where they were also often employed for decades and in some cases enrolled as students, often the beneficiaries of scholarships.

Throughout my schooling at St John's, the headmaster was Deane Yates, later awarded an OBE in recognition for his work with young people in Botswana. As a pupil I was nervous of him. He was an imposing and intimidating individual. He had some widget on the heels of his shoes and you could hear him approaching a long time before you saw him, his academic gown flying behind him.

Yates tried very hard to turn St John's into a non-racial, multicultural school by enrolling students of colour, but the odds were always stacked against him. Purely and simply, it was against the law. Having said that, he would be exceedingly proud of St John's College today which is considered one of the great private schools of the world. Today the college is superbly led by Stuart West and accepts boys of all race and religion from across the continent and, horror of horrors, even has girls in sixth form!

CHAPTER 3

FAMILY BUSINESS

The South African branch of the Dearlove family started in 1854 when my great-grandfather, Jos Dearlove, arrived in Durban from England. The reason for his migration has been long forgotten but he did not seem to have been hard up, being one of the first churchwardens in Pietermaritzburg, surely quite a status symbol in Victorian times. Family history reports he was a man of some culture and carried a Bible and a volume of Shakespeare on all his travels. After the discovery of diamonds and gold up-country he went north to the Transvaal where, instead of becoming a 'digger', he became a trader with several wagons supplying both the goldfields and the diamond fields. His children were born across the provinces of the Union of South Africa and Rhodesia. Most were British citizens but some were born in the Boer Republic and were called up for service in the 1899 Boer War. This must have caused some rifts within the family since my ancestors still identified strongly with the land of their birth. One of the sons was deeply and emotionally involved in the Boer cause and rose to be commandant in the Boer commando fighting unit. Another, fighting for the British, was killed in the siege of Ladysmith. It must have been a very difficult time with members of the family fighting on opposing sides.

Apart from the well-known generals such as Jan Smuts, Louis Botha, Redvers Buller, Baden Powell and Lord Kitchener, two other men who were to become giants on the world stage were also deeply involved in the war. A young Winston Churchill was a war correspondent who was captured by the Boers just two weeks after he arrived in South Africa in October 1899 and was held in a prisoner of war camp. With the assistance of an English mine manager, he escaped and returned to Britain hailed as a hero, while at the start of the war, Mahatma Gandhi supported the British in the hope that the conditions of Indians would improve in South Africa. He created the Natal Indian Ambulance Corps for use by the British as stretcher bearers, with all expenses met by the local Indian community. In 1914, having spent twenty years in South Africa helping fight discrimination, Gandhi decided it was time to return to India with his family where he then led the successful campaign for India's independence from British rule and later inspired movements for civil rights and freedom across the world.

My great-grandmother's family was descended from an Irishman and there is little detail available about him. He arrived in 1781 with the British military to fight in the early Cape Frontier wars. These were a series of nine conflicts that continued from 1779 to 1879 between the Xhosa Kingdom and Britain and European settlers in what is now the Eastern Cape in South Africa. He withdrew his services soon after he arrived, and for some reason he found it expedient to change his name to Hill.

My grandparents, Henry Walter Dearlove born in 1875 and Blanche Hill born in 1879, were married on 13 May 1903, soon after the Boer War ended. My grandfather had a public house named the Wayside Inn between Johannesburg and Germiston. It was apparently extremely lucrative, but my grandmother decided she didn't want her children brought up in a bar atmosphere so they moved to a farm between Nigel and Springs on the edge of the Far East Rand goldfields.

Either the farm wasn't much good or my grandfather was not much good as a farmer and they had difficulty in making ends meet. However, my dad and his two brothers, Arthur and Roland, had a wonderful time enjoying the freedom of farm life. There was excellent duck shooting and plenty of partridges, so they could live fairly well off the land. All were able to ride, shoot and swim from a young age. To my grandfather, these three attributes were necessary for the appropriate development of any man, but fortunately or unfortunately, my grandmother felt their education should extend a bit further and the lads were sent to the Sunnyside School in Pretoria. One of their fellow students was a boy called Japie Smuts, son of Jan who was later to become prime minister of South Africa.

They were at this school when the Great War started in 1914. Many of the Boers decided this offered a good chance for going another round with the Brits, and in what was called the Rebellion, my grandfather was called out with the burghers, named for those who were fully enfranchised citizens, to suppress it. To his great regret he was rejected and sent back home because he had a claw hand from a badly treated fracture of the forearm when he was a child. Even so, he was a good shot and anxious to play his part.

The boys were then sent to a school in Nigel which looked quite imposing to these young lads from the farm since there were deadlines to be kept and to their absolute surprise, all pupils were required to wear shoes. It was a comprehensive school with girls and boys, Dutch and English, from ages six to fourteen. The headmaster was quite impartial since, as a Welshman, he seemed to equally dislike the English and Dutch. The curriculum required students to learn the Dutch language and their teacher was a big guttural upstanding woman who was said to have fought as a man against the British. The young boys didn't doubt it and, on just on that one example, they wondered how on earth the British had managed to win the Boer War.

The daily ritual was the same for Dad and my uncles. They would rise early, catch the horse, harness the trap, load up some hay and drive to school. Initially they had a horse, but all the best horses in the country were soon commandeered for the war effort, so they used donkeys.

Grandfather always had a nostalgia for the bushveld and eventually bought a farm in the Springbok Flats near Naboomspruit, some 200 kilometres from Johannesburg. At the same time my dad and Uncle Arthur were enrolled at St John's College in Johannesburg. In Arthur's final year the family finances were low and Grandfather had to give notice that Arthur would be leaving to give his younger brother, my dad, a fair run. Fortunately, the headmaster had sufficient confidence in the family to offer Arthur a year's schooling on the 'hire purchase system'. Study now and pay later. Somewhat unusual at that time.

Because of the tragic circumstances of their death, I never got to meet my father's parents who died in the same night on their farm in January 1928. Both had recently suffered from attacks of influenza which in the case of Grandpa developed into pneumonia. While he seemed to be well on the road to recovery, during the night his condition worsened. It is understood that Grandma got up to attend to him and this effort brought on a heart attack from which she succumbed almost immediately. They died within hours of each other. My dad was only nineteen and he and his two brothers must have been devastated.

On one of our trips back to South Africa, Margie and I took our children to the cemetery in what was previously Naboomspruit, now Mookgophong. It was something of a challenge to find my grandparents' graves but once we found them, we were pleased they seemed to be well cared for by the local church.

There were sad echoes of this tragedy when ninety-two years later my sister Yvonne succumbed to the dreaded COVID-19 pandemic that swept the world in 2020. Yvonne suffered from advanced dementia and was in a nursing home in Dorset in England when the angels came. It was a terrible shock for all of us but obviously, in particular, her lovely children Hazel and Chris. Although her mind had gone, she had been in good health.

Despite the highs and lows of being on the land, Grandpa and Grandma must have been relatively well off since they sent all three sons to private schools. Dad went to St John's in 1922 and left in 1924 at the age of fifteen, without any qualifications, to help his parents on the farm. He must have been quite a good cricketer since at that tender age he played for the First XI alongside future Springboks Bruce Mitchell and Ronnie Grieveson.

Ronnie later played in the famous 'Timeless Test' which started on 3 March 1939 and ended twelve days later after forty-three hours and sixteen minutes of play; 1981 runs and 5447 balls bowled. After all that it still lacked the one thing it was supposed to have, a winner. The match was the longest ever played and was declared a draw only because the England team had to catch their ship home at the end of the tenth day of play.

Bruce Mitchell went on to be one of South Africa's greatest all-rounders. I got to know him well when I was at school. He was the bursar, but he was always at our practice sessions in the nets where he spent hours helping me master the art of bowling googlies.

Four years after leaving school and working the family farm my dad joined Barclays Bank, Dominion, Colonial and Overseas (DCO) in 1928. He spent his entire forty-one years' working life with the bank.

Mum was born in Vredenburg in the Cape Province to

William and Mary Caldwell in 1914. She was one of thirteen children – a good Catholic family. I don't remember much of Pater and Mater, as their children called them, but I do remember that when we visited there were lots of children running around.

Mum and Dad married in June 1939 just before war broke out. They settled in Pietersburg in what was then known as the Northern Transvaal. Dad served his country from 10 October 1940 to 15 October 1945 as a gunner in the 42nd Infantry Brigade of the South African Airforce. Mum worked in the War Records of the South Africa Department of Defence. It must have been an extremely stressful job as her unit had the complex and emotionally taxing task of tracking the whereabouts of the 335,000 South African men and women who served in different theatres of war in Europe and North Africa.

On 22 June 1940, my dad was sent a telegram from the War Office in London saying his brother, 'Medical doctor Lieutenant Arthur Raymond Dearlove, Royal Medical Corps is believed missing in action'. One can only imagine the shock. A long three weeks later another telegram was sent from the Under-Secretary for War in Liverpool in the UK. Unfortunately, it was sent to Pietermaritzburg rather than Pietersburg so it was another week before Dad received the news, 'Lieutenant Dearlove previously reported as missing, is a Prisoner of War'. There was a subsequent telegram, also sent to Pietermaritzburg, from the London Committee of the South African Red Cross in South Africa House, confirming Uncle Arthur, 'Was a POW in Oflag 9A'. This was the German prisoner-of-war camp located in Spangenberg Castle in the small town of Spangenberg in north-eastern Hesse. The camp was used for housing RAF and British Army officers. On 29 March 1945, as the tide of war turned, the Germans marched the Spangenberg prisoners 100 kilometres east to the village Lengenfeld unterm Stein. The American forces liberated the camp's inmates a week later and Arthur could finally go home to resume his practice as a highly regarded doctor.

After the war, Dad resumed his career with Barclays Bank in Pietersburg, while Mum cared for Yvonne and me. In 1957, Dad was posted to Messina as branch manager and then four years later was appointed the manager of the Middelburg branch. He retired in 1969 and he and Mum lived out their years in the town.

Middelburg has a somewhat dark past. During the Boer War, the British led by Lord Kitchener introduced concentration camps. At first the British were not able to beat the Boers who were always on the move using classic guerrilla warfare tactics. The British reacted by cruelly placing the Boer fighters' family members into concentration camps. This meant family members could not give food, shelter or any assistance to the Boer fighters. The British soldiers also burned down the Boers' houses and farms and destroyed all the crops they could find, again to prevent the Boers being given sustenance to survive. They built a large concentration camp in Middelburg, one of more than forty-five tented camps which were built for Boer internees, and a further sixty-four camps which were built for black South Africans. In itself, an early version of apartheid.

This was not the first appearance of internment camps, as the Spanish had used internment in Cuba in the 'Ten Years' War twenty years before. The Boer War concentration camp system however was the first time a whole nation had been systematically targeted and the first in which entire regions were depopulated. An early example of a scorched earth policy, attributed to Lord Kitchener.

By far, the majority of Boers detained in the camps were women and children, with more than 26,000 perishing. The camps were poorly administered and conditions were terrible for the health of the internees, mainly due to neglect, poor hygiene and bad sanitation. The supply of all items was unreliable, partly because of the constant disruption of communication lines by the Boers. Food rations were meagre and there was a two-tier allocation policy and, almost unbelievably, families of men who were still fighting were routinely given smaller rations than others. The inadequate shelter, poor diet, bad hygiene and overcrowding led to malnutrition and endemic contagious diseases such as measles, typhoid and dysentery, to which the children were particularly vulnerable. It was a desperately cruel system and is still remembered with bitterness by many Afrikaner descendants of the detainees.

My parents are buried at the same cemetery as the 1381 women and children who died in the Middelburg concentration camp. Each time we visit, the tiny graves of the children bring tears to our eyes. Man's inhumanity to man.

CHAPTER 4

THE DURBAN YEARS

After leaving school in 1965, I was totally unprepared for what the following year would hold for me. I was keen to do a post-matric year at St John's but another year's school fees were out of the question. I didn't even bother raising it with my parents.

Each year, approximately 20,000 young white men were subject to a ballot system to do nine months' military service. Like all other school-leavers, I was resigned to doing mine until one day in November 1965, I received notification from the South African Defence Force saying my name had not come up in the ballot. In all honesty I wasn't sure if this was a good or a bad thing. I had really enjoyed school but wasn't sure if another nine months of being in a highly structured and strictly enforced disciplined environment had much appeal. In truth, I felt rather guilty that I was not balloted along with pretty much everyone I knew. On the other hand, I had no idea what I wanted to do career-wise. Medicine had always interested me but the two medical schools at the Witwatersrand and Cape Town universities had by this time closed their enrolments and I enrolled at the University of Pietermaritzburg for a science degree with the goal of then transferring to a medical school. Dr Dearlove sounded quite cool.

I felt really important wandering around the campus in my long white coat, along with friends like Christine Lang and Genee Botha, but in truth I was a bit of an imposter. Physics and chemistry had not been my strong suits at school and I was quickly found out at varsity. After the closeted teaching environment at school, I was certainly not skilled at working on my own. I didn't trouble the exams scoreboard much at the end of year then repeated the year with much better results, but came to realise entering the medical profession was not the way forward.

I switched to a commerce degree which was far more interesting and this showed in my results. My parents had put some success milestones in place which in essence were for me to pass all the exams or move on. I just missed this goal and somewhat reluctantly came to the conclusion that the Pietermaritzburg campus of Natal University definitely didn't see what Ray Dearlove had to offer academically. At the end of 1968 my parents strongly suggested, and I agreed, it was time to pick up stumps and do something else, and, as added by my dad, 'something meaningful'. Neither Mum nor Dad had been to university and it was only much later that selfish me realised how much I had disappointed them by squandering their money and my time. In Maritzburg, the favoured student watering holes were the Imp (Imperial) and the Ans (Ansonia) hotels, the latter being slightly more upper class, where they put on a dance every Saturday night. I would work most Saturdays at the Scottsville races to enable me to accompany the current girl of my dreams to the Ans dances where every evening concluded with Engelbert Humperdinck's 'The Last Waltz'. Very romantic.

One of the regulars at the Imp, Staf Naude, had a glass eye and whenever he needed to visit the bathroom, he would remove the eye and place it alongside his drink saying, 'Watch my beer'.

It worked every time, nobody dared touch his drink. The hotel management was at best tolerant of the students' behaviour given the amount of money they spent, but seemed to have the local police on speed dial in case of any 'excessive' frivolity. I spent far too much time at both establishments and I'm pretty sure their profits would have dipped until a new crop of students arrived.

Moving to Durban was a logical change for me; my intentions were to complete a degree and Maritzburg and Durban fell under the University of Natal banner. In addition, I knew a lot of people in Durban and it was still far enough from home to live my own life. Living in Durban was a lot of fun. Apart from the great beaches and golf courses, there were many more opportunities for getting a job in Durban than in Maritzburg. In addition, I was dating a lovely young lady named Mary from my Maritzburg days. She was probably my first true love. Her parents were members of the seriously upper class, the ODF, the Old Durban Families. As hard as I tried, I couldn't convince them this lad from Middelburg who had bombed out of university was a good match for their only daughter. I was probably my own worst enemy by continuing to enjoy more than the occasional beer, going surfing, playing rugby, golf, not taking my job particularly seriously and generally being a bit of a prick. Many years later Mary and I met in Johannesburg. She was genuinely astonished that I had become a fairly normal member of society. In fact, her exact words were, 'I thought you would land up dead or in jail'.

In Durban, I landed a job with the accounting firm Silburn, Castleden and Joubert. In one strike the firm covered all three 'white' tribes in South Africa. Silburn the Jewish fraternity, Castleden the English and Joubert the Afrikaners. A winning formula. While my parents still harboured hopes I would fulfil my newly chosen path of being a chartered accountant and a respected member of the establishment as befitted a St John's College alumnus, I wasn't so sure. Even so, I turned up for work as an articled clerk determined not to let myself, or my parents, down. Again. I had some credits from Maritzburg University and signed up with the sister campus of Natal University in Durban to do a bachelor of commerce.

At Silburn, Castleden and Joubert I was assigned to work under the firm's senior auditor, a man of British background with the imposing name of Mr Highton-Jones. I never knew his first name or where the gentrified addition of the Jones moniker came from. In his sixties, he was straight out of a Charles Dickens novel, complete with bowler hat, specs, umbrella 'just in case' and a briefcase the size of a suitcase. He was a rotund fellow but waddled along at a rapid rate, doffing his hat to anyone who looked twice at him and there were plenty of those, with me trailing him trying hard to give the impression we were not together.

Mr Highton-Jones and I spent hours checking invoices, payments, credits, debits and on and on and on. Always with a green pen. 'Good auditors always use green pens, Raymond.' We had nothing in common so there was no small talk. My hours were 8 am to 5 pm and I was paid a paltry sum, but with the benefit of hindsight it was probably fair for the contribution I made to the firm. On the dot of 5 pm I would be out of the office like a scalded cat and off to the beach or to play sport. Partner Silburn enjoyed his sport and probably saw right through me, but tried to encourage me to at least pursue the academic side by finishing my degree.

At the time I was playing good rugby for the Berea Rovers Club in Durban. It was a strong club with many provincial and Springbok players. Some trivia: Andrew Mehrtens, one of the All Blacks' finest, was born in Durban where his dad Terry and his lifelong Kiwi mate Peter Hatchwell plied their trade at Rovers. Both represented Natal against many of their All Black contemporaries in 1970.

Rovers was one of the oldest sporting clubs in South Africa, but like many sporting clubs it had fallen on hard times. After much angst on both sides, the club merged with the Natal Airforce Club based in the middle of the Durban CBD. The Airforce Club was started by World War II South African Airforce veterans and while the club had made strong efforts to become a businessmen's club, the competition from long-established clubs such as the Durban Club was too much and it was forced into a merger. I was good friends with George Carrick who did the books for the combined entity and I watched as club managers came and went, often caught with their hands in the till. One evening over a few beers George, himself a chartered accountant, asked me how my job was going. It was a rhetorical question because he knew I hated it. He then said, 'You love sport, you're honest, you hate your job, why not take over as manager of the combined Rovers Airforce Club?' And as a sweetener, 'I'll give you a salary increase.' That clinched the deal. The following day I told Mr Silburn I was leaving. He asked me if I was going to a competitor. When I told him about the Rovers job, he smiled and winked saying, 'Mr Highton-Jones will be devastated.' I nearly choked.

So, there I was, twenty-two years old doing a management job which had long hours but was not overly onerous. George was a great backstop and we worked very well together. In the quiet times and with the exception of life member Julius, who arrived to take up his seat at opening time and left on the dot of 6 pm, there were many hours where there were no customers. The barmen Allan and Lennie and I would then sharpen our snooker and darts skills. In no time at all, I was the best snooker and darts player in the club, building my life skills.

The two Indian barmen were so different. Allan was a smooth, suave, good-looking man and butter wouldn't melt in his mouth, whereas Lennie was a hard man, a man of the streets. I enjoyed their company immensely, but at the same time I knew somehow one or the other or both were skimming some of the profits. Mainstay cane spirit, a drink much like rum and enormously popular at the time, was the one drink that seemed to 'disappear' in volume. George and I tried everything but could never work out how they were doing it. Bear in mind this was the late 60s. No CCTV or sophisticated digital tracking systems then. I thought Lennie was the team leader while George was convinced it was Allan. We never caught them out.

Because of a large influx in the 1860s when Indians were transported to work on the sugarcane plantations of the Natal Colony, Durban has the highest population of Indians outside of India. In total, approximately 200,000 Indians arrived as indentured labourers over a period of five decades. This had grown to a population of about 1.6 million in 2021. Many years later, I met up with another Indian barman at one of Durban's luxury beachfront hotels and told him the story of Allan and Lennie. He was a very amusing fellow and responded, 'You know, Ray, when my ancestors came to South Africa, they planted the cane and cut the grass ... nowadays, my people drink the cane (spirit) and smoke the grass.' He thought it was very funny and so did I.

At the time I was sharing a house on the Berea, a lovely leafy suburb overlooking the Indian Ocean. My housemates were all older than me and all had failed marriages, so it was a true bachelor's house. We all got on very well but Billy Hall in particular became a good friend. He was a slight, quiet, bespectacled man, who was a printer at the *Natal Mercury* newspaper.

One of the best sportsmen I have ever played with was John 'Dumpy' Dyer. He excelled at all sports and was flyhalf in the same team I played for at Rovers. Dumpy was, and still is, happily married to Carol who like so many wives I have met, was long-suffering. Billy, Dumpy and I would often meet for a few beers after work, generally on the Durban beachfront. One day Billy mentioned he had on good authority that the monthly

1820 Settlers reunions were worth attending. The 1820 Settlers was a group of mainly English ex-pats, many of whom were descendants of the British colonists who settled in the Eastern Cape of South Africa that year. The gatherings always took place at one particular beachfront hotel. Despite it being a ticket-only affair we managed to talk our way into the party. The room was pumping. There was a rock band, dancing, plenty of single women and plenty of drinks; an ideal combination for a Friday night. Billy was wearing his smart multi-coloured shirt and slacks while Dumpy and I were dressed in our best safari suits, the outfit of choice in steamy Durban. We were irresistible. The room was set up in a square around the dance floor with the band at one end and trestle tables at the other. The tables were groaning under the weight of food and drinks and the prizes for the novelty events.

We seated ourselves at the edge of the dance floor and tried our best to engage with some of the fairer sex, with very limited success. I suppose our heavy South African accents were a dead giveaway to the Brits. The MC then announced a musical chairs competition and we decided to participate. It was good fun and I ended up as the winner with a particularly pretty young lady. I didn't see, or chose to ignore, the ring on her wedding finger. As the victorious couple, the MC cheerfully invited us to help ourselves to some of the goodies on the trestle tables and I tucked in with tins of ham, mushrooms and asparagus. I thanked my 'partner' and rejoined Billy and Dumpy at the table sharing the spoils with them.

I was seated with my back to the dance floor and suddenly, out of the corner of my eye, I saw this fellow running across the dance floor. He gave me a helluva whack to the side of my head and yelled, 'This one is for getting cute with my wife!' No guesses as to who his wife was. Anyway, I fell to the floor taking a few trestle tables with me and then it was on for young and old.

Dumpy was a good man to have at your side in a fight and while we were heavily outnumbered, we held our own. That was until one of these Poms jumped on my back and I fell to the ground. These blokes were all over me. Fingers going for my mouth, my nose, my eyes and somewhat cruelly, my balls. To say the least I was in trouble. That was until my quiet, bespectacled friend Billy, who had been a passive observer, sidled up to the fellow on top of me and executed a beautifully placed kick to his ribs and innocently retreated to the sidelines. Job done. By now the room looked like something out of the Wild West. Tables down, fruit and food all over the floor, as more and more of the 1820 Settlers got involved. Possibly trying to avenge the British defeat at Rorke's Drift.

Suddenly we heard police cars approaching and we bolted. My treasured blue safari suit was in tatters, the comb from my long socks missing and there was blood dripping down my chest. We ran for a back alley, stopped, and then burst out laughing at the incongruity of it all. Dumpy's wife Carol was convinced I was the one who was always leading her husband astray in these innocent pursuits. If she only knew.

As my darts and snooker improved, I got to know more members and I felt I was making a contribution to the club. There was unease and suspicion between the World War II veterans and the young, rowdy testosterone-filled athletes but both sides knew they needed each other. Despite my youth I got on well with the older members and was able to build trust between the two very different groups. No random breath testing in those days, so the club was open and busy most nights until 11 pm.

One morning I was sitting in my office with the bookkeeper reconciling the takings from the previous night, and thank God not playing snooker, when in walked my parents. Completely unannounced, I got a helluva fright. I was happy to see them but the feeling was obviously not mutual. I asked the bookkeeper to leave and invited my mum and dad to sit down. They kept standing. I could see my dad was seriously angry. My mum, always my ally, stood quietly in the corner. The mainly one-way conversation went something like this, 'What the hell are you doing here?'

'Just working away, Dad, would you like me to show you around?'

My dad was a big man, probably 1.93 metres, and he advanced towards me saying, 'Raymond, (how I hated that name) your mother and I have sacrificed a great deal to send you to the best, and if not the best, certainly the most expensive school in South Africa and then sponsored three years of parties at university and what do you have to show for it working in a bloody pub? I believe you are the champion darts and snooker player at this joint? We want you to put in your resignation today and move to Johannesburg and get a job, a real job. Are we clear?' Mum and Dad had travelled the 800 kilometres from Middelburg to deliver the message. 'Are we clear?' 'Yes, Dad.' I didn't think it was a good time push my luck and to respond like Tom Cruise did to Jack Nicholson in *A Few Good Men*, by saying, 'Crystal'.

They returned to Middelburg the following day, turning down my invitation to have dinner at my club.

To the surprise of some, I am not that stupid. Within a week I was back in Johannesburg, but having lost contact with most of my school mates I asked a friend, Laura, if I could stay until I found a job and a flat. I had met Laura, an ICU nurse at the Lady Dudley Hospital, at a party in Durban a few months before and it developed into a long-distance relationship. She agreed, so I moved into her abode in Hillbrow which was the heart of entertainment in Johannesburg.

Not long after, things rapidly deteriorated with my dad. Long before mobile phones, I had given him the phone number of Laura's flat in case of any emergencies, having told him I was staying with a school buddy. Early one morning the phone rang. Laura sleepily answered, 'Hang on … I'll get him … it's for you,' and passed the phone to me across the bed. It was a short, very sharp phone call. I had never heard my dad swear. Until that morning.

Thank the Lord, later that week I got a job with the highly respected international company IBM. Relationships with my dad improved. Sort of. Needless to say, I never introduced Laura to my parents.

CHAPTER 5

THE 1970s

Living in Johannesburg as a bachelor in the early 1970s was idyllic. Once I had joined IBM, I could afford to rent an apartment and found a studio in a block named Doromo in Hillbrow where good friends Mary 'Bunch' Le Roux and Margaret Argue and my sister Yvonne also resided. All the action was in Hillbrow. There was an active nightlife with restaurants, bars, even a theatre and of course, Des and Dawn Lindberg, the popular folk singers playing 'Die gezoem van die bye' and 'The seagull's name was Nelson' at the Troubadour. We played plenty of sport, mostly at the Old Johannian Club where the facilities were excellent. Many of my friends were single and we'd think nothing of heading off for the weekend to the Drakensberg for hiking or the Kruger Park to see the wild animals in their natural environment.

Communal houses were very popular in Johannesburg and contrary to the views of our parents they weren't nests of hippies with long hair and smoking 'boom', the colloquial word for dagga, pot or cannabis. It was a cheap way of living with six or more young men and women sharing a large house which would usually have a large garden, swimming pool, tennis court, several servants, and importantly, everyone had their own bedroom.

Through Bunch, I became very friendly with Jock McLean, son of the legendary New Zealand rugby author and journalist, Sir Terry McLean. Jock lived in a house in Klip Street in Observatory with five others, all New Zealanders, male and female. Despite living in the same house, everyone lived his or her own life. The rule of the house was that if a couple fell for each other they had to move out. This may seem like a tough rule but it prevented conflict.

I spent a lot of time at Klip Street, mostly on weekends where there would be plenty of braais and the occasional failed Hangi, lots of laughs and music like Neil Diamond's *Hot August Night*, plus a fair amount of drinking of Castle and jugs of cheap Amorosa red wine. On Sunday nights we would hire a movie projector and watch the latest hit movies. No television in South Africa until 1976. The state-controlled South African Broadcasting Corporation (SABC) saw the new medium as a threat to the Afrikaans language and the Afrikaner volk. They claimed television gave undue prominence to English and created unfair competition for the Afrikaans press. Prime Minister Hendrik Verwoerd compared television with atomic bombs and poison gas, claiming, '… they are modern things, but that does not mean they are desirable. The government has to watch for any dangers to the people, both spiritual and physical'. The mind boggles. Dr Albert Hertzog, Minister for Posts and Telegraphs argued, '… South Africa would have to import films showing race mixing and advertising would make (Black) Africans dissatisfied with their lot'. The new medium was regarded, by him, '… as the devil's own box for disseminating communism and immorality'. Hard to believe I know, but this was South Africa in the early 70s.

In 1973, one of the New Zealand girls left Klip Street to

continue her world travels and the vacancy was advertised through the communal house network. I was visiting the house one Sunday afternoon when the interviews for the vacancy were taking place. Obviously, Kiwis would be given preference, but the final applicant was an Aussie. She walked in, beautiful long red hair and equally beautiful long legs. She was wearing a little blue number, miniskirts being all the rage at the time. Well, I don't know about this love at first sight business, but I was cooked. I was sitting behind the interviewee, Margaret Kinnane, so she couldn't see me giving the thumbs up to the interviewing panel of Jock, Tom and Malcolm. Sadly, I don't think Ms Kinnane even noticed me. I'm delighted to say the panel took my advice and about eighteen months later, Margie became Mrs Dearlove.

When she was twenty-one, Margie had left Australia, as many of that generation did, to explore the world for what was often referred to as the Kangaroo Hop via Europe and Africa. She headed to London where she worked part-time as a teacher and as a secretary. These jobs funded her travels around Europe. She flatted with Australian friends, Robyn and Deirdre, both nurses, in the favoured area for colonials of Earl's Court and Kensington and they remain good friends fifty years later. After a few years Margie got sick of the grey skies and rain and on a whim decided to return to Australia via South Africa. She had some dramas at Johannesburg airport because she didn't have an onward ticket and was detained at the airport overnight until a friend bailed her out. Welcome to South Africa.

Margie and I were married in 1974 and trust me, I had to work really hard to win her hand since she had planned for the South African stopover to be just that, to see the country and then to return to Australia. She hadn't planned to spend the next fifteen years of her life in South Africa. She did some part-time work and then joined Canadian Bill Mounsey in his events management company which traded under the grand name of

Festivals and Conventions Trust (FACT). This role opened all sorts of opportunities for her in terms of travel. FACT arranged international conferences and, almost without exception, delegates wanted to visit Cape Town and also see wildlife in the country's famed game reserves.

I first met Dr Ian Player in 1977 when he and Sir Laurens van der Post, godfather to Prince William, conceived the first World Wilderness Congress. It came about at the suggestion of Player's friend and mentor, game ranger Magqubu Ntombela. Margie and her business partner Mounsey had the privilege of being selected as the event managers for the conference which was attended by 2700 delegates from thirty countries. What was quite extraordinary was when Margie and I met with Ian shortly before his death, he remembered not only her name and Mounsey's, but also the name of their company, Festivals and Conventions Trust. That was almost forty years later.

One of their most memorable events was the International Equine conference that took place in the Kruger National Park. Margie gave me the job of ferrying overseas delegates from the airport to Pretoriuskop Camp. This was not exactly onerous. It gave me opportunities to see plenty of wildlife and to enjoy the 'oohs' and 'aahs' of the tourists and some very funny comments, 'Is that a tiger, Sven?' 'Shh, Ingrid, no tigers in Africa.'

As described, by sheer chance (or fate), Margie landed up at the Klip Street shared house, not at all a 'commune' as all of our parents thought, and over time, as our relationship developed, I moved into the house. It was cheaper than where I was living and the occupants of the house had all become good friends.

As above, one of the rules of the house was that if any relationship developed, one or other or both parties had to move out to maintain the harmony among the members of the house. It was a sensible policy and in due course, Margie and I moved into a quaint little house in Linden. Today it would be described as 'rustic'. It was simple, but it was ours and we had our dogs and we could entertain without upsetting anyone else.

I was playing a lot of cricket and it became a bit of a weekly ritual that after several post-match drinks at the Old Johannian Club on Sundays our team would repair to our house and Margie would cook scrambled eggs for the team, most of whom were bachelors. That was how Margie earned her nickname of 'mother', courtesy of Tom Lawless. She continues to be called that by many of our South African friends.

One of my abiding regrets is that none of Margie's family attended our wedding in Johannesburg. We didn't have enough money to pay for tickets, nor did her parents. Margie was 'given away' by Bill Mounsey who was as much a friend as a business partner. Margie was skilled in shorthand typing and Bill would dictate all his correspondence. The problem was he had the habit of lengthy pauses between sentences and more than once, he had to raise his voice because Margie had dozed off.

During our planning for the wedding, we arranged an appointment with the priest at our local Catholic church in Linden. As we sat down, he said he did not recognise us and asked how often we attended Mass. We were irregular worshippers and the question threw us. We were left speechless when he told us that, as a result of us not taking our faith sufficiently seriously, he wouldn't marry us. It was both embarrassing and annoying for a young couple who were trying to do the right thing, so we stepped out and headed for another Catholic church in Rosebank where the priest welcomed us with open arms.

A month or so later, IBM friends Clive and Janine Badenhorst who never missed Mass, were about ten minutes late for the service at the same Linden Catholic church. They quietly ushered their five children into the pew as the same priest who had refused us stopped the service mid-sentence and just stared/glared at them. He then made the general but pointed comment that he would like his parishioners to be more respectful and be on time. A big man, not to be trifled with, Clive gave the priest a long look and then silently led his family out through the front door walking straight past the priest never to be seen again in that church. Be very careful what you wish for.

We had a wonderful wedding at the historic Eton Arms estate which was interrupted for a while by a classic highveld summer storm with plenty of thunder and lightning. As MC Peter Auld said, 'If rain at your wedding is considered lucky, you two are going to be bloody lucky.' And so we have been.

My parents really enjoyed the wedding and Margie and I enjoyed introducing them to our friends.

In the same year we decided to spend Christmas in Australia. South African Airways (SAA) flew from Johannesburg to Sydney via Mauritius and Perth. It was a long flight and we then had to get a connection to Brisbane in order to meet the family in Ipswich.

I approached the meeting with Margie's parents with quite some trepidation. Her dad was a former Australian boxing champion and although this was in the lightweight division and I was 193 centimetres tall and fit, I was still a bit nervous. As it turned out, Annie and Owen Kinnane were lovely people. Knowing this a decade or so later made the decision to emigrate that much easier. Both came from large families. Owen was one of nine and Annie one of eight. Their family bonds were strong and they all made me very welcome and were wonderful role models for our children. I tell the story, only slightly exaggerated, that there was a sizable queue around the block of their home with 'friends' visiting to check what colour this African was who had married 'our Margaret'.

One of the first 'we have to show you Australia' escapades was a visit to the local pub, which was owned by the famous McLean rugby family, where I was introduced to a 'pony' sized glass – all

140 millilitres of it – by my brother-in-law, Les. It would take quite a few to get in any way tipsy. Also, glasses being kept in the fridge, 'otherwise the beer would not be cold for very long, mate'. Somewhat sobering, but sadly familiar to me, was noting the serving of drinks to Aboriginals through a hatch at the back of the pub.

There was very little local knowledge about South Africa and most Australians referred to Africa as if it were a country rather than a continent. Many still do. Given the highly contentious White Australia Policy was officially terminated just one year before, there was a lot of interest in apartheid. I had to explain it wasn't 'apart-hate' but an Afrikaans word literally meaning 'being apart' or 'separateness'.

To the disappointment of most sports-mad Australians who relished the tussles in rugby and cricket, the international sports boycott of South Africa was now in full swing. This was even more bitter for Australian cricket lovers because their teams had been towelled by the Springboks in the two most recent series in 1966 and 1970 and they wanted revenge. Little did we realise it would be a long twenty-plus years before the countries would again compete.

While none of Margie's family could join us for the wedding the following year her brother Les and his wife Trish from Ipswich in Queensland spent several weeks visiting us. Neither Les nor Trish had been overseas before and were understandably nervous about 'darkest Africa'.

Margie and I had planned the trip carefully to show them as much of Southern Africa as we could while also giving them a holiday. Both were school teachers so they had read plenty about what to expect. Nevertheless, Africa still managed to spring a few surprises.

One of the planned highlights of the trip was to the Victoria Falls, one of the seven modern natural wonders of the world.

Given Rhodesia was in the middle of what was known as the Rhodesian Bush War, Les and Trish were approaching the visit with considerable apprehension. The war was a civil conflict from July 1964 to December 1979, which pitted three forces against one another. They were the Rhodesian government led by Ian Smith, the Zimbabwe African National Liberation Army, the military wing of Robert Mugabe's Zimbabwe African National Union, and the Zimbabwe People's Revolutionary Army of Joshua Nkomo's Zimbabwe African People's Union.

Les and Trish were unusually quiet during the flight from Johannesburg to the quaint Victoria Falls airport. Their apprehension jumped another level when our tourist bus to the hotel was accompanied by two heavily armed armoured cars. One in front and the other behind. A loud American on the bus asked if we all knew some tourists had recently been shot from the Zambian side of the Victoria Falls. He was referring to a group who had been hiking along the Zambezi River on the Rhodesian side of the Falls who, when they saw what appeared to be some workmen across the river they waved, with no warning of what was to come, the men suddenly opened fire. The tourists tried to hide but the shooting continued. The firing started just after 2 pm and continued until 4 pm by which time two young Canadian women were dead.

I obviously knew about this incident but had chosen not to mention it to Les and Trish. There was a hush on the bus and if looks could kill that American would have been on his way back to Boise in Idaho or wherever the hell he came from.

That same afternoon we enjoyed a wonderful 'booze cruise' along the Zambezi seeing lots of animals. Unlike the previous times I had done the boat trip, this time we were accompanied by fully armed police speed boats speeding between us and the Zambian side. More alerts.

The following morning, we had our first visit to the Falls

getting soaked in the rain forest and marvelling at the 110-metre-high mass of water tumbling over the width of 1708 metres. As the proud locals will tell you, Victoria Falls is roughly twice the height of Niagara Falls and well over twice the width of the Horseshoe Falls – the largest of the three falls making up Niagara.

It was a very hot December day and we decided to have lunch at the grand and historic Victoria Falls Hotel, a truly colonial establishment which was built by the British in 1904. As we sat sipping our pre-lunch drinks at the swimming pool, seemingly out of nowhere, a platoon of Rhodesian soldiers ghosted in. We gasped and stared as these young men carefully placed their guns against the trunk of an old Msasa tree and stripped down to their shorts and dived into the pool. As they emerged the waiter brought them cold soft drinks which they thirstily gulped down. They got dressed, put on their boots, picked up their rifles and melted into the bush. As they left, there was spontaneous applause from the people gathered around the pool. Trish spoke for all of us when she said, 'They are all so young.'

The following day was New Year's Eve and we had booked for the dinner dance to be held at our hotel. Fittingly for those days it was a formal affair, black tie and long dresses. Les and Trish's room was next to ours. They knocked on our door as they made their way to the lounge for pre-dinner drinks and when Margie and I joined them Les was already on his second beer and had a strange, slightly twitchy look. Trish was unusually quiet. Les explained that as they were coming down the stairs, they noticed this not so young couple entering the reception area dressed in their finery, the man in his tuxedo and the woman in a pretty, long frock complete with an elegant stole. They headed for the cloakroom but instead of handing in his coat he handed in his sub-machine gun. It turned out they were farmers who lived about 20 miles from the Falls and when we spoke to them, they reminded us there was a war on. Les was speechless, there was so much to take in. Africa can be very confronting.

That New Year's Eve will always remain fixed in our memory. ABBA were at their peak and the local band obviously loved the Swedish group but had a seriously limited repertoire and belted out the song 'Fernando' over and over again. 'Can you hear the drums?' Yes, I can. Almost fifty years later.

There was another reason to remember New Year's Day, 1975. We had booked a flight in a light airplane over the Falls and were picked up from the hotel, as planned, at 6 am by a young man with long blond hair. Trish noted his normally blue eyes were seriously bloodshot and he was accompanied by an attractive young woman with similar long blonde hair. We assumed he was the driver for the company and they had collected us on their way back from a big New Year's Eve celebration.

We thanked them when we arrived at the airstrip but he replied, 'No need for goodbyes, we are coming with you'. So far so good, until he hopped into the pilot's seat and the blonde sat next to him. 'Jesus!' exclaimed Les as we clambered aboard the six-seater. 'Welcome aboard,' said our long blond-haired driver-cum-pilot. 'It's a beautiful day for flying but I need your help. We don't have any radio or radar on this plane and there is a plane from the opposition which will also be in the area so if those of you on the left could keep a lookout for him and the same on the right.' Trish reached for the brown bag.

The 'Flight of Angels' is an amazing journey over the 1700-metre vast curtain of water known locally as the 'Mosi oa Tunya' translated to 'The smoke that thunders', then along the Zambezi River and the Zambezi National Park. The views are spectacular. I'm pleased to say we didn't encounter the other plane and our pilot did remarkably well for a man who could barely see. Returning to the airport, our pilot went home to bed with the blonde while we headed for the closest watering hole.

Another highlight of the trip was when we took Les and

Trish to Swaziland, now Eswatini, one of the smallest countries in Africa. Gambling was prohibited in South Africa so, for something different, we decided to have dinner at the Mbabane Casino. Les was resplendent in his in-fashion – at least in Australia – green safari suit, complete with long pants. Les was dismayed when told he was not suitably dressed and would not be permitted to enter the restaurant without a tie. Fortunately, one of the waiters came to the rescue and loaned him a spare. My brother-in-law was getting used to the foibles of Africa and to his credit he actually developed a bit of a strut with his safari suit and tie. Trish just rolled her eyes.

CHAPTER 6

THE CITY OF LIGHT (AND LOVE)

I loved working for IBM in Johannesburg. Not having any real experience or any qualification, read degree, I started at the bottom of the pile as an accounts receivable clerk. Obviously, no computers then, so we used punch cards to record and balance the debtors' accounts. IBM was growing like Topsy and hiring people left, right and centre and I quickly took to the company's distinct culture. As then CEO John Akers described so well, 'We were very square, we wore the blue suits, white shirts, ties and black shoes.' In his view, that image came to stand for something, 'Our customers felt they could count on us.'

The IBM catchword of the day was THINK, and it was on every communication from the company. Our competitors came with their own version. While they're thinking, we're drinking. Touché.

In 1977, IBM South Africa celebrated its twentieth anniversary of operating in the country. The milestone was marked with a memorable cocktail party at the Carlton Hotel across the road from the IBM Centre. All spouses were invited and it was a very enjoyable event. Despite having been well watered and fed, a group of us thought we were still thirsty and needed more and repaired to Norman's Grill at the Grand Station Hotel in the suburb of Jeppe. Norman's was a very popular restaurant with plump Australian king prawns with peri-peri sauce and Irish coffees being the specialities of the house. We continued to toast IBM and just about everyone else and then hopped into the car for the drive home. Somewhat predictably, I fell asleep at the wheel and had a serious car accident. It was entirely my fault. I was very, very fortunate nobody was killed, including my wonderful wife. I landed up in court and was given a three-year suspended sentence which was a real wake-up call.

Still shaken by this accident and also the sentence, I was called in by my manager at IBM the following day. Jeez, I thought, what more could go wrong, are they going to fire me? The news, however, was good. In fact, it was better than good, it was bloody wonderful. I was offered a three-year assignment to work in Paris for IBM Europe. Was I interested? Was I what! Three years out of the country had huge appeal after the suspended sentence and of all places, in Paris. It was the stuff of dreams.

The role was an internal auditor. At my interview with Englishman Martin Jones to whom I would report, he stressed the job required 100 per cent international travel. He emphasised it really was 100 per cent travel and that I would not be spending much time in Paris. It was the nature of the job. I discussed the offer with Margie, and we had no hesitation in signing up.

We were invited by IBM for a look-see week in the City of Love and what a week it was. We settled into a lovely hotel on the Champs-Élysées near the Arc de Triomphe and had the services of a driver to help us find somewhere to live. Martin owned a late-model Porsche and on the first evening he took us for dinner at the Gare de Lyon restaurant where we feasted on rare lamb for the first time. It was magnificent. After dinner, Martin took us for a spin through the cobbled streets of Paris with me in the front and Margie curled up in what was laughingly described as the back seat. It was exhilarating.

One is often asked, where were you when this or that happened? We will never forget walking down one of the grand Parisian boulevards hand in hand and seeing a newspaper poster, *Elvis est mort*. That was 16 August 1977.

We had both had previous fleeting visits to Paris but this was different and we had time to enjoy observing how the Parisians lived. We were captivated by the cafés which have existed since the 17th century and serve as a meeting place and somewhere to relax or to refuel. They are not your local Starbucks but rather offer a restaurant menu with meals for any time of the day. Often, we would enter a dimly lit café and be assailed by the smells of the locals smoking Gauloise or Gitane cigarettes, but also by the strong, almost hypnotic coffee aroma and the dulcet tones of Edith Piaf, the Little Sparrow, playing quietly in the background and Le Patron and the waiting staff in their white, starched aprons and the locals who always greet each other by shaking hands or with a peck on each cheek. In the early mornings for the shift workers on their way home, the first stop was to the local neighbourhood café where, after a cheerful 'bonjour madame et monsieur' greeting, the order may be 'un demi biere' or 'une pression' and occasionally 'un pastis' and 'un espresso'. We found out early that drinking at the bar is cheaper than doing so at one of the tables requiring service. The entire experience could only be described as magical and exhilarating.

We were given a generous allowance to cover our rent and we inspected several places before deciding on a modern and spacious fourth-floor apartment in the Paris suburb of St Cloud overlooking the Seine River, the Bois de Boulogne, the Arc de Triomphe and the Eiffel Tower. Beat that. Our settling-in allowance enabled us to tastefully furnish the apartment and also to buy a new car. We both enjoyed the unusual experience of spending 'other people's' money, and eventually settled on a Peugeot 304. Then the challenges started. In the mid-19th century, Baron Haussmann set out to make Paris the grandest city in Europe. The twelve arterials radiating from the Arc de Triomphe were part of his master plan. The creation of a series of major boulevards, intersecting at diagonals with monuments such as the Arc de Triomphe as centrepieces. Clearly the Baron did not anticipate the popularity of the automobile. We were warned by the Peugeot salesman, 'Allo, if there is an accident, each driver is considered equally at fault. This is the only place in Paris where the accidents are not judged. No matter what the circumstances, insurance companies split the costs fifty/fifty.' He sniffily added, 'In Paree, a good driver gets only scratches, not dents.' Thanks for that.

The Peugeot showroom was on the Champs-Élysées and since I was overseas, Margie had to collect our brand-new, left-hand-drive treasure and drive it home. Getting out of the showroom was a piece of cake but she then had to join the twelve lanes of traffic around Place de l'Étoile and edge her way to the Bois de Boulogne exit. In the words of American travel writer, Rick Steves, 'My car plunges into the grand traffic circle where a dozen boulevards converge on this mightiest of triumphal arches. Like referees at gladiator camp, traffic cops are stationed at each entrance to this traffic circus, letting in bursts of eager cars.' Being immersed in this crazy traffic boiling pot made Margie giggle.

Cars entering the circle have the right of way. Those already in the circle must yield. Parisian drivers navigate the circle like a comet circling the sun making a parabola. They drive so fast and with such confidence it's a game of chicken, and he or she who hesitates is definitely lost. Margie could see herself in that maelstrom until midnight. Eventually, after much hooting, yelling, finger-lifting and pointing, she burst through the pack onto the serene Avenue Foch heading for home. We would later take our overseas guests for a spin around what must be the fastest and most exciting merry-go-round on earth.

During our stay we obviously had lots of friends and family to visit, and on one occasion Margie's parents Ann and Owen spent a week with us. Accompanying them were their great friends from Brisbane, Dawn and Henry Kingston. Henry was a hoot. He had the loudest voice of anyone I have ever met. This was their first trip out of Australia and they were buzzing when we collected them from the airport and took them to Chez Dearlove in St Cloud. The next morning was clear and warm and Henry went out on the balcony to admire the view which we thought was pretty special. The next thing we heard this hellishly loud Australian-accented voice trumpeting, 'Hey Margaret, what's that creek over there?' I just hoped there weren't any locals within a 10 kilometre radius who could understand English. They would have been mortified at their mighty La Seine being referred to as a creek.

When Martin Jones had said the job was 100 per cent travel he was not exaggerating. I would leave home on Sunday night or if I was lucky, Monday morning, and travel to whichever IBM country where we were conducting an internal audit. On Fridays we were not permitted to leave for the airport for home before 1 pm. Everyone knows the difficulties of travelling on Friday afternoons and Paris Charles de Gaulle airport was no exception. I soon learned the French definition of a queue. There is no such thing. Look straight ahead and push.

Margie must have been lonely in Paris and to help fill the time between museums and art galleries she taught at the American School which was conveniently located in St Cloud, the same suburb as we lived. Now that was an experience. Being used to fairly conservative school environments in both Australia and South Africa, the Parisian students were significantly less formal and much more relaxed.

My audit territory was essentially Western Europe so the UK, Spain, Portugal, Germany, France, Switzerland, Austria, Belgium, Italy, the Netherlands and Scandinavia. Because I travelled on a South African passport, I was not welcome in any Eastern Bloc, Middle Eastern or African countries. The one notable exception was Israel. All this travel may sound terribly exciting, and most of it was, however the endless queues, delayed flights and irritable and voluble French taxi drivers all took their toll. A huge plus was I had the choice of travelling back to Paris each weekend or Margie could join me wherever I was working. The result was we travelled extensively and had a wonderful time.

During our three-year assignment in Paris, exercise was hard to come by. I travelled internationally every week and weekends were spent with Margie, us often being tourists in our hometown. Being a cricket tragic, I was always on the lookout for a game. I worked with a fellow from the Netherlands who introduced me to the Standard Athletic Club situated on the outskirts of Paris in the Meudon Forest.

The club was founded in 1890 and in its early days was a loose association of young Brits who wanted to play sport together. It gradually grew to a size where playing fields were required and in 1922 the historic decision to ensure a permanent home for the club led to the purchase of the scenic grounds in the Forêt de Meudon. During World War II the club was taken over by the Nazis and used as a radar jamming station. Just prior to the liberation of Paris in 1944 the entire top storey was blown up.

The club has an illustrious sporting past, supplying most of the French team who played the only cricket match ever to be held in an Olympiad at the Paris 1900 Olympic Games.

59

Playing for and at the club was probably some of the most enjoyable cricket I've ever played. Being the oldest cricket club in France it attracted cricketers from all over the Commonwealth and Europe. Thanks to apartheid, I had never played with or against Indians, Pakistanis or West Indians. It was so refreshing to have the opportunity. The multitude of nations and languages resulted in more than the occasional mishaps in running between wickets resulting in the oft heard yes, no, wait, sorry calls.

Everyone enjoys a visit to Paris so we regularly played against touring sides such as the Diplomats from the Foreign Office, the Lords Taverners, Lloyds of London, the Australian Embassy, the British Law Society and the Gents of Hampstead.

The 1978 club autumn newsletter records that against Geneva Cricket Club, established in 1872, leg-spinner Ray Dearlove excelled with 7/69 and he will remind cricket connoisseurs of the great Doug Wright who *Wisden* rated as the finest English leg-spinner, perhaps the most dangerous of all English bowlers, in the years just before and after the war. High praise indeed, or maybe he didn't know much about cricket.

Because the audit team covered so many diverse countries, each with its own language, IBM team members were recruited from different countries. We had Germans, a Spaniard, Brits, the occasional American, a Swede, a Frenchman, a chap from Lebanon, the lot. The common bond was everyone spoke English. We had one fellow from the Netherlands, Wencel Welling, who could fluently speak eight languages – Dutch, Flemish, French, English, Spanish, Portuguese, German and Italian. Maurice Karam, from Lebanon, spoke French, English, Arabic, Italian and Spanish. It was amazing to hear these guys effortlessly switch languages. I added just a wee bit of value since I am fluent in Afrikaans, and could easily understand Dutch and get by in German. The American, Tom Lawler, made no attempt to speak anything but American English. Now there's a surprise.

Because I travelled so much, my French was only just passable. Margie became fluent in no time at all, partly because IBM generously covered the cost of French classes and partly through sheer necessity. It was the only way she could make herself understood when shopping or elsewhere. Pointing could only get her so far. Her learning circle had an interesting approach. The group consisted of multiple nationalities wanting to learn French, and another group of French ladies who wanted to speak or improve their English. The first hour would be a lesson in French, and the second hour the conversation was strictly in English and the last hour only in French. It was a novel and highly successful approach. This was very different from our bachelor friend Gerry Smit who claimed to have learned his very good French 'on ze pillow'.

We had some interesting experiences within the audit team. On one occasion we were doing an audit of IBM Germany headquarters in Stuttgart and it was a big one. We had discovered what seemed to be fairly serious 'anomalies' which really annoyed the responsible German manager. He demanded we 'prove' it. This was at about 9 pm. We hadn't had any dinner and had been working to a gruelling schedule. Our fellow German auditor suggested to this fellow, in German, that we should pick it up again in the morning. He was less than impressed with the request, saying, 'Zere is twenty-four hours in ze day and after that zere is ze night,' and marched out. We soldiered on and duly produced the required evidence.

The following year I led the German audit and by this time the same manager had been promoted to managing director. The standing protocol was that on the morning we arrived we would meet with the IBM leader of that country. This chap obviously remembered the earlier incident and decided to lighten the moment by asking if I knew the two biggest lies in audit? I shook my head. He triumphantly enlightened me, 'The first lie is when you say you are here to help me, and the second is when I say that I am pleased to see you!' He was highly amused at his own joke. There was a similar exchange when the managing director of IBM UK told me the definition of internal auditors was, 'Those who come in after the battle and shoot the wounded'. You can certainly tell how welcome we were when we arrived for an audit and how popular we were as we said our farewells.

Margie and I travelled a lot both before and after our son Paul was born. We spent five weeks in Tel Aviv during the IBM Israel internal audit. Our first challenge was boarding the El Al flight from Charles de Gaulle airport to Tel Aviv, bearing in mind aircraft hijackings were at their peak. We were required to be at the airport five hours before our flight to undergo security checks and had to present letters of introduction from the CEOs of both IBM Europe and IBM Israel. Even with these we were each personally questioned by a security man. It was both unnerving and assuring given the well-founded rumour there was an armed security guard on every El Al flight.

The audit was a particularly complex assignment because pretty much everything was in Hebrew. We were assigned a translator but we never knew whether the translation was in fact true to the script.

We were entranced with Israel and visited all the tourist sites including Jerusalem, Bethlehem, Nazareth, Masada, the Dead Sea, Jericho and the Sea of Galilee. We drove to the border with Lebanon and agreed it would not be a good idea to mess with the Israeli soldiers guarding that border. Having said that, the men and women in uniform all seemed so young. We had a swim in the Dead Sea. It was a very different feeling floating in what felt like a bowl of salt. We didn't spend much time in there!

There is a town in South Africa named Bethlehem and a trivia question often asked is why Jesus was born in Bethlehem in Palestine rather than in Bethlehem in the Free State in South

Africa? The story goes they couldn't find a virgin or three wise men in Bethlehem in South Africa.

On a far more serious note, as we walked the Via Dolorosa steps, visited Jerusalem and other biblical sites, irrespective of one's religious beliefs, we felt there was 'something' there. As Christians, it was uplifting.

We had some characters in the audit team. The Spaniard Alberto Ibbarondo was a walking time bomb. His very short fuse didn't make for the patience required of an auditor. He and a colleague had completed an unenjoyable audit of Zambia and were on their way home. At the airport customs desk at Lusaka, he was asked if he had any Zambian kwacha currency. He did, and was told to hand it over. Asking if he could instead spend the money at the airport, the official told him he couldn't. Alberto erupted, 'Maldito sea eso', meaning, 'Bugger that'. The volatile Alberto then proceeded to tear up the notes in front of the official. Well, all hell broke loose since defacing the head of state, President Kenneth Kaunda, was a serious crime in Zambia, as it is in most countries. Alberto was swiftly arrested, handcuffed and jailed. Because Spain had no consular representation in Zambia, it took the intervention of the United Nations to spring Alberto out of the Lusaka jail. After that, his IBM audit contribution was limited to Western Europe.

The American, Tom Lawler, fancied himself as a bit of a lady's man. He was single and very well paid in US dollars. His killer line when charming lasses from London to Lisbon to Lugarno was, 'How would you like to spend this weekend in Paris?' Irresistible.

What was so refreshing, and comforting, about being an internal auditor with IBM was no one person was exempt from scrutiny, irrespective of rank. Clearly, as an auditor, you had to be 100 per cent certain of your facts. If you were, you had the full support of management.

An audit experience which reinforced the line IBM management had drawn in the sand, in terms of ethics and the principles of good governance, took place in 1979.

In May 1968, a period of civil unrest occurred throughout France lasting some seven weeks and punctuated by demonstrations, general strikes as well as the occupation of universities and factories. At the height of events, which have since become known as May 68, the economy of France came to a halt and the protests reached such a point political leaders feared civil war or revolution. The national government briefly ceased to function after President Charles de Gaulle secretly fled France to Germany. Global organisations like IBM, which had their European headquarters in Paris, were spooked. There seemed to be a real risk the Communist Party may gain power in France.

The IBM executive moved quickly and quietly and set up an exact replica of the IBM Europe organisation in Brussels. It was simply called the IBM Office. This little-known entity could immediately take on the role of IBM's Europe, Middle East, and Africa headquarters in the event of IBM Europe having to shut down in Paris.

Ten years later I was asked to conduct what was the first-ever internal audit of the IBM Office. It was a very small organisation with approximately six staff headed by a titled English aristocrat. Given the IBM Office did not manufacture or sell anything this should have been very straightforward. I thought I would be home in a few days. This, however, was not to be. Brussels is the headquarters for the European Union or Common Market and the IBM Office managing director was perfectly suited and very comfortable in these diplomatic circles. As I probed, the pattern became clear. The main activity of the office was the seemingly endless round of parties attended and or hosted by our man. He clearly enjoyed his role because he threw a few humdingers of his own with the tipples of choice being Veuve Clicquot, Dom

Perignon and the finest French wines. Naturally, the catering was of the highest standard.

IBM at that time was a dry house. To understand why, Tom Watson Jr, son of IBM founder Thomas Watson, wrote in his autobiography, 'One day my dad went into a roadside saloon to celebrate a sale and had too much to drink. When the bar closed, he found that his entire rig – horse, buggy, and samples – had been stolen. He was fired from his job and fined for the lost property'.

Watson Sr would enforce strict rules at IBM against alcohol consumption, even off the job. According to Tom Jr, 'This anecdote never made it into IBM lore, which is too bad, because it would have helped explain Father to the tens of thousands of people who had to follow his rules'.

As IBM employees, we certainly did. I remember attending a major IBM conference in New York in 1979 and there was no alcohol served. Instead, some revolting drink called Near Beer. American food critic, Waverley Root, described Near Beer as '… such a wishy-washy, thin, ill-tasting, discouraging sort of slop that it might have been dreamed up by a Puritan Machiavelli with the intent of disgusting drinkers with genuine beer forever'. Waverley was my kind of man.

Writing up the IBM Office internal audit report was tough. The MD and his wife were lovely people and had been very welcoming and, as far as he was concerned, all of this entertainment was not only normal but actually expected on the diplomatic circuit in Brussels. I knew this practice would be considered excessive by the powers that be in IBM headquarters and I was proven correct. The MD was encouraged to return to London and the IBM Office closed.

Not surprisingly we loved Paris. In 1979 our first child Paul was born at the American Hospital in Neuilly and we made great friends such as Bruno and Anne Ganter and Donal and Mary

65

O'Shea. The only sad memory I have of those three years was that my dad died suddenly from a stroke a month after Paul's birth and he never met our son. When Dad died, I was eternally grateful I worked for an organisation like IBM because the South Africa managing director Brian Mehl could not have been more thoughtful and considerate. He swiftly arranged flights, transport and accommodation for Margie and me to attend the funeral in South Africa.

Dad's death caused me to reflect on my relationship with him. As I look back, I realise I didn't know him or my mum particularly well which is something I deeply regret. I was at boarding school from the age of eight, then to university in Pietermaritzburg, then working in Durban and Johannesburg and then living and working in Paris. During the school holidays and afterwards we would have a game of golf and a couple of beers but the conversations were at best superficial. Perhaps it was that stiff upper lip British heritage, but he would seldom, if ever, show much affection. Having said that, I would receive a letter from him most Thursdays when I was at St John's. These letters were generally more newsy than personal. I never got to ask about the six years he spent 'up north' during World War II or about his parents and brothers, how he met Mum, all really important details now gone forever. It also made me think, and it still does, was I too selfish and caught up in my own little life to explore his or my mother's lives more deeply?

When our Paris assignment ended in 1980 and we returned to Johannesburg it was a very much changed place from when we had left three years earlier.

CHAPTER 7

THE DARK SIDE OF SOUTH AFRICA

In today's society police are spat on, abused and assaulted with little respect for authority or fear of retribution. In contrast, during the 1980s police brutality was constantly in the news. I am certain I was not the only South African, white or black, who was scared of the South African Police. How things have changed.

Like every other middle-class family, we employed a gardener. His name was Johannes Ramafalo, a Zulu by birth. At our house in Woodmead we had two sets of servants' quarters and Johannes lived in one of these. It was fairly rustic with a bedroom, a toilet and a bathroom with a shower and a bath. He did odd gardening jobs around the house and did the same for several of our friends in the suburb where we lived. In 1984 and 1985, there were two incidents with Johannes which shocked and angered me and prompted me to write to the then Minister of Police Adriaan Vlok. My letter read,

'I would like to inform you of two recent incidents which occurred concerning an African man who has been known to me for the last three years. On a Saturday afternoon last month, Johannes Ramafalo was picked up in Lincoln Street in Woodmead by the Morningside police and taken to the police station. I was advised about the incident on the Monday and I phoned the station to be told that he had been taken to the Alexander Courts. It was not until the Tuesday that I managed to find him and have him released. He had been badly beaten but no charges were laid against him or fines paid.

'Last week, for no apparent reason, he was again picked up, this time in Singer Street in Woodmead, where he had been doing a gardening job, this time by the Bramley Police and taken to the Bramley station. He was again beaten and was asked if he had any money to pay the fine. He said that he had and was forced to hand over all of the money that he had which amounted to R60.00. He received no receipt and was not charged but released.

'As stated above, I have known this man for three years and in that time his behaviour has been above reproach. He is a hard-working and conscientious employee and I am extremely distressed that he has been subjected to treatment of this kind. I would be grateful if you could investigate this matter and let me know the outcome.'

I copied the station commanders of both the Bramley and the Morningside police stations.

Friends told me I was wasting my time, that I was pushing my luck and 'what was the point anyway'. I had a different view. If everyone who was touched by the strongarmed tactics of the South African Police raised their voices, somebody might listen and take action.

I mailed my letter on 3 August and received an acknowledgement on 15 August. Two weeks thereafter I was contacted by a senior police officer. The experience was unnerving because of his threatening and aggressive attitude. He told me the alleged assault was being thoroughly investigated. He insisted on speaking to me in Afrikaans. Fortunately, I am fluent in the language but I'm not sure how the conversation would have gone if I, or anyone else, was not.

A month later, I received a letter on behalf of the Minister of Law and Order, Adriaan Vlok, and signed by a Brigadier Dippenaar saying, *'The averred assault on and robbery of Mr Johannes Ramafolo had been thoroughly investigated ... and ... the South African Police have been unable to trace the assailants in either of these allegations.'*

Of course they couldn't. The poachers had turned into the gamekeepers. Then and now I had one regret, that I had not taken photos of Johannes' face when he had been hammered. Margie dressed his battered face for days. I know this was not an isolated incident. Within a decade, the Truth and Reconciliation Commission would shine a light on the brutality of the South African Police. Give a man a uniform and he will grow a metre in height.

As an aside, the same Adriaan Vlok was a member of the South African Bureau of State Security appropriately known as BOSS, which was alleged to have planned and implemented drastic repressive measures including hit squads, carrying out bombings and the assassination of anti-apartheid activists.

IBM was a model employer. At the time one of the largest corporations in the world and the leader in technology, IBM was also a pioneer in employee practices in South Africa.

In the early 1980s, the IBM Corporation in New York decided to 'force' change in the profile of the IBM South Africa workforce. The government's apartheid system classified the population as being Black, White, Indian or Coloured. Coloured referring to people of mixed race.

In truth when hiring new staff, the easiest option was to hire a white person. Why? Because their background, education and experience were easily verified and their integration into the workforce almost seamless. For Blacks, Indian and Coloured applicants it was far more difficult. As a result, very few of the latter were hired and an impatient and frustrated IBM Head Office decided to impose targets on IBM South Africa to 'encourage' change in hiring policies. The local IBM CEO Jack Clarke was given two years to have an employee profile that would include a minimum of 15 per cent 'non-whites'. A terrible expression, I know, but this was the language of the time. That 15 per cent was then split into Blacks, Indians and Coloured targets. All headcount hiring restrictions were lifted to ensure compliance and to speed up the process.

'IBM can do business in South Africa in a way that provides a model for a society in which black, white, Asian and Colored might someday enjoy peace and freedom. It may be an impossible dream. But I'm not ready to give up on it,' IBM President John Akers said in a *New York Times* article in March 1986.

As an example of this 'model', he pointed to IBM's equal-opportunity employment practices and grants for black education in South Africa. He also said IBM had a strong business interest in ending apartheid and had committed itself to actively work for change. He described IBM's primary mission in South Africa as a moral and not an economic one, saying, 'The IBM Corporation could depart with very little financial sacrifice, but we believe the right thing to do is to remain and to redouble our efforts to advance social equality.'

Jack Clarke called a meeting of all senior managers and laid down the law. 'Make it happen, or you will be asked to succeed elsewhere,' he said, puffing away at his Texan cigarette.

I was proud to do my bit and hired Nomsa Mlangeni as my secretary. Nomsa was a mature woman and on her first day, she was clearly terrified. Whichever way she looked at it she was in the minority. In time, she became a maternal figure for new black employees. A lovely lady.

A few months later, I was introduced to another recent hire, Mandla Mtsweni. A slightly built man, whose name in Zulu means strength, was impeccably dressed and in contrast to Nomsa he was quite at ease and comfortable in his own skin with an ever-present smile. In fact, I was probably more nervous than he was. With these quotas, as managers we all knew we had to make good choices in terms of hiring, but we also had a business to run.

Mandla was a star, he rapidly understood his role in the business planning department and became one of the best in my team to the extent I arranged to bring him to the attention of Roley Clark, head of personnel, as it was known then. Roley carried responsibility for ensuring the employee quota targets were met. Also, IBM had a program termed 'high potential' employees and I told Roley by any measure the dapper Mandla fitted the bill to be included in this program. The program involved fast-tracking men and women through the key areas of the business such as sales, marketing, engineering, customer service and so on into leadership positions. Roley enthusiastically agreed and started planning Mandla's program. Mandla was the first of his race to be in the program.

Everything was going swimmingly until the day Mandla did not turn up for work. This was highly unusual since he was normally first in and last out. He lived with his sister on the East Rand in a racially segregated area about 35 kilometres from IBM. This was before mobile phones and there were few landlines in the townships so communication was always difficult. At about 4 pm I had a call from Mandla's sister saying he was in hospital and their house had been fire-bombed the previous night. Apparently Mandla was asleep in his bedroom when a Molotov cocktail was thrown through the window. As he ran from the bedroom his feet and legs were badly burnt. This was serious, and IBM did everything possible to assist him through his rehabilitation.

When Mandla returned to work I asked him what had happened. He looked me in the eye and quietly and calmly confided he was a senior executive of the Pan African Conference (PAC). The PAC broke away from the ANC in 1959. Rightly or wrongly, PAC were seen as far more militant and violent than the ANC in pushing for change in South Africa. This threw me since I had always seen Mandla as a quiet, industrious fellow, not a political activist. When I asked him who had attacked him, he said, 'It's the Third Force, Ray.' I gave him a blank look. I had never heard of the Third Force. I did some research and it was reported that the South African government allegedly had a centrally directed, coherent or formally constituted 'Third Force', a network of security and ex-security force operatives, frequently acting in conjunction with right-wing elements, which was involved in actions that could be construed as fomenting violence and resulted in gross human rights violations including random and target killings. After his release, Nelson Mandela was incensed by a spate of murderous attacks on black people in areas such as the East Rand, the same area where Mandla had been attacked. These attacks, Mandela believed, bore the hallmarks of organised, covert government death squads, named the Third Force. The government denied any involvement in, or knowledge of, such an organisation.

Mandla and I didn't discuss this any further but I did brief Roley about the conversation. Like me, he had grown to like and respect Mandla but was sceptical about the existence of such an organisation.

This scepticism evaporated a few months later when, after two days of Mandla being absent from work, his sister called saying, 'Mandla has disappeared'. Naturally, she was distraught and said she had checked with the local police who had no interest in her enquiry. I told her to move out of the house and stay with family or friends but to keep me posted. I hotfooted it to Roley's office where he was meeting with CEO Jack Clarke. Jack didn't take kindly to being disturbed saying, 'This had better be good, Ray.' Hearing the news, Roley immediately picked up the phone and as Jack and I sat there, called every police station and hospital in the area. It was a case of, 'Who? Mandla who? Never heard of him'.

Jack Clarke was a fairly fiery fellow and said to Roley, 'Leave this one to me.' He then called the Minister of Police's office. The minister was none other than Adriaan Vlok, the same man with whom I had previously locked horns. Some lowly secretary lazily took a message and undertook to pass the message onto the minister. The next call Jack made was to John Akers, president of IBM in New York. At this point, I was asked to leave the room. Things moved quickly from here. The US government summonsed the South African Ambassador Johannes Beukes and told him to find Mandla, alive or dead, within forty-eight hours or the matter would be taken to the United Nations.

Miraculously and mysteriously, Mandla was found. He had been detained at the notorious John Vorster Square in Johannesburg CBD which was a detention centre for political activists. Those sent to detention were not allowed to have any contact with family members, lawyers or seek any outside help. They were cut off from the world. Detention could last for a few hours to a few months depending on the whims of the police.

Mandla was subsequently reunited with his family and returned to work a few weeks later, but he was a different Mandla. Already slim, he had lost a lot of weight. Instead of the bubbly, smiling man he was now sullen and withdrawn. He and I had a strong and easy relationship, but now he seemed to avoid me. Seemingly I was just another white man in a cruel system.

Over time, Mandla was appointed as personal assistant to IBM's country general manager. Today he runs his own successful management consultancy in Johannesburg, proving the good guys don't always finish last.

*

Each year around Christmas time, Margie and I would host my IBM team which included so-called non-whites at a braai at our home. This was illegal under the apartheid laws but that didn't deter us. We had a lot of fun and certainly got to know each other better in a relaxed social environment. It was usually a hot summer's day and after lunch and a good few beers most of us would have a swim.

One year our son Paul had just returned from school and, cozzie on, he dashed out and dived into the pool joining his siblings Kevin and Hayley and others. Joe Marulen, a Zulu man of small stature, had feasted well and was sitting on the edge of the pool dangling his feet in the water. I was in the pool keeping an eye on the children when out of the corner of my eye I noticed Joe jump in the water. I wasn't sure how well he could swim and very quickly it became obvious he couldn't. He came up gasping for air and then went down again. As he sank, I swam over, pulled him out and sat him on the side of the pool. He then threw up his lunch and several pints of alcohol and pool water. He soon recovered and, clearly embarrassed, he said, 'Jeez Ray, I saw Paul jump in and I thought it was a sooooo easy. You saved my life.' As much with relief as anything else we both had a good laugh. A few years later when Joe heard I was emigrating, he came into my office and closed the door. He said how sad he was the Dearloves were leaving South Africa and closed with the hint of a tear in his eye by saying, 'Ray, always remember that I owe you a life'. It was a totally unexpected and startling comment but stated with absolute sincerity. A good man, Joe Marulen.

As I write, today is 16 June, a date that is indelibly etched in my brain. On this day in 1976, a series of 'demonstrations' and protests led by black school children in South Africa took place in what became known as the Soweto Uprising. Students from numerous schools began to protest in the streets of Soweto in response to the government's introduction of the Afrikaans language as the compulsory medium of instruction in local schools. Afrikaans was known then, and still is, as the language of the oppressor. It is estimated that more than 20,000 students took part in the protests. They were met with fierce police brutality. The number of protesters killed by police is given as 176 but estimates of up to 700 have been made. As with the Sharpeville massacre and Steve Biko's death, 16 June became a rallying date for anti-apartheid forces and everyone was on high alert for demonstrations which often turned violent. Paul was at the local primary school in the suburb of Rivonia and come 16 June each year the parents worked shifts patrolling the school perimeter to prevent any incidents. Sadly, several parents were armed so who knows what might have happened if there were to be any such action. In remembrance of these events, 16 June is now a public holiday in South Africa, named Youth Day. On a recent trip to South Africa, I hosted a group of golfers and conservationists from Pennant Hills Golf Club on a visit to Soweto. It was an eye-opener in so many ways.

Now, so many years later, I can look back at those troubled times with more objectivity. Given the racial ingredients of so many stakeholders in the country, South Africa was sitting on a tinderbox.

Noting that these are all generalisations, I will nevertheless plough on. The whites were split into two tribes, the Afrikaners and the English. The former, by and large, extremely conservative and desperately wanting to preserve their identity, language, culture, traditions and strong religious beliefs. The English meanwhile were more liberal and felt somewhat powerless given the dominance of the apartheid enforced by the largely Afrikaans

Nationalist government which had been in power since 1948. Both tribes were skittish about what the future might hold given the poor democratic and economic success rate of recently independent countries north of the Limpopo River such as Zimbabwe, Zambia, Uganda and the Congo and also the size of the disenfranchised South African population majority.

The Indians and Coloureds were treated as different racial groups by the government and were included in the searingly cruel classification of non-whites. Indians were generally seen as quiet and just going on minding and doing their own business. Often successful small business operators, they made a significant contribution to the economy.

As British journalist Alan Cowell wrote in *The New York Times* in September 1985,

> 'To be "Coloured" is to be neither black nor white, more privileged than blacks but less privileged than whites, living a segregated life drawn from roots that deny segregation, labelled "Coloured" by the authorities, as if that denoted a homogeneous group, yet drawn from disparate roots. The label of "Coloured" is one of convenience, lumping together those who do not fit elsewhere in apartheid's great racial divisions.
>
> 'The apartheid laws went further, but in its classification of "Coloured" the law includes many subclassifications – Griquas, Cape Coloureds, Cape Malays and "other coloured" – that defy the notion of homogeneous minorities on which apartheid is based. The Cape Malays practice Islam, while many other people of mixed-race worship in a branch of the Dutch Reformed Church, initially founded by their white Afrikaner overlords to institutionalize racially segregated religion.'

The Africans, or Blacks, were numerically superior by a huge margin and were totally disenfranchised by the apartheid system. Most whites 'felt sorry' for them, but did bugger all about it and often in the same breath expressed fear if ever there was to be an uprising. The press was relatively free, but the justice system seemed to be managed and often manipulated with occasional glimpses of the application of consistent fairness, generally found in the higher courts.

The fact that the 1994 new South African constitution entrenches eleven official languages, including Afrikaans, is indicative of the complexities of these nations within a nation. The approximate percentages of the main languages are Zulu 25 per cent, Xhosa 18 per cent, Sepedi and English both 9 per cent and Afrikaans 4 per cent.

South Africa and the world owe a massive vote of thanks to Nelson Mandela for navigating so many minefields to orchestrate a peaceful transition of government in 1994. Credit must also go to President FW de Klerk whose government became one of very few to voluntarily hand over power.

Both received the Nobel Peace Prize in 1993.

CHAPTER 8

FLANNELLED FOOLS
IN AFRICA

I loved cricket from an early age. My dad was a good cricketer and he would bowl or throw balls at me for hours. We had a vacant block of land across the road from our house in Vorster Street, Pietersburg, and Dad would mow it and cut the 'pitch' even lower. My friends and I would stage test matches against traditional rivals like England and Australia at every opportunity. We allowed girls to play but they seemed to spend more time chatting than fielding, probably because they rarely had the opportunity to have a bat. My mother would bring out the homemade lemonade and ginger beer between innings. My favourite cricket book and (still) treasured possession is *The Art of Cricket* by Sir Don Bradman.

For a country primary school, the quality of sport played was very good; cricket in summer and rugby in winter. Because of Dad's coaching I was a useful cricketer and turned out for the school's First XI. I vividly remember the day when Peter Heine, one half of the feared Springbok fast bowling combination of Heine and Neil Adcock, gave a coaching clinic at the school. As you would expect, Heine was a tall man and as most fast bowlers (erroneously) do, fancied himself as a classy batsman. I had been given a brand-new bat for Christmas and, since I was the tallest boy at the clinic, he borrowed my bat to have a hit. Well, on about the third ball he took an almighty swipe with my treasured willow. The ball and the bat flew off into the bushes while he held onto the handle. I was distraught. Despite having a well-paid job with South African Breweries, there was no offer of a new bat from Heine. From that day on Neil Adcock was my favourite fast bowler. Many years later I ran into Heine at the long bar at the Wanderers Club and by this time I was as tall as him. I asked him if he remembered the incident and was mortified as he just shook his head. Despite this slap I remained an enthusiastic supporter of his employer's products.

When we moved to Messina in 1958, the love of cricket continued but with a difference. Messina is 15 kilometres from the Limpopo River, the border between South Africa and Rhodesia, as it was known then. To all intents and purposes the borders were open, and regular travellers to and from Rhodesia knew the police and customs officers so well that they were simply waved through at Beit Bridge.

As bank manager, my dad had many clients across the border and twice a year there would be cricket matches played on one of the huge farms situated along the Rhodesian side of the Limpopo. A field would be mowed, logs and rocks moved to define the boundary, the pitch would be more closely mowed and rolled. If it so happened there was a tree on the field and the ball got stuck in the tree you were given out. The father of cricket, WG Grace, would have been proud to see these men all dressed in their faded creams playing cricket in the wilds of Rhodesia. Youngsters of all ages were encouraged to play and often had three 'lives' before being given out. It was accepted that the umpires were biased, resulting in much banter as decisions were vigorously challenged and debated. After the match there was always a braai with a freshly shot kudu or impala or both, turning slowly on the spit as the beer and brandy flowed and the highlights of the day were revisited. On one occasion an inquisitive elephant showed up at deep square leg with ears flapping and noisy trumpeting as he haughtily walked on.

Much later that night we would take the hazardous gravel road back to Messina with regular encounters with a variety of antelope and the odd elephant. Once again, we would be waved through the border by a sleepy police officer. A gentler time indeed.

In 2022, Margie and I retraced our footsteps and visited Keith and Wendy Knott on their vast citrus farm on the northern banks of the Limpopo. Keith's dad Bennie had been one of my dad's clients in the 1950s and Keith and I were in the same class at school and would travel on the train from Messina back to school in Johannesburg. Keith, Wendy and their family have done an extraordinary job in building what was once desert-like wilderness into a 220,000 citrus tree farm. They export their oranges and grapefruit into Europe. They have committed to the 1000-strong workforce that whoever is born on the farm has a job for life. There is a school and a hospital and not one life was lost during the COVID-19 pandemic. There are so many negative stories about Africa, but Margie and I were stunned at the whole enterprise, it is truly inspirational and offers optimism for the future.

After school I attended the University of Natal in Pietermaritzburg, one of two campuses, the other being in Durban. Other than at inter-varsity competitions, Natal University competed as one combined team and had an extraordinarily strong side which included Clive Rice, Vince van der Bijl,

Arthur Short, Dassie Biggs, John Traicos, Mike Smithyman, Pelham Henwood and David Dyer. All of these men went on to play provincial cricket and, in my view, all of them would have played for the Springbok team had the 1970 tour of England and the 1971 tour of Australia not been cancelled because of the South African government's apartheid policies. A real tragedy for these young men caught in the crossfire of the anti-apartheid campaign. South Africa would not play a test match until 1991, meaning a whole generation of cricketers missed out representing their country. Instead, players like Tony Greig, Clive Rice, Allan Lamb and Kepler Wessels successfully plied their trade offshore.

I played a few games for Maritzburg varsity First XI, then a friend who lived in the Natal Midlands asked if I could raise a social side to play against the Richmond XI. Richmond was a pleasant farming village about 75 kilometres from Maritzburg. I agreed and had no shortage of willing starters but certainly a shortage of (reliable) cars.

My mum's nest egg had come in handy when I wanted to buy my first car. It was a second- or maybe third- even possibly fourth-hand Ford Anglia and cost the princely sum of Rands200, and Mum paid for it. I can't remember but I hope I paid her back.

Over time, 'Ray's chariot' would become quite famous because the floor of the passenger seat was completely rusted and one had to tread very carefully as you entered or exited the vehicle on that side. Winter was a real problem since air-conditioning was unheard of and the cold air would sweep through the little car from the gaping hole. Girlfriends came and went but winter snuggling in the Anglia was in short supply. A passion wagon it was not.

So, we took off in our collection of old and dented cars, girlfriends on board, to take on the might of the Midlands. We had a marvellous day. It was village cricket at its best. Good quality players, relatively unbiased umpires, beer on tap and the hospitality and catering expertise of the farmers' wives. Although we won the match, the locals had such a wonderful time they invited us back for the return match the following Sunday. We obviously obliged.

The news of success and the social skills of our team spread far and wide to the point we were invited to play a few games in Rhodesia. There were many Rhodesians studying at Pietermaritzburg University at the time, many of whom were in the agricultural faculty, and most played cricket.

So once again this merry band of keen cricketers, this time without girlfriends, headed off to play our first game in Bulawayo, 1500 kilometres away. The quality and reliability of the cars continued to be highly questionable. My vintage Anglia was really put through its paces on this trip and I seemed to spend as much time under the bonnet as behind the wheel.

The convoy eventually rolled into Bulawayo where we were met by our hosts at the Bulawayo Athletic Club which was founded in 1894 and dated back to colonial days. It is in many ways the spiritual home of Rhodesian cricket. Rhodesians have a well-deserved reputation as being extremely hospitable people and our welcome matched that reputation. We were billeted out but before we went to our hosts' homes, we had to enjoy a few lagers and the inevitable braai. Knowing casinos were illegal in South Africa, the club had put on a special casino night for us. I spent more time under the tables collecting the money being dropped by the punters than actually betting.

I was captain for the game the following day and at about 11 pm one of my teammates whispered to me, 'Do you think that they are getting us pissed so that it will affect our performance tomorrow?' They needn't have worried. The club had been under the impression a full-strength Natal University side was touring with all the big names mentioned earlier. Given this, they chose their strongest side including Joe Partridge and Tony Pithey who until recently had represented the Springboks. I recall we chased leather for several hours and then had to contend with bespectacled Joe Partridge showing us no mercy with his lethal swing bowling. We batted twice and then headed back to the pub licking our wounds.

During the match there was a young woman who spent hours practising her tennis against the wall. She was obviously a player with much potential. When we asked about her, we were told she was Pat Walkden, who would go on to be one of Southern Africa's finest players. Practice makes perfect.

We then drove the 500 kilometres to Salisbury, where we scraped a win against Salisbury Sports Club and then set off for Wankie, now Hwange, 650 kilometres 'up the road'. Wankie was known for its coal mines and the world-famous game reserve. My co-captain, Glyn Evans, gave me the day off so the night before the match was even merrier than usual. I was billeted with Mick the Wankie captain who was also the local bank manager. He lived on a sprawling estate with ancient Mukamba trees, beautiful gardens and rolling manicured kikuyu lawns. On the morning of the match, Mick left me in the care of the house boy, who turned out to be a distinguished looking man in his sixties. 'Moses will look after you, I'm afraid we don't have a shower but if you have a bath just sing out to Moses and he'll bring you a beer.' This was at 9 am. Sure enough, as I settled into a steaming hot bath the phone rang. It was Mick, 'Good news, man, we are playing twelve a side. I'm sending someone to pick you up now.' Bugger.

Driving in Rhodesia had its challenges since most of the roads outside of the main centres were two strips of tar and a 'middelmannetjie' (the ridge between the strips). By and large people were courteous, but every now and then one would come across a driver who was either bloody rude or was in the mood for a game of 'chicken'. That game generally ended badly.

I had long had a love for Rhodesia but as time wore on and

independence loomed the pessimistic hardcore Rhodesians' catchcry was, 'Come to Rhodesia now and see the Zimbabwe ruins and next year come to Zimbabwe and see the Rhodesian ruins'.

When I returned to Johannesburg after my Durban adventures, I joined the Old Johannian Club which was originally only open to those who had attended St John's College, but subsequently became an open club. It was a beautiful place with a large clubhouse, several squash and tennis courts and two ovals which were used for cricket in summer and hockey in winter. It had two bowling greens and an Olympic-size swimming pool. It was a very social club and with the range of facilities available it had a wide spectrum of membership of both men and women. Apart from bowls, I played all the above-mentioned sports and made lifelong friendships. The club was very strong and produced several players who represented their country at different sports.

After the cancellation of the England and Australia cricket tours in 1970–71, South African cricket fell into a slump. It became increasingly obvious it was going to be a long time before we were readmitted into the international cricket family. Outstanding cricketers such as Clive Rice, Barry Richards, Mike Proctor and Garth le Roux joined overseas teams and competitions such as World Series Cricket. Others such as Arthur Short simply returned to build their careers outside of cricket.

Inter- and intra-company cricket matches were very popular in the 70s, and with my love of cricket I was often in the vanguard of organising these matches. One year, the IBM Durban branch manager challenged our head office to a match on their home turf. For us, raising a side was not a problem – who could turn up an opportunity for a weekend in Durban. So, the train tickets were bought and the team assembled at the (then) imposing Johannesburg Park Station, well stocked with the necessary provisions. By about four hours out of Johannesburg, the carriages were quite merry. Margie had never been to Durban so she was invited along as 'scorer'. She seemed still to be oblivious that I had fallen for her. We were on an 'all stops' train and at Standerton as we were playing a noisy game of cards, the windows all open, a cushion came flying through the window hitting one of our players on the head. There were not your soft cushion/pillows but hard and heavy – the green ones known to millions of South African train travellers. Well, two of us thought that this wasn't quite cricket and looking out the window noticed two railway guards walking away cackling with laughter, so we alighted from said train and approached these two, enquiring why they had thought fit to stuff up our game of poker with a dangerous missile? They laughed with a 'what are you going to do about it?' and one feinted a punch at me. I retaliated with one of my best, only for him to duck, and I hit the very sturdy train carriage behind him. More laughter as I withdrew trying not to show my now aching bowling hand.

There was some (but not much) sympathy from my teammates (who knew that I determined the batting order). At the next stop at Volksrust, we had some unwelcome visitors to our compartment being the railway police. These burly, unsmiling fellows found nothing amusing about the incident and marched off muttering all sorts of threats.

After not much sleep we arrived in Durban and set off for the field. One of the Durban player's wives was a doctor and her immediate diagnosis was two broken fingers of my now very swollen bowling hand. We were a bit thin on the ground with bowlers so I had to do my bit. Try bowling leg-spinners with two broken fingers. We lost the match (with our scorer being less than impressed) but we won the dancing and drinking competitions at the after-match party at Jack Quayle's lovely home.

Then back to Johannesburg to see my doctor who took some

convincing that I had sustained the injury by hitting a South African Railways train.

The Old Johannian Club was very much in the British tradition. If one did a poll of those who supported the Nationalist 'apartheid' government it is unlikely it would exceed 5 per cent. As a general rule, if you were Afrikaans you would support the government, while if you were English you would support any party in opposition to the government. If you were classified as 'non-white' being Black, Indian or Coloured, you had no vote at all.

Cricket administrators such as Joe Pamensky, Dr Ali Bacher and Don Mackay-Coghill worked very hard to 'normalise' cricket in South Africa. They tried uniting the various bodies running the game for Whites, Blacks, Indians and so on. This was no simple task given that within each of these national organisations there were autonomous provincial associations. There were many false starts, but eventually in 1976 with the support of Rashid Varachia, head of the South African Indian Cricket Board, it was announced that in the Transvaal province the two bodies would merge.

This opened up a whole new world. I was captain of the Old Johannian Second XI and we were chosen as the first all-white team to play a match in Lenasia against the local Indian side from the Kohinoor Club. Lenasia, near the Lenz Military Base, had been created by apartheid-era planners as a suburb designated only for Johannesburg's Indians. The name 'Lenasia' is thought to be a combination of the words 'Lenz' and 'Asia'. The Lenz in question was Captain Lenz who owned the original plot on which Lenasia is situated. The 'Asia' seemed to be a condescending nod to the origins of the residents who, in many cases, had left India one hundred years and more before. Many of Lenasia's early residents had been forcibly removed under the detested Group Areas Act from suburbs such as Pageview and Fordsburg, formerly non-racial areas close to the Johannesburg city centre. As segregation was increasingly enforced it became the largest township where people of Indian extraction could legally live in the Transvaal.

We were all aware of the historic nature of this match and, in truth, we approached it with some trepidation. The reader may find it extraordinary that none of us had ever been to Lenasia before although it was only about 30 kilometres west of Johannesburg. Following directions, we drove through the township and were surprised at the size and quality of many of the homes and gardens. This was certainly nothing like the black township of Soweto. We, in turn, were subjected to looks of surprise from residents as we made our way to the ground.

Arriving at the oval on which we were due to play, it was not what we were used to. We stood and stared at each other.

To explain, let me describe a match at our home ground at Old Johnnies. The oval is surrounded by magnificent gum trees and encircled with a gleaming white picket fence and tiered seating is available for spectators. We arrive ready for a 10 am start, with girlfriends, wives and children joining us later at the swimming pool. We might have a chat to Koos the groundsman about how the pitch might play later in the day. Decked out in our creams and club caps, the two captains walk out to the pitch dressed in their blazers for the toss. After shaking hands, we head to our changeroom and the visitors to theirs. The smartly dressed umpires in dark pants, three-quarter white jackets and ties then lead the fielding side out. At 1 pm, the umpires lift the bails and we all adjourn up the hill past the pristine gardens and lawns for lunch, all clad in our often-gaudy blazers. Lunch is a sit-down affair served by waiters in their purple jackets and smart black trousers. And ties. A few hardy souls will have a few beers which is frowned upon by their teammates. After all this is a serious game of cricket. The match resumes at 1.40 pm with stumps declared at 6 pm. We then have a nice hot shower and head off to the clubhouse for drinks. All very civilised in the British and colonial tradition.

At Lenasia, there was no clubhouse. We changed in our cars. We were quite concerned about security but we locked our cars. We had left our wives, girlfriends and children at home. Nevertheless, the match commenced on the dot of 10 am and was played in excellent spirits. We had no idea of the quality of their competition and we played our strongest side. Everyone wanted to play this match. Lenasia fielded first and their players were good. Very good. As you would expect they had two bowlers, one no more than fifteen years old, who were outstanding wrist spinners.

We hadn't been told to bring our lunch so as 1 pm edged closer we wondered what lay in store for us hungry athletes. It was actually very simple. We were paired with their players and drove to their homes for lunch. As captain, good friend Peter Auld and I were hosted by their captain. We entered his lovely home, took off our shoes and were seated on the carpet at a table that had warm naan bread, all sorts of spices, rich sauces and homemade lemonade. The captain introduced us to his wife, a very attractive woman dressed in a traditional sari, who glided in and out of the room with the plentiful food. I sensed that they were as excited as we were. It was a very hot November day and the lemonade was very welcome. What was not so welcome was the hellishly hot curry we were served. At the best of times, I am not too good with spicy food and soon my nose was running, my eyes were watering and my scalp itching. We had previously researched as many protocols as we could and learned that when eating you always use your right hand. Even if you are left-handed, you must use your right hand for eating since Indians consider the use of the left hand to be unclean and offensive. I'm pretty sure my fingers were burning as much as my mouth was.

It was a long afternoon in the field for us and one or two of the lads made it to the portable loo, but only just. There was relief when a typical highveld storm struck and the game was called off with the spoils shared. Very few of the Indian team drank alcohol but they were charming hosts and brought along a cooler box of beer. Photographs were taken and undertakings made to have a return fixture at the Old Johannian Club.

Soon after this ground-breaking match I approached Joe Pamensky, president of the South African Cricket Association, about recruiting an overseas professional player of colour to join our club for a season in defiance of the apartheid laws in force at the time. I had made some enquiries about Vanburn Holder, the former Barbadian cricketer who played forty tests and twelve One Day Internationals (ODI) for the West Indies from 1969 to 1979. He had an excellent reputation in county cricket, playing for Worcester. My thought was to employ him as a player and coach. I had sponsors lined up who loved the idea. Joe Pamensky was an excellent leader and said he would come back to me. A week later he called me to say Minister for Sport, Piet Koornhof, had approved the approach but there was to be no media coverage until the deal was done. Negotiations were well advanced and terms agreed but then Holder withdrew. His partner was white and they were nervous about how they would be treated in apartheid South Africa. I understood completely.

Richard Lumb, the prolific Yorkshire batsman who had opened the batting with Geoff Boycott, joined us that season and was a great addition to the club. Richard later settled in South Africa and years later his son Michael represented England.

A few years later in 1981, West Indian great Alvin Kallicharan who had played sixty-six tests was invited to play in South Africa by Joe. Perhaps because of our Vanburn Holder efforts, or perhaps because we were seen as the most liberal club in Johannesburg, Kalli joined Old Johnnies. One of my greatest memories was watching Graeme Pollock and Kalli two of world cricket's greatest left-handers, tearing a quality provincial attack apart at the Wanderers 'bullring' in Johannesburg. The word would spread into offices that Graeme or Barry Richards were batting and there would be an exit of cricket lovers to the Wanderers or Kingsmead. Sir Donald Bradman named Pollock as the greatest left-handed batsman he had ever seen while as an overseas player for South Australia, Richards scored 325 runs in a single day against Western Australia off an attack that included Dennis Lillee, Graham McKenzie and Tony Lock.

Kalli subsequently led the West Indies unsanctioned 'rebel' tour of South Africa in 1982. It was wonderful for the sports-mad South African public, but proved disastrous for the West Indian players who were banned from cricket and ostracised at home. The rebel tours and the aftermath have recently been superbly chronicled by friend Ashley Gray in his book *The Unforgiven*, published in 2020.

At the end of each season, the Old Johnnies Club have an awards dinner. It is a formal, stag affair generally joined by a well-known guest speaker. Our members keenly felt the cricket isolation and all we wanted was to see and play against cricketers from other countries. So, when it came to the annual dinner, we usually pushed the envelope by inviting controversial identities to be the keynote speaker. One such person was Abie Williams, a coloured man, who had been assistant manager of the ill-fated 1981 Springbok rugby tour to New Zealand. Williams truly was a change agent and he delivered his message at every opportunity.

In apartheid South Africa, it was illegal for any Black, Indian or Coloured people to be in a white residential area, particularly after dark. We chose to ignore that law and Abie was very happy to be invited to be the guest speaker. We covered ourselves to a degree by inviting some of Transvaal's cricket bigwigs and a member of the English-speaking media to the dinner. To this day, I can remember the passion, emotion and hurt with which

Abie spoke. The usually noisy audience was silent. Silent and embarrassed.

The following morning, *The Johannesburg Star* newspaper reported, 'Mr Williams received a standing ovation when he said, "If we can play sport together, fight together and die together, why can't we live together?"'

After the dinner we farewelled Abie as he drove alone to his home in an apartheid designated suburb as defined by the despised Group Areas Act. I don't even want to contemplate what he was thinking as he glanced at us through his rear-vision mirror.

The Old Johannian Club's strong anti-apartheid stance was probably also the reason we were asked to host a braai during the even more controversial Arosa Sri Lankan Tour in 1982. Another example of Joe Pamensky, Ali Bacher and Don Mackay-Coghill doing their best to keep the game of cricket alive in South Africa.

Late one night in September 1982, South African lawyer Colin Rushmere flew into Colombo, Sri Lanka. His most important luggage item was a briefcase, his constant companion. In the bottom of it, disguised by other things, were fourteen contracts. He was in Sri Lanka to have them signed through Tony Opatha, a former Sri Lankan cricketer, who was arranging the 'rebel' tour of the Republic from their side.

All the clandestine manoeuvring had started a couple of months before when Ali Bacher and Geoff Dakin, the chief executive and president respectively of the South African Cricket Union, were in London and arranged to meet Opatha. Negotiations commenced and Opatha asked for $US30,000 per player. Ali then said, 'You think we have that sort of cash. You must be in cuckoo land.' Opatha's quick-fire response was, 'So tell me, Ali, how many cuckoos are there to the dollar?'

A deal was struck and although Sri Lanka had previously played only one official test losing by seven wickets to England in Colombo that result or the quality of the team didn't appear to be overly significant to either Opatha or the South Africans. Carrying far more heft was the fact the Sri Lankans were a non-white team playing against apartheid-era white opposition. By their standards they were going to be handsomely paid and sure enough, a few months later a group of tourists from Colombo arrived at Jan Smuts airport. The tourists were shadowed by one Piet Kellermann, a South African government representative who saw to it there were no official incidents. The tourists were described as 'charming ambassadors' but were required to toe the petty apartheid line. There was to be little venturing outside of their hotels or 'see-for-themselves' furloughs. Seeing South Africa's darker side soon faded into insignificance as the tourists realised they had a looming crisis of credibility on the field. Although they held out for an early draw against a gun Western Province side, they lost their opening match to a Transvaal Invitation XI. The wide strength of South African cricket was confirmed after the first ODI where they could only patch together 102 in reply to South Africa's 291 for four, losing by 189 runs.

While South African cricket was formidably powerful at the time, it was also in the midst of a prolonged changing of the guard. Senior statesmen like Graeme Pollock, Barry Richards and Vince van der Bijl in their mid- to late-thirties were being gently challenged by a younger generation of players like Peter Kirsten, Stephen Jefferies and Lawrence Seeff. The elbowing for places made for a mutually watchful, competitive environment within the South African squad. Internal competition plus local hunger equalled abject Sri Lankan misery. On their fourteen-match tour they didn't win a game, frequently losing by an innings. In the second test, Seeff and Jimmy Cook both plundered centuries in an opening stand of 250 and Pollock scythed his way to 197 before Kirsten declared.

It had been suggested the Sri Lankans helped pave the way for the West Indies rebels of the future, demonstrating it was possible for a non-white team to tour the Republic without incident or undue hindrance. Most pundits doubt this was the case pointing out the tour was 'a flop' simply because the tourists were missing some of their best players. In addition, Sri Lanka certainly wasn't the cricket powerhouse it is today, in fact most of the South African supporters were not even aware the Sri Lankans played cricket and Ceylon was probably a better-known name than Sri Lanka. The conditions in which they lived and travelled in the Republic were often artificial and the hidden emotional costs of the tour profound. The reception faced when the Sri Lankans returned home was vitriolic and all fourteen players were given life bans by the Sri Lankan board, a setback the fledgling cricket power could ill afford.

Former Transvaal captain and administrator Don Mackay Coghill is a good friend who now lives in Perth. I asked him for his recollections of the Sri Lankan tour and perspective about the rebel tours.

'I remember the tour only too well because it was the last game of cricket I played. They started the tour with a warm-up game against the Nicky Oppenheimer XI and in the act of delivering my first ball my big toenail flipped back and I just kept running on to the change room. That was the end of the game for me. An ignominious end to a career if ever there was one!

'At the time I was all in favour of rebel tours for a number of reasons, "To maintain the public interest in cricket, to provide our top players with some form of international competition and as a break from what we thought at the time was the tedium of Currie Cup, and, perhaps most important of all, to try and encourage our top players to remain in the country". In fact, together with Ali Bacher and Joe Pamensky, I was also instrumental in negotiating the two Kim Hughes rebel tours. Ali was in Singapore staying at the same hotel as the Australian team which was on its way back to Australia from England, while Joe and I were on the telephone to him from Joe's office in the old Stock Exchange building on Hollard Street. It was a fascinating negotiation exercise.

'Having had time to reflect and with the benefit of hindsight I think we erred in bringing rebel tours to South Africa. The penalties handed out by the respective cricket boards to the rebel players were extremely harsh and we certainly didn't do ourselves any favours with the South African Cricket Board of Control (SACBOC) which was the body running non-white cricket in South Africa at the time. Furthermore, the standard of cricket in the Currie Cup competition at the time was extremely high with sell-out crowds over the traditional Boxing Day game against Natal at the Wanderers and against Western Province at Newlands over New Year. In fact, many more people watched Currie Cup cricket in those days than now watch Test match cricket in South Africa.'

The braai we organised at Old Johnnies in the Sri Lankans' honour was awkward in so many ways. Very few of them could speak much English and unlike their South African hosts didn't eat much meat. The main ingredient at a braai is meat, meat and more meat. I asked Gavin Bazley who succeeded me as chairman of the Old Johannian cricket club for his thoughts about the braai.

'I recall the braai quite well and remember the Sri Lankans to be almost timid in their social interaction, I suspect partly because of the language barrier but also because they were overawed at their grand treatment in South Africa.

'Ali Bacher always contended that the tour was for the cricketing benefit and upliftment of the Sri Lankans, personally, I'm not so sure.'

In October 1981, I reached out to Austin 'Ocker' Robertson who was Dennis Lillee's manager to enquire if Lillee would have any interest in spending a season playing for Old Johannians. International cricket was in turmoil after the launch of World

Series Cricket by Kerry Packer in 1977 and with that cricket was forever changed. Packer signed up the best cricketers in the world, including South Africans, and as far as I was concerned all bets were off. Anything was possible and Lillee was a massive drawcard wherever he played. I had sponsors queuing up to be involved.

My discussions with Robertson were cordial and he said he would have a chat to Lillee. From who knows where, the London *Sunday Telegraph* picked up the story on 8 November 1981. When Lillee was questioned, he denied any contact had been made and said, 'Somebody is just flying a kite'. This really pissed me off since my name was mentioned in the article. A week later in the *West Australian* newspaper the headline read, 'Lillee admits he had an offer'.

All hell broke loose slap bang in the middle of the world's sport ban on any contact with South Africa. The *Australian Cricket* newspaper claiming to be the world's first cricket publication headlined what it termed a World Exclusive, 'LILLEE MAY QUIT FOR JO'BURG'. Australian journalist Marshal Wilson wrote that Dennis Lillee could be lost to Australian cricket at the end of his 1981–82 benefit season.

My phone was running hot. Dennis Lillee was arguably the best bowler in the world and unquestionably one of the big characters in the game, and the possibility he may play in South Africa was big news. The South African Cricket Union was fully supportive but kept a low profile since this was an invitation from a club rather than from the administration. I did my best to play down expectations but also to keep the matter open. There were a few howlers in the media including a story that Old Johannians had Lillee under an exclusive contract. I wish. Interestingly this claim came from an Australian journalist.

Finally, on 8 December 1981, to bring the matter to a head, I wrote to Dennis. A certain Perth journalist was very helpful and gave me his home address. The letter provided some background about the Old Johannian Club and spelt out that we were prepared to offer airfares from Perth to Johannesburg for him and his family, accommodation and a car. With regard to money, I left it open for him to let us know what he would expect to be paid. As mentioned above, there was no shortage of potential sponsors.

No email then, so I had to rely on the postal service to deliver the letter. In the interim I decided to not contact either Lillee or Robertson. Franky, I thought by now the chances of getting him to South Africa were very slim indeed but where there is life, there is hope.

Eventually, I received a letter from Dennis Lillee in which he politely declined the offer citing the importance of the upcoming Ashes series. I wrote back wishing him well and noting ours was an open offer. Nothing ventured, nothing gained.

Within three years Kim Hughes would lead an Australian side on what was termed 'rebel' tours which included ten current Australian test cricketers (but not DK Lillee). While South Africa won both series, the International Cricket Council did not acknowledge the matches of being worthy of 'test match' status and it was only several years later in 1991 that the country was readmitted to the test playing brotherhood. South Africa had last played Australia led by Bill Lawry in 1970 and really put them to the sword by winning the series four-nil.

When South Africa next played and toured Australia in 1993, some wag had a very large banner at the Sydney Cricket Ground which read, *Welcome Springboks, unbeaten since 1970.* Half of the crowd loved it.

CHAPTER 9

EMIGRATION

Let me assure you, moving countries is not for the fainthearted. In the 1980s when the Australian dollar and South African rand were almost at par, the South African government introduced the 'financial rand' system which provided for two exchange rates for the rand. One for current account transactions and one for capital account transactions for non-residents. Limitations were placed on the convertibility of financial rand into foreign currencies. This meant you could only transfer a limited amount of money out of South Africa and what you could transfer was at a dreadful exchange rate. The system was highly successful as a deterrent. Once we had made the decision to emigrate it was not worthwhile to transfer money at this rate and we, like many others, tried to devise ways of getting money out of the country. The one-ounce gold Krugerrand coin minted in South Africa was a favourite among emigrants. Legend has it that all sorts of ingenious ways of secreting these coins were applied, including stashed away in works of art, furniture and even in a private yacht which sailed from Cape Town to Sydney.

Separately, immigrants to Australia were permitted to import a container of furniture and a car provided we owned it for a year in South Africa and then kept it for a year in Australia. With this, and given the penurious exchange rate, we did not have much 'wealth' when we arrived in Sydney as I approached the dreaded age of forty with a wife and three young children.

In April 1987, three months after we arrived in Sydney I wrote to South African friends. Reading some of these notes more than thirty years later is quite stark and revealing. Here are a few examples.

> 'The day we arrived, we moved into a rented house in Normanhurst, a suburb about 25 kilometres from the Sydney CBD. The house is built from a wooden structure, with brick exterior and what is called gyprock for the inner walls – they call it brick veneer.'

Most houses in South Africa were built of double brick. South Africans searching for a home in Australia were named 'The Knockers' by real estate agents because the moment they walked into a house they would knock on the walls to check if it was brick. I still do it today.

I went on, 'Our lease expires at the end of May. We have taken a very deep breath and decided to buy a house. The mortgage rates are a frightening 16 per cent and inflation is 9 per cent. Needless to say, Margie is looking for a job.'

Our primary reason for leaving South Africa with all its problems was to try to ensure a future with some certainty and security for our children. Margie and I had agreed we would give them the best education possible at whatever personal cost. Paul and Kevin started at Newington College, a private primary school, and both fitted in well. They excelled at sport and did particularly well at the first swimming gala or carnival, as it is called in Australia. After winning all his six races Paul, all of eight years of age, said to me he hadn't realised he was so fast back in

South Africa. I remained silent. He then said, 'Maybe the boys here are slower than in SA.' The innocence of youth. We put Hayley, aged two, into childcare. I hated doing this but we had no option and no money!

Margie's parents must have had some talented genes. Not only was her dad an Australian boxing champion, but three of their grandchildren represented Australia. Our niece Kerri Kinnane wore the green and gold as a sprinter and our sons Kevin and Paul at rugby, Australian Schools and Under 21s respectively. Paul also had a game for Scotland. The tradition continues with Kerri's son Hayden, representing Australia Under 21 at hockey. A talented family with an extremely strong bloodline. I married well.

I wrote about my job at IBM, 'IBM Australia has 3700 employees and turns over AUD1.1B. Contrary to general belief outside of Australia, they work bloody hard. It is a complete myth that all Australians are lazy and would prefer to be on the dole and on the beach.'

We loved Sydney from the start, and I commented, 'The beaches are magnificent and we have been to the beach most weekends.'

I finished by saying, 'Needless to say, there are many things that we miss very deeply. People here are friendly, but friendships will take time.'

In a letter like that you don't reveal the downside. It was difficult, very, very difficult. For the first two years, we were very short of money. So short that on weekends we would take the children to places where there were no entrance fees or costs, like the beach. We would also find some local tennis courts or cricket nets and spend hours playing with the children. That may not sound like fun but the kids loved it and they all turned out to be very good at sport. Ice creams for the children were a special treat. At work I was certainly the exception by bringing homemade sandwiches rather than enjoying the delights of the IBM canteen at the Cumberland Forest headquarters.

Buying a house in Sydney was not without its challenges. We started our hunt with what we thought was good research. Our first stop was at a real estate agency in Lane Cove, a lovely suburb about 10 kilometres from the city. Even before we could properly introduce ourselves the agent said, 'You are from South Africa, right?' We nodded. 'So, you are looking for a double-brick house with three or more bedrooms, two bathrooms, a swimming pool and double garage and you don't have much money, right?' We nodded. 'Sorry mate, you're in the wrong suburb.' He thought it was an hilarious comment. We didn't.

We finally found a house in Pennant Hills double the distance from Sydney. Compared to our Johannesburg home it was modest but it was handy to IBM's offices and we owned it. We had to borrow $17,000 from Margie's parents to put down a deposit. That hurt our pride but again there was no alternative and we agreed that as soon as the year was up, we would sell the Mercedes-Benz we had brought with us to repay the loan. This was particularly hard for Margie. She went from driving a late-model Benz to an old Toyota with no air-conditioning. In the first week with the Toyota, sons Paul and Kevin asked if they could be dropped around the corner from their posh private school rather than at the front gate. That hurt a bit too but later we all found it quite funny.

On day 365, we advertised the Benz. To our chagrin the car had neither compliance plates, which I'd never heard of, nor the required five safety belts. As a result, car dealers wouldn't touch it. We finally had a call from a chap whose English was not that great asking if he could come and see the car on the weekend.

So, there we all were on the Saturday morning waiting nervously with an occasional furtive look through the curtains.

Eventually four young men of 'Asian appearance' were knocking at the door. I told the family to stay inside and I spoke to these Cambodian lads who owned a bakery in Canberra. We went for a drive. Margie later said she wasn't sure if she would see her husband again! Could they pay cash, they asked?

I stuttered, 'Yes, sure.' They said they would be back the following week. It was a long week for us not knowing if they would return. We just had to sell the car and these chaps were the only game in town. True to their word they arrived on the Saturday and we sat in our lounge room, blinds drawn, carefully counting $25,000 in cash. All good and off they went in our lovely Benz. Our tears were as much of relief as anything else. We repaid Margie's parents the following week.

We struggled financially. Margie, in her quietly determined way, more than pulled her weight by utilising her teaching qualifications. She lectured at a local Technical and Further Education (TAFE) college as well as working at Tara Anglican School for Girls and part-time at IBM at various times. She also built a little business doing picture framing for friends. As an accomplished seamstress, Margie made a number of her and Hayley's clothes. This was not a chore because she enjoyed it, although I know that, deep down, she would have much preferred to be looking after Hayley and buying her nice clothes. Her income was crucial for us in those early years. Despite this, we still battled financially. In July 1988, I responded to an advertisement for the position of executive director of the New South Wales Rugby Union. With the benefit of hindsight, I probably had no chance at all but what the hell, Margie and I were in a financial hole. I was not enjoying working for IBM in positions I had held ten years earlier in South Africa and Margie was working every day to keep the wolf from the door. I didn't get the job but little did I know how many times the New South Wales Rugby Union would cross my path in future years. In the meantime, on weekends, I ran a series of part-time coaching clinics for aspiring young cricketers which (slightly) helped the cash flow.

For many years, I had aspired to join the IBM sales team. This didn't eventuate until we got to Australia. The career change had gone from desire to necessity because we just could not live on the salary I was being paid. When we arrived in Sydney, I was given a leg-up by IBM South Africa managing director Jack Clarke, who wrote a surprisingly glowing introductory letter to his counterpart Brian Finn at IBM Australia. I also received support from one of the IBM Australian divisional sales executives, Malcolm McMurray, who was a fellow South African. Malcolm was famous for describing selling as a 'belly-to-belly' engagement. Not quite PC in today's world. All this support paid off and at last I became a member of the IBM Australia sales team.

The first account I was given to manage was the state-owned Sydney Water Board. Malcolm thought he was doing me a favour in that the organisation was an exclusively IBM installed account: a 'blue' account as it was termed in the industry. What seemed like a soft landing into computer selling soon evaporated as the NSW Member of Parliament John Hatton accused both IBM and the Water Board management of collusion and corruption. All hell broke loose in the media – a journo's delight – a multinational and a government department. Accounting firm Price Waterhouse was engaged to investigate the matter. I had no idea what he was on about. The accusations were proven to be completely without substance but some of the mud stuck. The result was that we, as a sales team, had to then fight tooth and nail for every bit of business both new and installed. The Water Board, probably understandably, took the path of least resistance by acquiring competitors' products. Chief information officer Dennis Furini was fair all the way through, but it was a lesson hard learned as I built my career as a sales guy.

In late 2002, another advertisement appeared in the media

calling for applicants for the chief executive officer for the ACT Rugby Union. My application was again not successful and Andrew Fagan was appointed. Again, who was to know that ten years later we would work together at the Brumbies.

Arriving in Australia with a young family, a container of furniture and not much else, I was determined there and then I would focus on building relationships and a network. Not just for Margie and me but also for our children. I did not regard this as a burden, I like people and I like meeting new people. In the years to come, my time as general manager at the Sydney University Football Club (SUFC) certainly gave me a head start. It is the epitome of a high-quality networking organisation.

Over time, with our sons playing a lot of rugby, Margie became something of an expert in the game, her speciality being the offside rule. At a memorable Bledisloe Cup test match between Australia and the All Blacks in Sydney, we were seated with Sir Graham Henry, the New Zealand Rugby World Cup winning coach. I had arranged for Graham to be the keynote speaker at a fundraiser and having spent most of the previous day with him, I suggested Margie sit next to him. Points to note. Point one, Margie is a passionate, long-suffering fan of the Wallabies. Point two, All Black captain Richie McCaw is acknowledged as the best flanker, if not the best ever player in the world, and he often plays right at the edge of the offside rule. By the beginning of the second half, it was obvious the Wallabies were in for a long, back-pedalling night. Richie was dominating the game at the breakdown and elsewhere. Margie's agitation grew, and at the next breakdown, she yelled out, 'Look, look that Richie McCaw is offside. Again!' Seated in front of us were several All Black legends, including Andy Haden, Grant Fox and former coach, John Hart. As one, they turned and glared at Margie. Graham leaned back in his seat with a wry smile, and I pretended to talk to the chap sitting alongside me. The ref couldn't have been listening because the All Blacks continued on to a comprehensive victory. Margie was unrepentant.

In the 2018 Shute Shield rugby final, the University of Sydney played sparkling running rugby to dismantle a gallant Warringah side. As Margie and I left the ground we ran into Cameron Clyne, then chairman of Rugby Australia, and his CEO, Raelene Castle. Margie already knew Cam and I introduced her to Raelene. Margie and Raelene walked on together while Cam, an enthusiastic Sydney Uni supporter, and I discussed the match. As we went our separate ways, I asked Margie how the conversation with Raelene went. She replied airily, 'Oh, I just said to her, wouldn't it be great if the Wallabies could play like Sydney Uni?' I nearly choked and asked if she knew who Raelene was. She said she hadn't heard my introduction and who exactly was she? 'She is CEO of Rugby Australia and has responsibility for the Wallabies.' Margie's cool response being, 'Oh well, at least she now knows what true Wallabies supporters think about their performance.' Gulp.

The voice of Australian rugby, Greg Clark, is a good friend and the ultimate professional when it comes to research in preparing for his next call. When it came to pronouncing some difficult Afrikaans, Zulu, Xhosa, etc names, he would call me for advice. It was good fun as I tried to phonetically spell out a van Schalkwyk or a Aphelele Fassi with Clarkie. Very few commentators went to this trouble to get the pronunciation right.

CHAPTER 10

SOUTH AFRICANS IN AUSTRALIA

Superficially, South Africans and Australians are very similar; they love the outdoors and their sport, but if you scratch below the surface they are quite different.

John Cundill, a highly respected journalist who attended the same school as I did in Johannesburg, emigrated to Perth in 1994 and wrote an interesting article of 'explanation' about why so many South African private school-educated men and women made their way across the Indian Ocean. He wrote about attending a St John's College Old Boys' reunion at the Zebra Steakhouse in Perth where the menu included South African specialties such as bobotie, boerewors, kingklip and deliciously sweet koeksisters, with Castle or Windhoek Lager to wash it all down.

Many years later I was invited to meet the Sjamboks rugby team in Perth at the same restaurant and pub. The Sjamboks claim to be the only club in the world permitted to use the leaping

Springbok emblem. It was a wonderful evening with a group of young men and women who treasured their roots but loved living in Australia.

In John Cundill's article he poked fun at the St John's, St Andrew's and Michaelhouse products dressed in their natty cravats and old school ties. He described my alma mater as being a chillingly accurate reproduction of a Victorian English public school, right down to such archaic details as atrocious food, cold showers, autocratic prefects, bare-bottom canings and 'Gaudy' days. When I started at St John's a short six years after Cundill left not an awful lot had changed.

Cundill referred to Perth as, 'This remote corner of a vast, empty continent where nothing significant untoward had happened since it emerged from primordial sludge 500 million years ago,' and finished the article saying, 'We Saffas have found not only the ultimate refuge but a place that suits our style.'

In August 1988, a year after we arrived, Alison Stewart wrote a blistering article in *The Bulletin* magazine, entitled, 'South Africans in Australia – Racists, radicals or victims of prejudice?'

She opened the article by saying, 'South Africans are a growing migrant group in Australia – visible only because of their funny accents and their penchant for foods with unpronounceable names.' Presumably she was referring to biltong, koeksisters and boerewors. Really not that hard to pronounce.

She went on, 'A diverse lot, South Africans variously describe one another as arrogant, adaptable, opinionated, excellent migrants, victims, brainwashed, hardworking, psychologically damaged, highly skilled, racist and professional shoppers.'

About the immigrants, 'Mainly English-speaking, middle-class, white South Africans who are traditionally jittery about their place in Africa and that this jitteriness has earned them such sneering titles as "soutpoes" (Afrikaans for "he/she who straddles the ocean between England and Africa so his/her genitals hang in the sea")'. I had never heard this expression although 'soutpiel' or 'soutie' are common epithets for English-speaking South Africans with the same meaning.

She continued that former Rhodesians and Zimbabweans came to be known as whenwes, as they reminisced about 'When we were in Rhodesia'. Another popular name for any Southern Africans moving overseas was 'the chicken runners'.

Stewart went on to suggest a common Australian concern being voiced was, 'Are white South Africans importing their conservative, if not racist, views?' Stewart clearly had a selective memory since it was only thirteen years earlier the Whitlam government did away with the White Australia Policy, and in 1975 passed the Racial Discrimination Act which made racially based selection criteria unlawful.

One size certainly doesn't fit all immigrants from South Africa.

In my case, there were multiple reasons for leaving. Both my parents had passed away while Margie's parents in Queensland were much younger and in very good health. In fact, both lived well into their nineties so our children had more than twenty-five wonderful years with their grandparents who were excellent role models in every way. Another powerful reason was Margie and I had no intention of having our two sons do their compulsory military service supporting an apartheid regime we detested. Also, Johannesburg in the mid-80s was not a pleasant place to be. There were bombs going off in major shopping precincts such as the Carlton Centre directly opposite the IBM Tower where I worked.

Margie worked in the Kine Centre on the other side of the Carlton Centre. On 29 April 1975 there was a terrorist attack on the Israeli Embassy which was just east of the Carlton Centre. Margie and I were in our respective offices, both on the upper floors, and we could both clearly see police snipers on the top of buildings, trying to get a clear shot at the individual or individuals holding hostages in the embassy. Most of the CBD was in lockdown and we could only communicate via telephone. To say it was scary is an understatement. The strict government censorship laws meant we never knew what was true or false, but according to *The New York Times*, four people were killed and thirty-two injured by a 'disillusioned' South African–Jewish man.

Then there was the South African Prime Minister PW Botha, also known as 'Die groot krokodil', the big crocodile. He was adamant there would never be majority rule in South Africa. It is interesting to note that this extreme hardliner Afrikaner's parents both had anti-British backgrounds. His father Pieter Willem Botha Sr fought as a commando against the British in the Second Boer War and his mother Hendrina Botha was interned in a British concentration camp. His constant finger-wagging at his opponents was enough to push anyone to consider emigration.

Finally, who could have foreseen Nelson Mandela would be a free man within three years of us leaving South Africa?

Getting back to Alison Stewart's *Bulletin* article, she explored the situation where at that time nearly a quarter of the South African immigrants to Sydney were Jewish and more Jews were heading to Australia than to Israel. She quoted former South African book editor and now Sydney resident Lynne Segal as being highly critical of the Jewish school system in Australia, which was heavily patronised by South Africans, saying, 'I have a theory about (these) schools, I think it is a throwback to apartheid. The South African government encourages separation and Jewish schools perpetuate this. For many people who come here, nothing is quite as good as it was in South Africa.' Strong words indeed.

In December 1993, the *Australian Financial Review* published a piece by Valerie Lawson entitled 'The South African Wave'. Lawson opened her article by quoting a story by stockbroker and former South African Neville Miles at a meeting of Fairfax

Publishing. Among those present were South Africans Geoff Levy, David Gonski, Roy Randall, Stephen Chipkin and Miles. There were a couple of Australians including Trevor Kennedy and investment banker Malcolm Turnbull, later to become prime minister.

Lawson continued, 'South Africans in Australia are, without a doubt, the most visible, privileged, noisy, successful, demanding and wealthy migrants this country has ever had.' She quotes South African-born Professor of Politics at Macquarie University Colin Tatz, 'They are the hardest workers, they bring their own money and are never a drain on social security.'

Based on conversations with many South Africans, Lawson said the Joburg dinner party or braai conversations revolved around how to migrate, how to sell the house, and how to get money out of the country. The South African exchange control limit was R100,000 which didn't and still doesn't go very far in Australia.

Lawson's unflattering comments about South Africans go on to list many who made their mark in Australia, including Steve Mulholland CEO of the Fairfax Group; Sammy Linz the founder of Barbeques Galore; Brian Sherman of Equitilink; Robert Holmes à Court, Australia's first billionaire, Peter Wilkinson CEO of Coles Myer; the Hammerschlag brothers Ivan and David of Freedom Furniture; the Shein brothers David and John founders of ComTech; Meyer Rosenblum OAM lawyer and sportsman; Professor Colin Tatz AO; Robin SC and Jill AM Margo barrister and journalist respectively; Bernie Liebmann CEO of Waco International; and Geoff Levy AO, chairman of Investec.

I did further research into this topic, and in later years Southern Africans who have had significant success in Australia include David Gonski AC, known as 'the chairman of everything'; author JM Coetzee, Nobel Prize for Literature; designer Collette

Dinnigan AO; Platinum Asset Manager Founder Keir Neilson; the late author Bryce Courtenay AM; banker Gail Kelly; BHP CEO Marius Kloppers; Anton Enus, SBS Broadcaster; Brad Banducci, CEO Woolworths; Raphael Geminder, chairman of the PACT Group; Giam Swiegers, CEO Deloitte; Gary Wingrove, CEO KPMG; Ivan Glasenberg, CEO of Glencore; Trevor Loewensohn, founder Babcock and Brown; Brian Schwartz AM, CEO of Ernst and Young; Dr Brian Clark, chairman of Boral; Dr Jerry Schwartz, entrepreneur and owner of what was Sydney's most expensive house; Andre Louw, chairman Jardine, Lloyd Thompson; Andrew Reitzer and Doug Jones, both CEO of Metcash; Cliff Rosenberg CEO of LinkedIn; Larry Diamond, CEO of ZipMoney; Hein Vogel, entrepreneur; Julie McIntosh, CEO of Classic Safari Company; Ian Curlewis, international AFL Referee; Trevor Gerber, chairman of Sydney Airports; Professor Prem Ramburuth of the UNSW Business School; Richard Enthoven, owner of Hollard Insurance and the Nando's chain of restaurants. (Coincidentally, Robbie Brozin, the co-founder of Nando's, was born in Middelburg where my parents rest. Robbie's dad, Max, was a family friend who owned the Ford franchise for the region.) Then there is Ronni Kahn, best known for founding the food rescue charity OzHarvest, and Jonny and Di Schaffer who owns the dominant toy company, Plum Products. The list is long.

On the sports field, Australia has benefitted strongly from the Southern African exodus with rugby players Tiaan Strauss, Clyde Rathbone, David Pocock, the Haylett Petty brothers and the late Dan Vickerman, Craig Tiley, CEO of Tennis Australia, while Australian cricket has benefitted from the likes of Tony Greig, Kepler Wessels and Marnus Labuschagne, while Australian cricket coach Mickey Arthur gained unwanted fame with the infamous 'homework gate' saga which cost him his job.

Former cricket player and administrator Don Mackay-

Coghill is chairman of the Gold Corporation and David Duchen, former Springbok squash player, was chairman of Arrow Pharmaceuticals. Champion athlete, John Steffensen, is one of many second-generation South Africans who have made and who are making their mark in Australia. Devon Conway, educated at my alma mater St John's College, scored a record 200 runs for the New Zealand Black Caps in his first test. Born in Malawi, Cate and Bronte Campbell are the holders of several world swimming records and Cate carried the Australian flag at the opening ceremony of the Tokyo Olympics in 2021. David Payne was South Africa's top jockey before moving to Australia and making a highly successful transition, becoming a racehorse trainer with more than 100 Group One winners. Born in Johannesburg, Scherri-Lee Biggs was crowned Miss Universe Australia in 2012.

There are many more examples of former South Africans succeeding in Australia such as Launa Inman CEO of Billabong and now a Commonwealth Bank director; the Sher family, founders of Chargrill Charlies; Patrick Allaway, formerly dux at Hilton College and now chairman of the Bank of Queensland; Giselle Roux, chief information officer at JB Were; Mark Simkins, art director; Patrick Forth, partner at Boston Consulting Group; David Harris, CEO of the Hastie Group; Lorna Raine, CFO of George Weston Foods; Paul Naude of Billabong; and Kim and Tyron Brant of Kooga.

In the medical field, Sydney has plenty of dentists, radiologists and doctors and at the Seventh Day Adventist Hospital – which I know well – every second clinician seems to have a South African accent. Vikesh Ramsunder, formerly CEO of Clicks, has been appointed CEO of Australia's biggest pharmaceutical, Sigma Healthcare.

Australia isn't the only beneficiary from the skill, experience and business acumen of South Africa émigrés. In the US, South African immigrants such as Elon Musk have risen to such key leadership roles they have changed the US and, in some cases, the world.

What is it that makes these and other South Africans so successful and such valued immigrants to their host countries? With few exceptions most had a high standard of living in South Africa with an excellent education system. That is, if you were white. It was a highly competitive society best demonstrated by the intensity shown on the sporting field. Innovative technology was part of the environment with inventions such as the Kreepy Krauly pool cleaner, the computerised diagnostic tool, CAT Scan, and the Speed Gun as used in cricket and in tennis.

The Cybertracker is a hand-held computer providing a high-technology method of tracking animals in the field. The unit is connected to a satellite navigational system and the graphic interface makes it possible for unskilled people to enter very detailed information which helps scientists carry out their research into endangered species.

Finally, the first-ever successful heart transplant took place at Groote Schuur Hospital in 1967 by Dr Chris Barnard, a true pioneer.

Most immigrants left Southern Africa somewhat reluctantly but were negatively influenced by escalating crime and an uncertain future. Once the move was made, often with little money and a penurious exchange rate, they were determined to regain their standard of living and they worked very hard to do so.

Of course, the competitive spirit kicks in in suburbs such as Rose Bay and St Ives, known locally as 'St Africa' where, after the initial 'Howzit' greeting, the introductory questions include, 'What school does your child attend, which car(s) do you drive, which Shul do you go to, etc, etc?'

Saffas are often accused of being arrogant but unsurprisingly I don't see it that way at all. The clipped way of speaking possibly gives that impression but in truth they are highly focused on getting results and by and large, they live their own lives, are not a burden on the social security system, work and play hard, and have embraced Australia as home with gratitude and pride.

As I have mentioned on several occasions, emigration was tough, but there were also plenty of lighter and joyful moments.

I like this quote from President Theodore Roosevelt, 'Here is your country. Cherish these natural wonders, cherish the natural resources, cherish the history and romance as a sacred heritage for your children and your children's children. Do not let selfish men or greedy interests skin your country of its beauty, its riches or its romance.'

CHAPTER 11

FLANNELLED FOOLS IN ASIA AND AUSTRALIA

Within weeks of arriving in Sydney, we were invited for lunch with Margie's sister Carmel who lived with Steve and their family on the western side of Sydney. To get there we drove down Pennant Hills Road and I could not help but notice this beautiful cricket field with shining pickets and a very traditional clubhouse. I said to Margie we must find out the name of the cricket club since I really wanted to play on that oval. On the way back we turned into the gates to find it was not a cricket club but actually the King's School, the oldest private school in Australia, established in 1831. From that day onwards, whatever the sacrifices, Margie and I decided we would send our sons to this magnificent school.

We were very fortunate when they started at King's. All the parents were extremely welcoming and friendly. What we particularly liked was the mix of boys. There was a strong cohort of boarders most of whom were very grounded but also a blend of lads from very wealthy backgrounds and also those who were solidly middle-class. The boys loved it and so did we.

As I had done so many times in the past, it wasn't long before I started a cricket team, this time comprising teachers and parents at King's. We called ourselves the Kingfishers. We had a specially designed cap and were ready for allcomers with the ultimate goal being to play on that magnificent cricket ground, the White Oval. I repeatedly asked the headmaster Jon Wickham if we could have a game. He held out saying, 'What would the bishop say, if he drove past on a Sunday and saw a game of cricket in progress? And not even King's boys.' What indeed.

Eventually, the headmaster relented and we had dads and teachers queuing up to play on the hallowed turf. Former Wallaby great and teacher at King's, Bob Egerton, celebrated by scoring a hundred in our first match. Thereafter we were permitted to play on the White Oval three or four times a year.

There was a similar story about the Bradman Oval, a heritage-listed cricket ground in Bowral in the Southern Highlands of New South Wales. It was named after the great Sir Don Bradman who lived locally and who played there in the 1920s. It is a lovely ground with a white picket fence and an old-fashioned pavilion which houses the Bradman Museum.

I'm sure members of the Kingfishers got sick of me raving about playing on the Bradman Oval. Once again, I was told to dream on, we would never get onto it. Yet another challenge to meet. I made some enquiries, met with curator Richard Mulvaney, and what do you know the following year the first annual King's School Cricket Club Bradman Challenge took place at the Bradman Oval. Watching these fifty, sixty and seventy year olds in their ancient, faded creams warmed the heart. It was always a special occasion and all of the players appreciated and respected the tradition of the oval.

Lou Armstrong, one of the King's dads from the country, is a keen cricketer. Over a beer, Lou issued the challenge to arrange an annual City vs Country match in Dunedoo. The town with the distinctive name is in the central west of New South Wales about 350 kilometres from Sydney. It has a strong farming community with many families having sent their sons to board at King's for generations. Challenge eagerly accepted by Rick Symons and me.

Talk about rustic, the match was played on the ninth fairway of the local golf club. It was a great weekend for city families as we were billeted out with the local farmers and our children had the opportunity to milk cows, ride horses and chase kangaroos.

The standard of cricket was fairly average but the rivalry was intense. It was an ideal opportunity for the locals to bowl a few bouncers at the teachers to sort out any real or perceived grudges followed by a few lagers after the match in the local Chinese restaurant.

When our boys moved on to the senior school, the headmaster of the prep, Geoff Grimes, wrote to me thanking me for arranging the matches. He said the City vs Country matches had significantly improved understanding and relationships between boarders and dayboys. It also gave his staff a better understanding of some of the issues country families face and how much the parents missed their sons.

At one match, not unusually, I was having problems with my legs and limping around when a grizzled, wrinkled grazier sidled up to me and said, 'Ray, you're a lovely bloke but if you were a bloody horse, we'd shoot you.'

In 1994, I decided to combine two of my passions (and an additional one for Margie) and take the Kingfishers to Hong Kong to coincide with the Hong Kong Rugby Sevens. Since wives were included and the lure of shopping strong, it was not difficult to raise a team.

Our first game was against the historic Hong Kong Cricket Club (HKCC) established in 1851 in Chater Road. It is the oldest cricket club in Asia and a truly colonial experience with players drawn from members or former members of the Commonwealth including West Indians, Pakistanis, Rhodesians/Zimbabweans, South Africans and Indians. It is a wonderful institution, and it was easy to see why there was a seven-year waiting list for membership.

When we arrived we were met by the gentleman who managed all the matches played at the club. Impeccably dressed and with a pukka English accent he enquired who was captaining the Kingfishers. I responded that I was. He said we could store our valuables in the club safe and asked me for our batting order. Here was the catch; the batting order in the Kingfishers was very fluid and depended on many factors, including how big and late a night we had, whether or not we had breakfast, the state of the pitch and, if we were batting first, how quick the opposition bowlers were, the level of pain in the hammie or the knees and importantly, whether the opposing teams had any 'youngsters' since we had none of those. I politely enquired why he needed it and he explained the scorers were situated in the grandstand and the scoreboard was directly opposite on the other side of the oval. The chaps in the scoreboard needed the batting order and counted every run and 'we do not like making mistakes'.

We soon found out the HKCC had raised a pretty good side for a weekday. We were skittled for 160. It was only thanks to Peter Luffman that we got to this semi-acceptable total assisted by same lusty tail-end hitting by the late Rick Symons. We stunned them early with Dick Headley's seamers but they were altogether too strong and we had an early finish, with the ladies from both teams joining us for sunset cocktails on the verandah. As one does. We dressed for dinner which was held in the club's superb restaurant to round off a special day at the genteel Hong Kong Cricket Club.

The following match against Kowloon Cricket Club was

so very different. The club was established in 1904 and as the website accurately describes it, 'Our green cricket field is an oasis in the heart of Hong Kong'. The oval was surrounded by high-rise buildings as opposed to the Hong Kong Cricket Club which had the feel of a country club. The players also seemed different. Several turned up late sprinting to the changerooms from their late-model cars dressed in smart suits and white shirts. These were very definitely busy men taking the afternoon off.

Thanks to some excellent seam bowling by Ron Guthrie, we enjoyed a welcome win. Our hosts were very gracious, grabbing a quick beer before dashing off to their next appointment. We then packed the cricket kit away and the shoppers gave truth to the adage the more you spend, the more you save.

If you are a sports lover, you just cannot miss the Hong Kong Rugby Sevens. It is a festival of entertainment with often outrageous dress by the spectators and with the atmosphere of a rock concert. The songs and anthems pierce the eardrums and the beer flows in copious quantities. The year 1994 was special, it was when the magnificent physical specimen that was the late Jonah Lomu made his debut while the 'The Fijian Wizard' Waisale Serevi mesmerised defences. The Australian team, which finished runners-up to the Kiwis, included young players like David Campese, Tim Horan and Jason Little, all of whom would become household names in the next decade.

The whole event was a memorable spectacle and thoroughly enjoyed by all. Everyone loved Hong Kong and one can only hope the current troubles there are peacefully resolved and the beauty, magic and uniqueness of the place can continue. Somehow, I have my doubts that Hong Kong will ever be the same again.

*

In 1996, the King's School First XI went on a tour of South Africa. Coach Ross Chapman asked me to give him a hand with the planning and better still, would I like to come along? I jumped at the opportunity since both Paul and Kevin were in the team and I hadn't been back to South Africa since we left in 1987.

South African-born Bryce Courtenay's *The Power of One* was the bestselling novel in Australia that year. I had met Bryce on a few occasions and I called him asking if he would say a few words to the touring party. Ever obliging, he agreed to meet the team at his office in North Sydney. Ross was delighted and suggested as a condition of the boys attending, they must read about PJ and his exploits in Bryce's book. On the dot of 3 pm the sixteen young men in full uniform trooped into the boardroom followed by Bryce. He was an absolute master storyteller and held the boys spellbound for almost an hour. He finished by asking if there were any questions. There were none. He then said, 'You chaps are about sixteen or seventeen, right?' They all nodded. 'So, the hormones are running hard and fast, right?' They all blushed. 'You've all heard of AIDS?' They all nodded. 'Lads, let me tell you that AIDS is rife in South Africa so I strongly recommend that you keep your pecker in your pocket.' Pandemonium ensued.

At another unrelated event, Bryce told the story of receiving a large royalty cheque and deciding to buy himself a Porsche. As the sixty-something was driving through Double Bay, one of Sydney's most affluent suburbs, the Porsche's top down on a lovely summer day, he stopped at a set of traffic lights. In his words these two young beauties were 'eyeing him off'. He smiled and waved invitingly but they just laughed at him with the one saying to the other, 'Look, menoporsche!' To add to Bryce's embarrassment, he stalled the car as he tried to make a quick getaway.

In the mould of past cricket writers Sir Neville Cardus, John Arlott and EW Swanton, Peter Roebuck was considered one of the greatest of all time. As a cricketer he was a consistent county performer scoring more than 25,000 runs and captaining the English county side Somerset between 1986 and 1988. I first met Peter in the mid-90s when he coached my son Kevin who showed promise as a batsman. He was an excellent technical coach and brooked no nonsense. I next caught up with him at the Pietermaritzburg College Invitational Cricket Week during the King's tour in 1996. He was easily recognisable by his ubiquitous tatty straw hat. When I joined him circling the oval, Peter mentioned he was staying with a family who knew me. I was puzzled until Johan Volsteedt joined us.

Johan was headmaster of Grey College in Bloemfontein, known as the 'Springbok Factory' because of all the international rugby and cricket internationals the school had produced. He reminded me that I had been billeted with his family when I represented Transvaal Primary Schools on a cricket tour in 1960. Apparently his red-headed sister whose nickname was Vonk, meaning flame, took a shine to me. She thought Vonk Dearlove sounded quite cool. The innocence of youth. We all had a good laugh.

Over the years I would occasionally see Peter, usually eyes down under that well-worn straw hat, and we also regularly exchanged emails. In 2011 when the Australian cricket team was touring South Africa and Peter was covering the tour for the *Sydney Morning Herald*, we compared notes about the merits of the two teams. Peter wrote to me from Cape Town on 11 November saying, 'Hi Ray, it was an action-packed day. I really enjoyed watching Amla and Philander. Such a pity it is only a two-test series!'

The next day, as Margie and I were following Tiger Woods on The Lakes course during the Australian Golf Open, my phone rang. It was my son Kevin who said, 'Peter Roebuck is dead.' I was stunned. It could not be true. I had sent him an email that very morning, 'Peter, we have a house at Ingwelala Private Game Reserve – right in the middle of the Timbavati. A bit out of the way – about five hours from Joburg – but if you ever had the time, you'd be very welcome to use it. Please let me know.'

Peter never received my invitation. He had committed suicide by jumping from the sixth-floor bedroom window of his hotel in Cape Town the previous night. A month or two later I had dinner in Brisbane with good friend Jim Maxwell, known as the 'voice of Australian cricket', who was the last person to see Peter alive. We both shed a few tears as we chatted about Peter, a complex but truly gifted and also very kind man.

A desperately sad and unexplained end to one of the great wordsmiths of our time.

Above: St John's College, Johannesburg.

Above: Jos Dearlove Hotel and general shop – circa 1889.

Left: The death notice of Grandpa and Grandma.

Below: Grandpa and Grandma's graves in Mookgophong.

1924

Back Row: D Duncan, H Hoar, Mr Dixon, C Dearlove, R Grieveson
Middle Row: D Beckingham, B Mitchell, E R Jones (Capt), A Dearlove, J Stevenson
Front: P Richardson, G Routledge

Above: Two Dearloves in the St John's College 1st XI in 1924.

Above: Forty-one years later, the St John's College 1965 1st XI. The author second from the right in the front row.

Above: The graves of the 1381 men, women and children who perished in the Middelburg concentration camp.

P.O. BOX 1419
JOHANNESBURG
2000

DECEMBER 8, 1981

MR D.K. LILLEE
C/O DENNIS LILLEE CRICKET CLINIC
18 SANDRA PLACE
WELSHPOOL
WESTERN AUSTRALIA

DEAR DENNIS,

YOU MAY CONSIDER THIS LETTER SOMEWHAT BELATED, BUT I HOPE THAT
YOUR WIFE DID TELL YOU THAT I HAD TELEPHONED YOU. I WAS RATHER
SURPRISED WHEN YOUR WIFE REFUSED TO LET ME TALK TO YOU.

ANYWAY, I THOUGHT THAT IT WAS TIME THAT I TRIED TO CLEAR THE AIR
FROM MY SIDE. DISREGARDING ALL THAT HAS BEEN WRITTEN IN THE PRESS,
THE OLD JOHANNIAN CRICKET CLUB WOULD VERY MUCH LIKE TO ENGAGE YOUR
SERVICES FOR THE FIRST PART OF THE 1982 / 1983 SEASON. THAT IS
FOR THE MONTHS OF OCTOBER, NOVEMBER AND DECEMBER. THE CLUB FIELDS
THREE SATURDAY SIDES, ONE SUNDAY SIDE PLUS OF COURSE THE 1ST XI THAT
PLAY ON SATURDAY AND SUNDAY, GIVING US A PLAYING STRENGTH OF
APPROXIMATELY 65. WE FORM A SUB-SECTION OF THE OLD JOHANNIAN CLUB
WHICH ALSO CATERS FOR HOCKEY. THERE ARE FOUR SQUASH COURTS, TEN
TENNIS COURTS, TWO BOWLING GREENS AND A SWIMMING POOL ON APPROXIMATELY
20 ACRES OF GROUND. (TWO CRICKET FIELDS). RICHARD LUMB OF YORKSHIRE
IS THE CLUB PROFESSIONAL - IT IS HIS BENEFIT YEAR IN YORKSHIRE NEXT
YEAR AND WILL NOT BE RETURNING IN THE FORESEEABLE FUTURE. APART FROM
HIM THERE ARE NO "NAMES" IN THE SIDE THAT YOU WOULD RECOGNISE,
ALTHOUGH PLAYERS SUCH AS CLIVE RICE, DON MACKAY-COGHILL AND RUSSELL
ENDEAN HAVE REPRESENTED THE CLUB. GOING BACK A LITTLE, JACK CHEETHAM
AND BRUCE MITCHELL. UNFORTUNATELY, THESE DAYS IN SOUTH AFRICAN CRICKET
WE TEND TO LIVE IN THE PAST A BIT, FOR OBVIOUS REASONS !

NOW ON TO THE ARRANGEMENTS. WE WOULD PAY THE AIRFARES TO AND FROM
PERTH FOR YOUR FAMILY, AS WE DISCUSSED. IN ADDITION, WE WOULD
PROVIDE YOU WITH ACCOMODATION AND A CAR. ALSO, OBVIOUSLY A FIXED
AMOUNT OF MONEY AND THIS IS WHERE I LOOK TO YOU TO GIVE ME AN INDICATION
OF WHAT SUM YOU WOULD CONSIDER.

..... /2

Above and following: Dennis Lillee correspondence.

IN ADDITION TO PLAYING FOR THE CLUB ON WEEKENDS, YOU WOULD BE
EXPECTED TO DO SOME COACHING AT THE NETS ON TUESDAYS AND THURSDAYS
BETWEEN 16H00 AND 19H00. ANY OTHER ACTIVITIES WOULD BE UP TO THE
SPONSOR.

ON THE SUBJECT OF SPONSORSHIP WE HAVE "TESTED THE WATER", BUT
NOBODY IS PREPARED TO COMMIT HIMSELF UNTIL WE HAVE SOMETHING FIRM.

THAT'S ABOUT ALL I CAN TELL YOU AT THIS STAGE AND LOOK FORWARD TO
YOUR REPLY SO THAT WE CAN TAKE MATTERS FURTHER. I AM SENDING A
COPY OF THIS LETTER TO YOUR HOME ADDRESS TO ENSURE THAT YOU GET IT.

YOURS SINCERELY,

RAY DEARLOVE
CHAIRMAN,
CRICKET SECTION

CHAIRMAN: David Hope-Johnstone,
1A Armstrong Road, Applecross, PERTH. W.A. 6153
Phone: (09) 322-4865

COMMITTEE

SYDNEY:
Geoff Forsaith,
Unit 10,
99 Darling Point Rd.
Darling Point,
SYDNEY. N.S.W. 2027
Ph: (02) 232-2822

•

MELBOURNE:
Leon ? Yeggard/
Davi   Job.
843 King Street,
WEST MELBOURNE
VIC. 3003
Ph: (03) 328-2271

•

BRISBANE:
Ron McConnell,
Ron McConnell
  Holdings Pty. Ltd.,
Gabba Towers,
411 Vulture Street,
WOOLLOONGABBA.
QLD. 4102
Ph: (07) 391-8511

•

ADELAIDE:
Graham Ferrett,
Stillwell ? ord,
1-11 S   North Rd,
Medindie,
ADELAIDE. S.A. 5081
Ph: (08) 269-4333

•

PERTH:
Dennis Tobin,
18 Lachlan Street,
Crestwood, Thornlie,
PERTH. W.A. 6108
Ph: (09) 327-2284

•

NEWCASTLE:
Kym Butler,
P.O. Box 957,
NEWCASTLE.
N.S.W. 2300
Ph: (049) 26-2499

DKL:jlp

19th January, 1982

Mr Ray Dearlove,
P.O. Box 1419,
Johannesburg
2000
South Africa

Dear Mr Dearlove,

Many thanks for your somewhat belated letter.

I am glad that you have also decided to make contact with me, as you may be aware, items did appear in the press here regarding our negotiations which were not correct.

I enclose a copy of the story which appeared in a leading cricket magazine in Australia which I found most embarrassing.

You were quoted in the story as saying that you had me under an exclusive contract. I found that remark particularly galling in the light of our one telephone conversation.

At this stage of my career I am uncertain about my arrangements for next summer. In fact, over the past four or five seasons, I have always considered myself a game-to-game proposition, rather than season-to-season.

In any case, on deeper reflection about coming to South Africa, I must say that I would find it extremely difficult to be out there playing for the Old Johannians Cricket Club, while Australia are at home preparing to do battle with England for an Ashes series.

It is on this note that I can now definitely say that I will not be coming to South Africa next summer.

Thank you for your interest.

Yours sincerely

Left: Opposing captains in Dunedoo – Lou Armstrong and the author – City vs Country.

Above: Michael Holding, Jeff Thomson, Ray and Margie Dearlove, the late Dean Jones, Greg Matthews.

Above: Minister Josh Frydenberg squaring up to the Muscles from Brussels.

Above: Minister Frydenberg turns a whiter shade of pale.

Above: Clive Kluckow and the author on the Zambezi. Photo credit Dr Gwilym Mumford.

Above: Bath time on the Zambezi. No names, no pack drill.

Above: Stephanie Gilmore assisting with the insertion of a microchip in the rhino's horn. Photo credit Linda Lee.

Right: Dr Chris Brown with the author. Photo credit Phil Hines.

Above: Johnny Young, the sixties heartthrob.

Above: A more 'mature' Johnny Young and the author in 2018.

Above: Brothers Ian and Gary Player.

THE BLAIR ATHOLL HOMEOWNERS ASSOCIATION NPC *Blair Atholl* Reg No. 2006/005664/08 Vat No. 4420228084

To all my Aussie supporters.
I love Aus so much and miss
visiting your great country.
Visited atleast 30 times and am
proud to have won your Open
7 Times, and still the record score
with old equipment. 264.
Have a great stay in SA and enjoy
our fabulous course 'Blair Atholl'.
Sincerely,
Gary Player
2018

Above: A message from the Black Knight.

Above: Rhino notching. Note the armed guards. Just in case.

Above: Fellow tourist Lesley Roberts showing some enchanted children photos of themselves. Photo credit Michael Eyles.

Above: Grade One children performing at Obakeng Primary School, with 180 kgs of donations carried by DHL in the foreground. Photo credit Michael Eyles.

Above: Margie, Dame Jane Goodall and the author. Photo credit Nancy Moloney – JGIA.

Above: The author with Major General Johan Jooste. Photo credit Julia Salnicki.

Left: The author with a framed poem presented to Bruce Leslie.

CHAPTER 12

THE AUSTRALIAN RHINO PROJECT – THE BEAT GOES ON

The date 25 November 2016 is indelibly stamped in my memory.

In May 2013, Margie and I were attending our niece's wedding on beautiful Hamilton Island in the Australian Whitsundays when I received an SMS from an unknown South African number. It was from Humphrey 'Humph' McAllister with whom I had worked many years before at IBM in Johannesburg. Humph was desperately concerned about the plight of the rhino population in South Africa and, out of the blue, he suggested I establish a breeding herd in Australia. I was certainly aware of the rhino poaching situation but this was now something else. Humph is a persuasive man and he moved fast following up with a well-thought-out note, reasoning why I should give this a go and why Australia seemed ideally suited as a destination. Humph finished his note, 'It will need movers and shakers like you to get things going, Ray.' Thanks, Humph.

With the full support of my family, I decided to give it a go. My first visit to the famous Kruger National Park had been when I was just four years old. I loved it then and have loved it ever since. In addition, I had 'sort of' retired but didn't really have the appetite to play golf five days a week or spend my years sitting in front of a computer swapping silly jokes with retired friends. So why not?

I had some early encouragement from Glenn Phillips, then CEO of Kruger, who confirmed the situation was indeed critical, pointing out that the ability to fight the poaching scourge in such a vast area with limited resources was nigh on impossible and adding that my type of solution could be one of the options in the toolbox. The number of rhinos slaughtered for their horns to feed the seemingly insatiable demand in some Asian countries had soared from approximately 300 a few years before to 1004 in 2013.

But where to start? Demonstrating just how naïve I was I reached out to a friend who owned a large property in the Hunter Valley, north of Sydney. To quote another Aussie mate, 'Ray thought he'd have a few rhinos running around the back paddock of some bloke's place.' Not quite, but not far off!

We contacted the Department of Agriculture who responded by saying if the animals were to be imported, they had to spend a year in quarantine. The ground rules were therefore very clear although over time they were regularly and inexplicably manipulated to make compliance exceptionally difficult, if not impossible.

And so, the Australian Rhino Project was born.

I soon realised this project had four critical components – getting the governance exactly right, obtaining Australian government approval, obtaining South African government approval to export the rhinos and finally, fundraising. Our baby steps moved into giant strides. Every day I felt the time would come when someone would lean across the table, pat me on the knee and say, 'Ray, this is a great idea and we admire your creativity and passion but sorry old chap, it just won't work.' But this did not happen.

I always knew the project would fail unless we were able to secure tax deductibility for donations and I spent an awful lot of time on getting this approval. In Australia this is called a deductible gift recipient (DGR) which is an entity or fund that can receive tax deductible gifts. This DGR status is granted by the Australian Tax Office. There were the cynics who told me we would never get the status; why would the Australian government permit a tax deduction for a non-Australian species for an issue taking place 10,000 kilometres away? A fair point perhaps but I took a completely different view; rhino poaching is a global issue and Australia could (and should?) play a key role in saving the species. I chased and chased our application. Once again, the 'experts' told me it would take two years to obtain approval that is if we were to get it at all. Game on. Through sheer hard work and persistence approval was granted in six months.

Over the years we gained support from many people, some famous, some wealthy, but mostly from those who were concerned at the strong possibility of losing one of the planet's most iconic creatures. We received several large donations, but the $10 we received from a twelve-year-old Sydney girl strengthened my view this was a battle we just had to win.

The 180-year-old wealth management firm JBWere was among our biggest supporters. They stuck with me through thick and thin and unfailingly invited me to their philanthropic events, meetings and presentations. It was at their invitation I met Emeritus Professor Warren McFarlan at Harvard Business School, who has devoted much of his sixty-year career studying and lecturing on not-for-profit (NFP) boards. Through JBWere executives Donna Gulbin, David Knowles and Shamal Dass's efforts, I was invited to attend a private and also an invitation-only session with Warren. Both were exceptional.

In Warren's presentation he repeatedly used the phrase, 'Give, get, or get off'. In other words, donate, get others to donate or find something else to do. He stressed there is no glory in serving on NFP boards, it is bloody hard work and if you are not suited for it, accept it and move on.

I asked Warren to sign his seminal book, *Joining a Nonprofit Board*, and to my delight he wrote, 'Best wishes for the most interesting Non-Profit I have ever seen'. I subsequently sent Warren a copy of my book, *The Crash of Rhinos*. He wrote back,

'It is a truly absorbing and impactful piece of work. I could not put it down once I started. You make the case for a self-sustaining rhino herd in Australia powerfully, while also capturing all the problems which made it so hard. You have done a beautiful job describing the plight of the rhinos and the extraordinary effort that your non-profit made to try to set up a self-sustaining Australian herd. It is a textbook case study of the challenges in building a non-profit, which stretches across multiple geographic boundaries and governments. In general, the book is intensely interesting. You have captured fully all the challenges of building and sustaining a board for a start-up organisation. You also have captured the complexities of trying to get an organisation off the ground as well as incorporating a very sad and informative section on how you lost control of the organisation and why it failed. There are many lessons on management of non-profit organisations embedded in your book and it is a real contribution. Oh, and your book should be mandatory reading for government civil servants.'

High praise indeed from a man who has spent a lifetime working with non-profit boards.

One of my ongoing concerns was the logistics and cost of

transporting the rhinos from South Africa to Australia. I had ongoing discussions with Gary Edstein, CEO of DHL Express for Asia Pacific, about how this could be achieved. Gary was an enthusiastic supporter and I knew as soon as we had the necessary approvals he and DHL would come through.

About a year later I picked up a story how DHL had flown a black rhino named Eliska from the Czech Republic to Tanzania. Somewhat triumphantly I gave Gary a call. He laughed, 'You never give up, do you? Send me the details.' It turned out DHL had used a specially modified aircraft for the flight during which Eliska was accompanied and monitored by a team of support staff including my old veterinarian friend, Dr Pete Morkel.

Gary shared with me how this had come to pass. Apparently, DHL Express Global CEO Ken Allen was toiling away in his London office one day when his mobile phone rang. 'Good afternoon, is that Mr Allen?'

'It is. Who's calling?'

'Mr Allen, it's Prince Harry.'

'Oh really? Nice try, mate. Look it's Friday afternoon, I'm exhausted and I'm also really busy right now so pull the other one. Who is it?'

'It's Prince Harry, Mr Allen. I want to talk to you about moving an endangered black rhino to Africa.'

Ken, to himself, 'Oh God!', stood up, took a deep breath and said, 'Of course, Prince Harry. How can I help?'

Who could resist such a call? A fortnight later Eliska was settling into her new home in Tanzania.

There has not been one day since May 2013 when caring for the rhinos before, during or after their journey from South Africa to Australia did not occupy my mind. It was always going to be a tough and complex journey and for that reason I assembled a world-class team of experts to make it happen. The team included South African vets Drs Pete Morkel, Pete Rogers, Will Fowlds,

Charles van Niekerk, Markus Hofmeyr and Roy Bengis. In Australia, we had access to Benn Bryant. These men are the best in their field of wild animal care. Having said that, some of the other advice that I received was about as useful as an ejector seat in a helicopter.

During my journey of getting the rhinos to Australia I met some interesting people. Jean-Claude van Damme has to be in the top five. To be perfectly honest I had heard of him, but having no interest in martial arts all he was to me was a name. I didn't know what he looked like, I'd never seen any of his movies and that's where it started and ended. As I was to find out, Jean-Claude has one of the most recognisable faces in the world and an enormous global following.

I will always go out of my way to assist anyone who is involved in the conservation of endangered species with obviously a preference for rhinos. JC, as he preferred to be called, was one of these. Out of the blue he contacted me saying that he was planning a visit to Australia and asked if I could assist him in setting up a sanctuary in Australia for endangered species. This seemed like manna from heaven, I was all over it and arranged a series of meetings with people of power. My focus was on the federal government which has responsibility for Australia's biosecurity and we set off to the country's capital Canberra. I was agog at the number of people in airports, hotels and coffee shops who recognised JC. He took it all in his stride. He was obviously used to the attention and proved to be an extremely charming and kind fellow.

We had a full schedule at Parliament House and our first meeting was with the then Minister for the Environment Josh Frydenberg. The meeting was on the Thursday before parliament rose for the Christmas break. There were Christmas trees, party lights and so on wherever you looked. We entered Minister Frydenberg's office, which was overflowing with his staff and the media, all of whom wanted to meet Jean-Claude van Damme. Josh was so excited. He is a big fan and there was much joking, posturing and teasing. The media wanted some photos and Jean-Claude duly obliged. The press was satisfied and off they went.

With the media gone there was more posing and more punches 'thrown' until Josh asked for a real action shot and without warning Jean-Claude kicked. Bear in mind he was wearing a tight-fitting suit but the kick whistled past Josh's head and there was an audible gasp from those present. Josh went white.

Vikki Campion, with whom I had formed a good working relationship when she was attached to NSW Minister Troy Grant's office, had kindly arranged for us to see the then Deputy Prime Minister Barnaby Joyce. (Vikki was subsequently relentlessly pursued by the media about her relationship with the same Barnaby Joyce.)

We were due to see Barnaby next so we made our farewells. Walking down the corridors my phone rang. It was Josh saying the media had heard about the kick and could we please return for another photo opportunity? I agreed, but after we had met with Barnaby Joyce. 'No worries,' came the reply, 'we'll wait.'

Our meeting with the deputy prime minister of Australia who was also the agricultural minister was a hoot. Jean-Claude has a very strong French/Belgian accent and English is very definitely his second language. He is the first to admit he is not very good with names, for example, he calls every woman he meets, 'Lady'. Always very politely, it is just easier for him.

When briefing him for the meeting with Barnaby he asked how he should address him. I said just use 'minister', he will be fine with that. Well, we walked into the boardroom where Barnaby was lunching with his National Party colleagues. It looked like a scrumptious feast with cold meats and salads. We were all starving but weren't invited to join in!

Barnaby Joyce is a fairly blunt fellow and it seemed he didn't enjoy having his lunch interrupted. Jean-Claude greeted the deputy prime minister with, 'Good afternoon, Mr Barnaby.'

The deputy PM replied, 'Joyce.'

'Good afternoon, Joyce.'

'My name is Barnaby Joyce.'

'My apologies, Barnaby Joyce.'

Diana Hallam, Barnaby's chief of staff, and I were in stitches hiding our mirth behind our hands. Not so Barnaby Joyce. 'How can I help you, Mr van Damme?' To which Jean-Claude responded, 'Please call me Jean-Claude or JC.' Diana and I exchanged glances. I'm sure she was thinking what I was thinking. Let's not start that again.

After the Barnaby Joyce meeting, we returned to Josh Frydenberg's office and the excited photographers. 'Ready?' asked Jean-Claude and kicked. It was so quick that not one of the photographers got the shot. JC had to repeat it to the accompaniment of nervous laughter. The photograph received nationwide coverage.

COVID-19 has caused so much disruption in the world, I am confident that once all the restrictions are lifted, some of Jean-Claude's dreams for protecting endangered species will be fulfilled.

As 2016 year-end approached, I was privately proud of what had been achieved. Awareness of the plight of the rhinos was at an all-time high locally and internationally. We had secured DGR status for successful fundraising and raised almost $1 million dollars. The Australian Rhino Project was fit-for-purpose and very focused. We had in-principle agreements with the Australian and South African governments and we had formal gold standard partnerships with organisations such as Investec, the University of Sydney and Taronga Zoo.

I was working on the project day in and day out and my health had suffered. I had been in and out of hospital for surgery in 2016 and according to my physician I had twice dodged a bullet.

Despite our achievements I sensed all was not well with my fellow directors and for reasons never made clear to me my input and influence were inexorably squeezed out. The day 25 November 2016 will go down as one of the unhappiest of my life. The pressure the three directors had put on me finally paid off (for them) and I tendered my resignation. My resignation was not, as suggested by some, due to ill health. Quite frankly, it was heartbreaking. I had given my all in this quest to assist in the fight against the extinction of an animal that has been on our planet for more than 10 million years.

Take a look at a rhino and apart from possibly a crocodile, it is the closest resemblance to a dinosaur we have on earth. My resignation was not a decision taken lightly nor in isolation. Great friends Peter Scott and the late Pod McLoughlin, both of whom I respect, advised me to get out and my family who had supported me from the get-go encouraged me to call it a day. When I was planning the Sydney fundraising dinner, I asked our three children to come along since I knew it was going to be a special night. Kevin and Rebecca, Hayley and Jeremy attended but Paul refused. I must confess I was surprised and deeply hurt. I wanted the whole family to be there. When I asked Paul why, he explained, 'Dad, I am not going to support something which is affecting your health.' Food for thought.

With time to reflect on my years with the Australian Rhino Project it was and is a massive and complex endeavour. All the way through I was driven by a number of factors. The world was running out of time to rescue the rhino species from possible extinction in the wild and I was convinced we were doing the right thing by attempting the seemingly impossible. As Larry Ellison, founder of Oracle Corporation, said, 'When you innovate, you have to be prepared for people telling you that you are nuts.'

Very occasionally I was told exactly that but I saw myself differently; rather as a catalyst for creating a safe and secure crash of rhinos away from the danger zone. I often used the analogy of children being moved out of London during the Blitz in World War II. From 13–18 June 1940 around 100,000 children were evacuated. When the Blitz began on 7 September 1940, children who had returned home or had not been evacuated were among the one million women, elderly and disabled people who were sent to safety elsewhere.

My journey was a rollercoaster of emotion. There were times my heart would soar and other times I would find myself in a very dark place. To the surprise of many I am quite sensitive. Personal attacks strike deeply but the encouragement of people like my family and the inspirational Pod McLoughlin would always lift my spirits.

While some did, I never saw myself as an activist, in fact I thoroughly dislike the label. In my view our cause was just and as Dr Jane Goodall said, 'It was an idea whose time had come.' Jane was a steadfast supporter.

I was very proud at what was achieved over the four years with the Australian Rhino Project. Since 25 November 2016, any number of people have encouraged or even urged me to challenge the existing board, assuring me that I have the support of the members. While there may be some personal satisfaction in such a challenge, the current directors were sufficiently confident that they could do a better job in bringing the rhinos to Australia without me and now, six years later, they appear to making progress. Despite all of the pain and hurt described above, I do believe we made a difference under my leadership. I certainly hope so.

In terms of the rhinos coming to Australia, when all is said and done it will all come back to the Australian authorities and the remaining directors' ability to navigate the challenges of dealing with government. I have the utmost respect for Australia's biosecurity laws and controls and for the authorities who do their job, but the foundations are in place for the Australian Rhino Project team to apply gentle but sustained pressure on the bureaucracy who are quite content to play the waiting game. The easiest decision for government is a no decision. If they persist with placing obstacles in the way, they run the risk of missing being in the vanguard of one of the greatest conservation accomplishments of the century. In the words of John F Kennedy, 'Change is the law of life. And those who look only to the past or present are certain to miss the future.'

Until the day I die, I will continue to believe persistence and constant constructive engagement will result in a crash of rhinos peacefully and safely breeding in a paddock in Australia under the Southern Cross far from the city lights and the threat of poaching and they could become a seed population back in Africa at the appropriate time. We owe this to the remaining rhinos on Earth.

After the crushing personal disappointment of being forced to resign from my board I face the world with renewed hope for the rhinos and a certainty that Australia will play its part. I just hope that I am around to see it since one of my cynical buddies has opened a book on whether or not I will be invited to attend the welcoming party when the rhinos get to Australia. Time will tell.

In the words of James Langston Hughes, *'Hold fast to dreams, for if dreams die, life is a broken-winged bird that cannot fly.'*

The headmaster of my old school in Johannesburg, Stuart West, introduced me to Stephen McGown. Stephen had attended the very same school. In November 2011, he was kidnapped by Al-Qaeda Islamists while travelling from London to Johannesburg by motorbike. He spent six years in atrocious conditions in the Sahara Desert held by this organisation founded by Osama Bin Laden. I was privileged to organise a dinner in Sydney where a full house heard, firsthand, Steve's extraordinary story of courage, resilience, mental toughness and determination to survive. He is a unique individual whose story is told in the bestselling *Six Years a Hostage*. Since the dinner, Margie and I have had the opportunity to spend time with Steve and his wife, Cathy, another extraordinary person.

As Nelson Mandela said, 'Courage is not the absence of fear, but the triumph over it. The brave man is not he who does not feel afraid, but he who conquers that fear.'

CHAPTER 13

WILDLIFE AND WILD TIMES

The Swahili word *safari*, meaning 'journey', evokes thoughts and images of Hemingway, *The African Queen* and *Out of Africa*. As a youngster I couldn't get enough of Humphrey Bogart, Katharine Hepburn, Robert Redford and Meryl Streep during their romance-filled, high-octane action romps through Africa. My good friend, safari operator John Mitchell-Adams, uses Richard Mullin's great quote, 'The only man I envy is the man who has not yet been to Africa … for he has so much to look forward to.'

Over the years, my family and I have been fortunate enough to enjoy safaris to Botswana, Kenya, Zambia, Zimbabwe, Tanzania, Namibia and, of course, South Africa. While the daily ritual of an early morning drive, a hearty brunch, a nap, an evening drive and dinner sitting around the open fire under the stars is idyllic, every lodge brings its own special and unique brand.

In 1983, I was invited by Nigel Hindmarsh, best man at our

wedding, to join him on a canoeing trip down the Zambezi River. Nigel and John Dawson, both extremely bright system engineers, had left IBM South Africa in the mid-70s to set up the IBM agency in Salisbury, Rhodesia. Given the ever-present threat of economic sanctions against South Africa this was a smart move and their business flourished.

The Zambezi, meaning 'great river' in the local Tsonga dialect, is the fourth longest in Africa, flowing some 2600 kilometres through six countries from its source in north-western Zambia to the Indian Ocean.

John's son Patrick, Clive Kluckow, Dr Gwilym Mumford, one of Zimbabwe's leading physicians and an avid photographer, and a couple of close friends joined us. There were four canoes in total and we had a young guide, Eddie Rouse. Since it was only a few years after the end of the Rhodesian bush war and there were still a number of related incidents going on, I was already somewhat nervous about the trip. This apprehension went up a notch when I noticed that Eddie was not armed. As it turned out I needn't have worried since he was extremely cautious and diligent and in years to come went on to be one of Zimbabwe's famed guides.

It was a five-day safari, paddling a two-man canoe down a river infested with Nile crocodiles and hippos. The reader may think that the word 'infested' is surely a bit of an exaggeration but Eddie's earnest advice was, 'Because hippos can sleep under the water, it's important we bang the sides of our canoes with our paddles as we journey downstream to wake them up … If a hippo is suddenly woken and gets a fright he'll likely upend us but having said that please be more aware of the crocs … they'll be the ones to finish us off.' Finally, under no circumstances, should we drag our hands in the river as we drifted along. For this city boy, no further explanation was required.

This safari was certainly not glamping. We took all our supplies, and once we had packed the beer and Marula liqueur, there wasn't much room for food. We started out from Kariba Gorge and had a dummy run around a calm part of the gorge which included some very gentle rapids. We easily conquered these in our Hiawatha-type Canadian canoes which had the reputation of being very stable, rugged and reliable. Mind you, as time would tell, the designers had definitely not stress-tested them on the Zambezi River.

As we meandered along downstream the thought occurred to me, shouldn't we be wearing life jackets? We were all in our thirties and fit, but what if? As we paddled around a bend in the river, we immediately noticed the group of young lads sitting patiently (or expectantly?) on the Zambian bank. We also heard the water tumbling over what was our first set of serious rapids. This was no gentle babbling brook; this was a rush of white water.

During our practice run Eddie had emphasised we needed to approach the rapids front on. This was really important so my partner Clive and I decided to hang back and watch the others go first. As the first canoe successfully went through the rapids there was applause from the lads on the bank. Very kind of them. Next was Dr Gwil with Nigel sitting at the rear. Dr Gwil had brought along a lot of expensive photographic equipment that only a physician could afford. Nigel is a big man, 1.95 metres tall and a powerful physique, weighing in at 115 kilograms. As we watched, they entered the rapids *sideways* into the raging torrent, oh all right, the fast-moving river. To the delight of the audience on the bank over the canoe went with Nigel, Gwil and all the photographic gear tumbling out. The lads hooted and clapped. This was obviously their daily entertainment watching the 'superior' white men gasping for air as they chased the canoe down river and tried to retrieve the gear. Nigel and Gwil are best mates, but there were no speaks for the rest of that day.

By day three we were relatively proficient and at our usual breakfast rendezvous of oranges and a beer Eddie warned us we would be going down Crocodile Alley later that morning. The alley is a narrow channel between the Zimbabwean riverbank and a long sandbank in the Zambezi. He explained he would not usually take novices that way but the river was flowing too fast to attempt other routes. The alley was so called because there were always plenty of crocodiles on both the sandbank and the riverbank. What Eddie failed to mention this time was the hippos. Hippos kill more people in Africa than any other animal and woe betide if you get between a hippo mum and her calf. In the first three days we had seen and heard lots of hippos and steered well clear of them all the while banging the sides of our canoes.

This was no time for bravado, we were all nervous and once again, Clive and I hung back as the first two canoes successfully paddled through the narrow stretch of water. Then it was Nigel's and Gwil's turn. We cheerfully waved them through as they entered the alley. Within seconds, despite Nigel's bulk, the back of their canoe lifted clean out of the water. Nigel looked back at us saying, 'What the fuck was that?' Thankfully, the hippo had lifted the canoe straight up not at an angle, which could have ended badly, and then waddled away up the riverbank. With our hearts in our mouths Clive and I broke some paddling records as we flashed through the alley.

Part of our daily routine was to stop at a convenient and 'safe' spot for our morning ablutions. Eddie would select the area and after beaching the canoes we'd get out and strip down to 'kaalgat' naked and have a wash. One morning we passed a particularly large crocodile sunbathing on a sandbank. One hundred metres further along the same sandbank Eddie pulled up and hopped out of the canoe announcing, 'This is a great spot that I often use.'

None of us moved and as we remained seated in our canoe, Clive asked, 'What about that bloody great flat dog over there?'

'Oh him,' Eddie said airily, '... it'll be fine as long as we can see him.'

Clive retorted, 'And what about his bloody brothers and sisters and mates?'

It was a quick wash that morning.

Evenings were spent chatting around the campfire debating whether rhinos actually do stamp out fires (they don't) or if black impalas exist (they do due to a recessive gene in the red impala).

One particular night, as usual, we camped on the banks of the river in a sheltered grove of tall wild fig trees in the Mana Pools area. We spread our sleeping bags on the flattest ground we could find and fuelled by generous doses of Marula liqueur we drifted off to sleep. Nigel is a very noisy sleeper who often woke us up with his snorting and choking snores. There was a full moon and Eddie suddenly awoke and noticed a honey badger scavenging close to a rubbish bin and even closer to us. The honey badger has a fearsome reputation as a fighter and will not think twice about attacking a lion if it or its young are in danger. It has also gained notoriety for attacking the genitals of the attacker or prey. So here was our mate Nigel out of his sleeping bag on his back with legs invitingly apart and a prowling adult honey badger getting closer and closer to the potential target. By now most of us were awake and as we silently surveyed the scene and the possibilities, I am certain we were all thinking the same thing. Decision time. Do we watch and wait or do we stop the movie? Eddie was the first one to crack with a loud 'Voetsek', to put it politely, 'bugger off'. Nigel and the honey badger almost jumped out of their skins. Over the years, we often reminded Nigel and wife Gill it was only because of our awareness and kindness his manhood remains intact. Gill just rolled her eyes.

The Lower Zambezi is a paradise for watching wildlife. As you glide quietly down the fourth longest river in Africa you see animals in their completely natural state. They seem to consider canoes of low risk and elephants in particular allow you to paddle very close to them as they bathe and play in the river.

We had decided to spoil ourselves by spending the last two nights of the safari at the luxurious Chikwenya Lodge in the Mana Pools National Park, a UNESCO World Heritage Site which is surrounded by a dense forest of albida and Natal mahogany trees. We were all looking forward to a shave and a hot shower and a few of life's luxuries. Instead, we were greeted with terrible news. Safari guide and lodge manager John Stevens and his wife Nicci were experiencing a blissful existence at Chikwenya with their two daughters Briar and Sarah. The week before we arrived John had returned from an early morning bush walk with guests and hearing them arrive, little Briar skipped along the path from their house to greet her dad. Suddenly John heard a grunt, 'I knew it was a lion ... don't ask me how ... and that it had taken Briar. I grabbed my gun, shooting into the ground. I couldn't see anything ... the grass was too long.'

A pride of young lions broke cover with one carrying Briar by the back of her neck. An excellent shot, John continued firing at the feet of the lioness carrying his little girl. After some 50 metres the lioness dropped the child and ran off. There she was, lying in the tall winter grass, a broken, flaxen-haired child. She had been bitten high on her back and her spinal cord was severed and a lung punctured. The pain would have been excruciating.

Nicci immediately put out a general radio call and soon two aircraft were racing to Chikwenya to save Briar's life. Within two hours they were in the intensive care unit of Harare's Parirenyatwa Hospital. The doctors and nursing staff fought for her unconscious life for three weeks while Nicci and John camped alongside her in the hospital trying to digest the news that her spine had been severed. Briar spent months in hospital and at three and a half years old she was a paraplegic.

Our highly anticipated visit to this beautiful lodge was obviously dampened by what had happened to Briar and we left Chikwenya with heavy hearts. While researching this book I caught up with Briar. Almost forty years later, this plucky young girl is now married with a young son and has a highly successful career in Melbourne. The family never returned to Chikwenya. Nor did we.

Astonishingly, a few weeks later Chikwenya was struck by yet another tragedy. In John Stevens' absence, we had been taken on bush walks by Russian-born Count Ura George de Woronin. He had lived at the lodge for years and was considered Zimbabwe's best-known hunter, guide and wildlife expert. The sixty-eight year old was quite a character with his mop of almost white hair and rangy physique. A highly intelligent and entertaining man, we sat around the campfire while he regaled us with story after story about the bush trying his best to lift the gloom after Briar's accident. He held the view you could have a 'bond of trust' with a wild animal you got to know. We city guys were somewhat sceptical about that theory.

Within a month of our visit Ura was strolling through the camp back to his living quarters when he came across a young elephant and tried to shoo it away, but he hadn't seen the calf's mother who was obscured by dense bushes. She suddenly charged out of the bush at Ura who had no hope of outrunning her and was gored and trampled. The lodge manager said Ura was armed with his rifle slung over his shoulder, he knew the bush better than anyone and one could only assume Ura didn't know the mother was so close by and didn't have time to use the gun. Two shocking tragedies in one month.

On the subject of honey badgers, a few years ago John and Peta Balderson joined us and friends at Ingwelala for a few days. I have known John for most of my life and he has a keen whimsical sense of humour. As is customary we all piled onto the game-viewing vehicle at 6 am sharp. Unusually, John and Peta were a little late and when they emerged John was obviously somewhat agitated and blurted out, 'Did anyone hear anything last night?'

Given that we were in the middle of a game reserve with no fences this seemed to be an odd question. Before anyone could respond John let fly saying that he and Peta had been fast asleep when they heard a noise coming from the adjoining kitchen. They both lay there awake and both jumped when they heard two more thumps and under the bedroom door, they saw the light in the kitchen go on then go off. By this time Peta's nudge had turned into a shove, 'Go and see what it is!' Now John is an equal-opportunity kind of guy and was about to suggest an alternative when once again the kitchen light went on. He sidled up to the door, opened it a few centimetres and in one movement he was back on the bed, breathing hard. John has a slight stutter which intensifies when he is animated and animated, he certainly was, saying to Peta, 'It's a bbbbbloody honey bbbadger – you know what they do to mmmmmen (as per the story about Nigel above), you're a female, you chase it away.' Peta finally persuaded/threatened him to grab the broom and shoo the honey badger out of the kitchen door to the patio outside and they returned to bed back-to-back to sleep, to sleep, perchance to dream.

What had actually happened is that the honey badger, one of the most resourceful animals on the planet, had managed to open the sliding door from the patio to the kitchen and headed for the fridge. He opened the fridge door and the fridge light went on. After helping himself to the lettuce the door closed of its own volition and the light went out, but then he decided he wanted something else and re-opened the fridge door and was enjoying a midnight feast of eggs until this crazy man in his shortie pyjamas with wild eyes wielding a broom appeared yelling, 'Unleash hell!' Despite the honey badger not having seen Russell Crowe in *Gladiator*, he certainly got the message.

*

In 1986, once we had made the decision to emigrate, Margie and I decided to cross off one of our bucket list items and visit the Okavango Delta in Botswana. The Delta is produced by seasonal flooding when the Okavango River drains the summer rainfall from the highlands of Angola and the surge flows 1200 kilometres in one month. The flood peaks between June and August when the Delta swells to three times its permanent size attracting animals from miles around and creating one of Africa's greatest concentrations of wildlife. We had long promised ourselves the trip to experience one of the Seven Natural Wonders of Africa and now not knowing when we would next visit Africa, it was time.

We invited old friends Ron and Cindy Hopkins and Bruno and Anne Ganter to join us. None had been to the Delta. Unfortunately, just before we left Anne became ill and could not join us.

The five of us travelled in my car and after packing the beer and wine, once again there wasn't much room for anything else. The safari was to be led by an experienced guide and we would camp in tents and all food was provided.

We departed early morning and spirits were high as we quickly cleared the South African customs post and arrived on the Botswana side. Immediately we noticed a change in attitude from the Botswana officials. At the time South Africa was at war with 'insurgents' from all the surrounding countries including Botswana and there were regular armed skirmishes along the long common border.

We were thankful we had made the early start since the paperwork took an age. As part of the customs process, we were told to empty the contents of the car's boot so officials could 'check the spare tyre'. This meant unpacking everything including the several cases of beer. There were some raised eyebrows when the officials counted the cases and asked how long the safari was to be and even more surprised when we told them it was for just one week.

Eventually we were given the all clear and off we went with plenty of time to cover the 20 kilometres to Gaborone Airport to catch the once-a-week flight to Maun, the entry point to the Delta. We had not travelled more than a kilometre when we were stopped at another roadblock, not by the police but by the Botswana Defence Force. This lot had no smiles and were all armed with AK-47 assault rifles. One of the soldiers wandered over and asked the same questions as the border officials, 'Show me your passports … why are you in Botswana? Where are you going? Why? For how long?' And so it went on. We answered the questions respectfully then he demanded we empty the boot. While Bruno and I lifted out the cases of beer we noticed the soldier had a little smirk on his face. 'Do you like beer?' Bruno asked. 'Yes, I do,' came the reply. We repacked the luggage and left a case under the car for our thirsty soldier.

The officer-in-charge then turned up. He was a mean-looking individual who seemed to undress the girls with his eyes. They hurriedly jumped back in the car. 'What is this?' he shouted seeing the beer under the car. Our now not-so-thirsty soldier made himself scarce and strolled away. For one wild dumb moment I was tempted to say it was beer, but I realised we were now in a real spot of bother. Instead, I lamely said, 'Sir, I thought you and your soldiers might enjoy a beer on this hot day.' He shifted his rifle to his right hand, looked at me with a 'Do you seriously think I am that stupid' look, told me to put it back and waved us on.

We drove to the speed limit although we all realised there was now a real possibility we were going to miss the once-a-week flight and the safari. Maun was about 1000 kilometres away. Too far to drive in time.

Driving through the town of Gaborone to our absolute dismay

there was yet another military roadblock just before the airport. After being asked the same questions, we pleaded with the armed soldiers to give us a break. They did and as we entered the car park, we saw our plane already on the runway. We left the car and sprinted for the terminal. Ron did a wonderful job of persuading the ground staff to radio the pilot and ask him to turn around. As a 'donated' case of beer gently did circuits on the carousel, five exceedingly nervous and relieved passengers boarded the plane. We all marvelled at the power of beer in negotiations.

The week in the bush went far too quickly. We saw a lot of game including many species seldom if ever seen on the eastern side of the continent such as sitatunga, springbok, eland, gemsbok and roan antelope.

Finally, we found ourselves back in Gaborone heading for the border post with more than a little trepidation. The previous week's events had really shaken us. We needn't have been concerned. It was a Sunday evening and everybody on the Botswana side seemed ready to go home. The same applied on the South African side. As we sailed through, we opened a beer celebrating that we were back in our country.

Well, the joy was short-lived. Almost unbelievably within 5 kilometres of the border there was a roadblock, this time manned by South African soldiers. We weren't overly worried. After all, we were back in South Africa and these guys were on our team. This was until Margie whispered that she could see an open 750 millilitre bottle of Black Label beer partly hidden by the STOP sign. A young man in full uniform with wild eyes, his automatic rifle cradled in his arms, ambled over to our car. He shone his powerful torch on each of us, lingering on the girls. I was driving and I was getting sick of all this. I was ready for a 'discussion' but I was told in no uncertain terms by Margie and others to shut up and behave. The same questions as before were asked. He then proceeded to give me a lecture. He sternly informed me he had previously been an officer in the elite Selous Scouts Special Forces during the Rhodesian war and he wasn't in the mood for 'any shit' from me or anyone else. He said this while pointing ominously to the soldiers standing behind him, all of whom looked keen for some action. The Selous Scouts had a formidable reputation as a fighting force. I assured him we were just a group of South African tourists returning from a safari in the Okavango Delta. Once he had established there was free beer to be had in the boot of our car, we parted the best of pals. Driving home to Johannesburg we asked ourselves why had we been so apprehensive about the dangers of wild animals.

*

In 1997, after a decade in Australia, Margie and I decided it was time to reintroduce our children to Africa. Paul was eighteen, Kevin sixteen and Hayley thirteen and they were all equally excited at the adventure. Some of our South African friends chided us when we told them part of the itinerary included canoeing down the Zambezi. They would exclaim, 'Surely Hayley is too young … don't you know how dangerous it is … etc, etc?' Fair questions indeed but every time I visit Southern Africa my senses are far more finely tuned and we studiously avoid any potential or perceived dangers. Margie and I had checked out the Shearwater Safari Company and were more than satisfied with the references provided.

Our guide's name was Biko after the anti-apartheid activist Steve Biko. He was a terrific young man, serious but with a good sense of humour. As we prepared to start paddling, I thought to myself he was going to need it!

We paired Paul and Kevin together, Margie and me and then Biko with Hayley. Because of the unstable political conditions in Zimbabwe (was it ever not so?), we launched from the Zambian side of the Zambezi and hugged the riverbank. The family soon understood why I loved this adventure. It was just you and nature, face to face, arm in arm, and in truth, sometimes in your face. And while danger was ever-present in varying forms, I felt we had tempered it with a qualified guide like Biko, even though he wasn't carrying a firearm.

The first day went smoothly and we pulled up at our overnight stop on the banks of the mighty Zambezi to be greeted by the cook/chef and various other helpers. They took us to our very well-appointed tents. We sat on camp chairs in a circle around the Zambezi redwood fire burning brightly, the bush bucket showers had piping hot water and the drinks were chilled. We had a lovely bush dinner with bread made on the coals and then drifted off to sleep marvelling at the closeness and brightness of the Milky Way and shivering at the distant roaring of a pride of lions.

After what we all thought had been an uneventful night, we rose at dawn to the chattering of a troop of monkeys only to be told that 'river pirates' had stolen all of the provisions for the trip from the canoes which had been tied to the makeshift jetty. This caused quite some consternation with Paul and Kevin who seemed always to be hungry. We were assured these would soon be replenished and oh, by the way, a couple of buffalo Dagga Boys had wandered through the campsite during the night. A pity they hadn't met up with the pirates.

Every day seemed the same on the safari and yet every day was quite different. After a hearty breakfast we would launch early. The mornings were generally calm on the river but a gentle breeze would come up in the afternoon. Despite paddling downstream, the breeze could make progress quite challenging. At around 9 am we would paddle alongside each other, 'link' the boats and while gently gliding down the mighty Zambezi we'd enjoy fruit and juice before continuing our journey. The serenity made us feel as if we were the only people on the planet.

146

The variety of wildlife and birds on both sides of the river was breathtaking. Because we were so quiet the animals seemed to ignore us and we saw some memorable close-up sightings of a wide variety of wildlife. We passed one sandbank and I was convinced the large croc sunbathing was the same one from the previous trip over ten years before. He seemed to gaze directly at me through those baleful yellow eyes. I thought of giving him the finger, but decided not to push my luck.

Biko was an excellent guide and he took particularly good care of Hayley. He was a quiet man with the ability to spot animals, hippos and crocs much earlier than we did. His knowledge was quite exceptional. He could identify animals, birds, trees and even insects and knew both their common and scientific names. It was a true learning experience for all of us. He did much of his communication through his paddle and hand signals. At one point, 'someone' dropped a paddle. It was a potential disaster but Biko surged ahead and retrieved the errant blade.

Our family is naturally competitive and inevitably there were canoe races down the Zambezi with much laughter, threats and encouragement which shattered the sounds of silence. Biko hung back as Mum and Dad took on the two boys. To this day, I will maintain Margie and I were the quicker pair although we did seem to crisscross from Zambia to Zimbabwe to Zambia fairly regularly as we strained to win the contest. On one memorable occasion we were well in the lead in the direction of a herd of elephants playing and bathing in the river on the Zambian bank. As we got closer, they got bigger. We did our best to veer away but we were going too fast and instead of gracefully slowing down we thumped into the riverbank just behind the startled elephants. There were gales of laughter from the other two canoes. After some trumpeting to remind us of the local pecking order the elephants continued with their frolicking in and under the water with Margie and I trying to work out how to reverse a canoe when the flow of the river was edging it closer and closer to the elephants.

A few days later we farewelled a surprisingly emotional Biko. As he headed home, we prepared for our next adventure, whitewater rafting on the Zambezi very close to the Victoria Falls. And there lie several other tales and close shaves.

As I reflect on this trip and the impact that it had on our children, Margie and I were very careful and the three children were acutely aware of the risks involved. In today's world so many teenagers live such cloistered and sheltered lives, often dominated by the curse of social media, that they miss out on adventures as a family and learn how to look out for people rather than taking the selfish and entitled approach. We would have no hesitation in doing it all again.

Early in 2016, the Sydney-based, Julie McIntosh-led Classic Safari Company built a tour for me to South Africa. We called it the Rhino Ray Endangered Species Safari. Incidentally, it was Julie who gave me the nickname of 'Rhino Ray' which has stuck. The trip was focused on spreading awareness about the crisis engulfing the world's rhinos. We had four couples from Australia and one from Hong Kong, all from very diverse backgrounds. It was an eye-opener for all involved. We saw a lot of game including my precious rhinos and everyone loved it.

While making the final preparations for the safari, Kirstin Scholtz, one of our keen supporters and the official World Surfing League (WSL) photographer, contacted me saying Stephanie Gilmore, then six-time professional world surfing champion, was keen to be involved. This was a wonderful opportunity to be associated with a world-class athlete with an impeccable reputation and a host of social media followers. Steph joined us for the Madikwe Safari Lodge sector of the safari and she was warmly welcomed by the whole group. This was a credit to her genial and friendly personality. A sensitive and articulate young woman, Steph had read extensively and quickly demonstrated her awareness of the poaching crisis.

A few months later I asked Kirstin if she could take some photographs of the rhinos that had been identified to bring to Australia as part of the Australian Rhino Project. The rhinos were being held at Hans Kooy's farm in the North-West Province of South Africa. I wanted to use the photos for marketing collateral and Kirstin jumped at the chance and penned this report after her visit.

'I was fortunate enough to visit the rhinos in what was supposed to be a safe haven in South Africa. Despite the electric fences, guard towers and watchdogs to protect the fifty rhinos, I quickly realised that nowhere is safe for rhino. As we skirted the inside of the large enclosure, staying close to the fence for safety, we noticed one large rhino lying under a tree away from the others who were feeding on a pile of hay. She was waiting for them to move before she made her way to the food and it was as she got up, that we noticed something was terribly wrong. She had been shot through the fence, just above her front left leg, leaving her crippled and in obvious agony.

'It is heartbreaking to think what an animal, with no natural predators and very poor eyesight, would go through during such trauma. Watching her trying to walk on three legs was one of the most distressing sights I have ever seen. Helplessly, we watched as she tried to inch forward to the feed. With each stumbling step, the top half of her body collapsed as her leg buckled under her enormous weight. A rhino simply cannot function with three legs, and as we watched with tears rolling down our cheeks, we knew that this beautiful animal stood very little chance of survival. A few days later we learned that she had died from her injuries. She was pregnant at the time.

'The cruelty of these poachers leaves me completely speechless. Absolutely heartbreaking.'

Dr Chris Brown, the Australian veterinarian and television

personality known nationally and internationally as the Bondi Vet, was the MC at our rhino fundraising dinner in Sydney and had become a good friend. While filming the TV show *I'm a Celebrity, Get Me Out of Here* in Hoedspruit in 2015, Chris invited his father, Dr Graeme Brown, a lecturer in veterinary parasitology at the University of Sydney, to visit the local rhino orphanage where they met the veterinary nurses. All UK trained, these nurses had responsibility for the rehabilitation of the young, orphaned rhinos. While working alongside Graeme they appealed to him for help. They really needed a microscope to perform faecal worm tests since outsourcing such testing to local vets meant delays in processing results and was also expensive. Graeme suggested that the nurses contact me for support. Their request was for financial support which I declined since I had a strong view that all of the people who donated money to us wanted it to go directly to the Australian Rhino Project, but I subsequently met with Graeme in Sydney and we agreed our best contribution would be to donate a microscope to the orphanage. I was sure the Sydney University Veterinarian Faculty would have a few spare microscopes and I was confident our great supporter, Roseanne Taylor, dean of the faculty, would support this request. She did. The microscope was duly shipped to the rhino orphanage.

During the Endangered Species safari, I included a visit to see the rhino orphans (and the microscope). While we were there, the nurses mentioned how grateful they were for the donation which was vital and central to their work, but they really could use a centrifuge to enable the team to independently complete basic blood analyses. Vivien Jones, a member of our group, pulled me aside and asked the cost. I told her it was $1000 and she immediately wrote a cheque. The nurses won't forget Vivien's generosity and nor will I. The equipment has been a significant step-change for the nurses in performing vital tests on the orphans.

In February 2015, the Channel Seven TV presenter Simon Reeve and I had ten days in South Africa filming what was planned to be a documentary for the Australian Rhino Project. At the last minute we were joined by the well-known *Sydney Morning Herald* journalist Sue Williams and photographer Julia Salnicki from the Classic Safari Company.

In recent years there has been a drive to tag rhinos and take their DNA samples to match a dead rhino with a poached rhino horn. I had arranged for the group to experience this rhino notching exercise which, while it is a necessary task in the Klaserie Game Reserve, by charging a fee it is also an opportunity to raise funds for protecting the rhinos. We were due to meet vet Dr Pete Rogers at 5.30 am for the notching. It was important that we were on time because of the increased stress on the drugged rhino in hot weather, so we excitedly left Thornybush Lodge at 4.15 am. Driving the hired Kombi vehicle I had received exact instructions from the lodge on how to get to the reserve gate. Bear in mind it was pitch-dark, no moon and there are no lights in a game park. Within minutes I knew we were lost. We had been instructed to turn right as we drove out of the lodge and I managed to get this simple task wrong by turning too soon. We travelled along all the while getting plenty of unsolicited advice from Sue and Julia in the back. One of the better suggestions was to travel along the fence line and surely, we would eventually come to a gate. This seemed like a good plan and as we drove along the electrified fence on my right the road narrowed and became progressively worse. It was starting to get light and I could just make out potholes and large rocks in the road ahead. I stopped the vehicle and asked Simon if he would mind hopping out and having a look to see if we should continue or not.

Ever obliging, Simon jumped out of the car and walked down the rocky road illuminated in the headlights. Stopping about 20 metres away he turned and gave me the thumbs down. I then beckoned him back to the car. He had taken just two steps when we suddenly heard, 'Fuck me, there's a lion!' As one, the three of us looked to our left and sure enough about 15 metres away on the edge of the road there was a crouching lioness between us and Simon. She sat perfectly still, intently watching Simon. We all knew the advice: if you came across a lion, the absolutely last thing you should do is run. Remain still. If you run, you are prey.

Forgetting or dismissing this warning Simon took off and covered the ground like Usain Bolt. He landed on my lap eyes wide and heartrate off the chart. The lioness had followed his unexpected and certainly unplanned movement and she just sat watching us, watching her. The atmosphere was electric. Not a word was spoken. We kept our eyes on her as I gently reversed the vehicle, she did not move. All I could think about was what I would say to Simon's dear wife Linda if the worst had happened. It would go something like this, 'Well Linda, you might find this hard to believe but we were travelling along in a private game reserve. Simon had hopped out of the car to have a look at the state of the road and then the lion pounced ...'

We eventually found the gate and by this time, the silence had turned to nervous chatter at the thought of what might have happened.

The next few hours will always be in my mind as I have no doubt it will with those fortunate enough to experience a rhino horn being removed or the rhino notched for future protection and identification.

We met up with the rhino notching team, led by Dr Pete Rogers and Colin Rowles, head ranger for the Klaserie Game Reserve, as well as a large group of specialists including the state vet and two heavily armed rangers for our protection.

Ear-notching is one of several different methods used to identify individual rhinos. In combination with micro-chipping, numbered ID tags and distinct physical markings, these tools help biologists and rangers monitor the movements, interactions, health and safety of all individuals within key populations.

Pete is not only a world-class wildlife vet, he is also a very funny man. As part of the briefing, he gave each of us a task. While Simon would be in the helicopter with the pilot and Pete with the gun to dart the rhino, Julia was to cover the tranquilised rhino's eyes with a blanket and Sue was given a special job. Sue is of English descent and has beautiful 'English rose' skin. 'Sue, your job will be to apply the ointment to the rhino's ear after it has been notched to stop the bleeding, prevent infection and so on.' I glanced at Sue and if it were possible, she was even paler than usual and also quite unsteady.

The helicopter thundered above, picked up Pete and Simon and took off to find a rhino. The rest of us were ready in the two Land Rovers with all the gear and the support team, our hearts in our mouths. Almost immediately, the radio call came in that they had found a rhino and we took off at high speed. We watched in awe as the helicopter hovered above the rhino with Pete hanging on from the side with his tranquilliser gun ready to dart. We had vertigo just watching. The helicopter then plunged down, swooping between the thorny branches of the acacia trees, as the pilot coolly pointed out the quarry – a fully grown white rhino with a pristine horn. The chopper kept pace with her as she ran and Pete unerringly darted her in the rump. It was immediately clear that the members of this team knew exactly what they were doing and were the ultimate professionals. When the rhino finally staggered to a halt the team raced to the 2000-kilogram animal and rolled it onto its tummy, inserted ear plugs and a blindfold to reduce stress so that the vet could take blood samples and start the notching and micro-chip implanting processes. Comfortingly but also disconcertingly, the rangers circled us, guns at the ready, just in case of any unwelcome visitors – man or beast.

Time is of the essence and the team had to minimise the

amount of time that the rhino was under anaesthetic. It was like watching a highly complex cardiac operation. Pete inserted a chip into the rhino's horn for future identification and then notched her ear, mentioning grimly in passing that this was the 227th rhino he had notched. All to prevent the animals from being poached.

As the rhino gave a quiet squeal, our team swung into action with Simon doing the filming and commentary, Julia helping wherever she could. We all watched as Sue was given the ointment to apply to the rhino's now heavily bleeding ear. She was ashen. I am not sure if her eyes were open as she applied the ointment but she was definitely swaying in the wind with tears streaming down her face. It was a powerful moment with all emotions laid bare.

Pete then turned to me and casually said, 'Oh Ray, I forgot to tell you that your job is to apply the antidote to bring the rhino back into full consciousness.' I gave him an incredulous look and said (epithet omitted), 'Pete, you can see that I have some issues with my legs and can't run particularly well. How far away will the truck be?' With a wave, his response was an airy, 'Oh, over there.' I said, 'Okay, well then I am going to apply the antidote as rapidly as I can.' His turn for a death stare and he responded, 'You'd better not bloody do that, you'll kill her.' As I inserted the syringe, I noticed the truck was moving further away for the 'safety' of the occupants. As Pete meandered off, I applied the antidote and as I removed the syringe he said, 'Okay, let's go' and jogged/sauntered off towards the truck. He must have had a lead of about 10 metres but bad legs or not I exploded out of the blocks and I'm sure I broke Simon's sprint record from the morning. I was already on the game viewer as this giant animal awoke, snorted and headed directly for us and at the last second executed a perfect sidestep that David Campese would have been proud of.

The entire experience was certainly another highlight of my life. I took a deep breath as I took in this life-changing experience and I certainly wasn't alone as Sue and Julia quietly wept.

Sue wrote an outstanding article about this experience which was published in the *Good Weekend* magazine in the *Sydney Morning Herald* and the *Age*. Sue writes from the heart and I could tell that she was deeply and emotionally touched during the darting of the rhino. Her empathy for the rhinos and anger at the poachers and the inherent cruelty of the killing was palpable.

I am a tactile person and as I rubbed the rough and wrinkled skin of the drugged rhino, I had this overwhelming sense of empathy and sadness for this massive animal whose ancestors had walked our planet up to 10 million years ago and is now completely defenceless against man and his guns.

*

Margie took up golf fairly late in life and is now a very good player. Some say I taught her everything she knows, but that would be a slight exaggeration. She sits on the board of Pennant Hills Golf Club in the Sydney suburb of Beecroft. I too wonder why it wasn't named the Beecroft Golf Club, but I digress.

We have met some wonderful people at the club and in 2018 we invited five couples to join us on the Golf and Game Reserve Safari to South Africa. In the two-week trip, we played five world-class golf courses and spent six days in game parks. The Australian contingent of Lyn and Phil, Joan and Michael, Lesley and Alun were joined by Leonie and Roger from the UK and Linda and Graham who seem to live in both countries. We had a blast. Only Michael had visited South Africa before and on that occasion, he was mugged in Cape Town. Given this, Michael and probably some others approached the trip with some trepidation.

Because of the complexities of lugging golf clubs on and off airplanes, I arranged for our group to travel around the country in a comfortable coach. As one of the ladies pointed out it wasn't that comfortable. It didn't have a loo. We had a lot of fun on the bus and while travelling through the Kruger National Park one morning my mobile phone rang. Margie had the phone and she handed it to me saying, 'It's Johnny Young.' Hearing the name, four pairs of smiling female eyes looked at me with surprise accompanied by giggling. All of them adored Johnny from *Young Talent Time* from a era when everyone was a lot younger. YTT as it was known ran on Australian television from 1971 to 1983 with a brief return in 2012.

I explained to Johnny why everyone was laughing. He loved it. At the time he and I were working on taking a group of his Radio 2CH listeners to game parks in Africa. We named it 'Johnny Young's Swinging Safari' which unfortunately never eventuated, but it elicited many memories for those on the bus about 'the good old days'.

In building the golfing trip I was told we would not be able to play the Gary Player course at Sun City because it was being prepared for the annual Nedbank Challenge tournament which attracted some of the best players in the world. Struggling to find an alternative quality course reasonably close to Sun City, I thought I'd give Marc Player, Gary's son, a call to see if he had any suggestions. Marc runs all of Gary's business interests under the Black Knight Enterprises label and is the nephew of the late Dr Ian Player, one of my heroes. Marc is a good friend and has always been very supportive of my conservation work.

Marc said, 'Why not play at Dad's course, Blair Atholl?' Because it is a semi-private course, I had never heard of it but it is one of South Africa's top ten courses. It was originally the Players' family home where Marc and his siblings grew up. I jumped at the opportunity but when I heard it was more than 100 kilometres from Sun City it became too difficult to arrange from a logistics point of view. I slept on it, but in the morning I thought why not get a helicopter to and from Blair Atholl? As you do. I made some enquiries. It wasn't cheap but if you split the cost between six couples it was a goer.

There was a great deal of excitement and nervous laughter as we waited on the tarmac for the two choppers. The helicopter flight was exhilarating. We landed at Blair Atholl and were welcomed by head professional Paul Marks, as many of the locals craned their heads trying to recognise any celebrities disembarking. Alas they were disappointed. We played the magnificent golf course, had a few lagers and were then ferried back to Sun City in the helicopters. The group felt like royalty. Marc, generous as always, had gone out of his way to ensure the group was well looked after and had arranged for a personal letter signed by Gary for each member. We also received a book about Blair Atholl signed by the Black Knight. It is so sad to now see the rift between father and son being played out in the media.

Another special part of the safari was the three days we spent at the five-star Madikwe Safari Lodge. As one of the highlights I had arranged for the group to go on a bush walk but there was an unexpected glitch when we arrived and were told those who were over sixty needed a medical certificate to join the walk. Well, that was all of us. Kevin the lodge manager was adamant. He would lose his job if we didn't comply. I pleaded with him pointing out we were all golfers who played at least twice a week and walked the course. It was to no avail. I broke the news to the disappointed group.

A few hours later Kevin told me he had organised to have a doctor from the closest town come to the lodge and do the medical checks. Given the town was three hours away on poor, dusty roads, this was exceptional service. The doctor duly arrived and each tourist was called in for an examination. One of our group, Roger, is British. And I mean British. A shaken, not stirred type of fellow. A lovely man, he could sometimes come across as a little distant and disdainful. I could see an opportunity and went for it. I sidled up to the doctor and asked if he would join in a prank. He agreed. After he had examined the last member of the group, he emerged from his room pulling on a plastic glove with his forefinger pointing menacingly upward. He then requested Mr Roger to join him for further examination. Roger's smile ran away from his face as the rest of us collapsed with laughter. He was a changed man thereafter.

Each time Margie and I go to South Africa – which was annually in pre-COVID-19 times – we stay at our little piece of Africa in Ingwelala Private Game Reserve and we take a suitcase of clothing for the local staff and their children. As I was planning this safari, I thought our group could do the same and donate some gear to a disadvantaged school along the way. I contacted Robert More, owner of MORE Travel who manages the Madikwe and Marataba lodges and enquired if they had any relationships with local schools. Rob said they sponsored the Obakeng Primary School just outside the game park. I offered to donate some clothing and various other items such as toys and stationery. Rob jumped at the offer. I told the group about the plan and they loved it and immediately commenced making beautiful quilts and clearing out cupboards of clothing in pristine condition but not to be worn again. Then came the discarded toys, card games and so on. Soon my garage looked like a second-hand clothing store.

On impulse, I reached out to Gary Edstein, senior vice president at DHL, whom I have known for years. I explained what we were planning and without hesitation he offered to transport up to 250 kilograms of clothing to South Africa. A stunning donation. I also contacted Christine Holgate, former chief executive of Australia Post, and asked if she could help. I had never met Christine who was on vacation in the US at the time, but she loved the idea and offered to transport clothing to the school in South Africa at no cost. Amazing. I then contacted Raelene Castle, CEO of Rugby Australia, Craig Tiley, CEO of Tennis Australia, and Rob Frost, GM of Eastwood Rugby Club, and all donated an astonishing amount of new but obsolete gear, balls and boots.

As we travelled to the Obakeng school there were no tarred roads and the extreme poverty was evident in whichever direction you looked. It was hot and dusty and yet when the children unexpectedly put on a concert for us, every child was dressed in sparklingly clean clothing. We eventually presented more than 180 kilograms of donations to the students and teachers at the school. It was an emotional visit and another life-changing experience for our generous group who subsequently also covered the cost of installing cooling fans in the fairly bare classroom.

*

As I write, Margie and I have just returned from South Africa after taking another group of Pennant Hills Golf Club golfers, Mark and Cheryl, Greg and Kim, Rob and Sue, Tack and Nerol and Greg and Bernadette. The itinerary was similar to that of 2018 but there was increased focus on the perilous state of the world's remaining rhinos.

After an emotional visit to Nelson Mandela's house in Soweto, the group visited the 1300 graves of women, children and babies who died in the Middelburg Concentration Camp during the Boer War. Once again Gary Edstein showed his incredibly generous side in arranging for DHL to donate more than 75 kilograms of clothing, stationery, toys and so on. These shipments were supplemented by our group who carried another 85 kilograms which we personally delivered to the 900-pupil Mpilonhle Primary School in Dullstroom.

The group proved to be avid, enquiring conservationists and deeply appreciated meeting some of the leaders fighting poachers and trying to ensure the survival of the rhinos. The K9 Centre where dogs are trained to find and track poachers was a winner while the opportunity to feed rhino orphans was a highly emotional experience. However, the opportunity to participate in the notching of a very large rhino bull will, I expect, be cherished for a lifetime. We named the rhino Henri, noting that the female rhino that the previous group had notched had not been seen for years and had likely been killed by poachers. We had given her the name of Raelene.

I have mentioned the Player family a number of times and my most recent dealings have been with Gary's son Marc. Many would know that Gary won seven Australian Open titles, one ahead of fellow legend Jack Nicklaus. Marc's company has built more than 400 courses around the world but none in Australia and this remains one of his goals. Marc has taken up the challenge and after much discussion and false starts because of COVID-19, I am really pleased (and proud) that after my introductions he has appointed his chief designer Phil Jacobs to work with my local Pennant Hills Golf Club to rejuvenate and refresh our course. Initial plans are really exciting. The power of relationships.

*

As mentioned elsewhere, I have met many interesting people through the journey of life. One of these was the late Tony Greig, former England cricket captain, who was born in South Africa, although he spent much of his life in England and Australia. He was a regular visitor to South Africa to keep in touch with his family and during those visits he would take as many opportunities as possible to get out in the bush and see the African wildlife. I recall one conversation with him at Sydney Airport when we were comparing life in Australia and South Africa and I suggested that Australia would be an even better place if we could see African wildlife such as elephants, lions, leopards, multiple antelope species and, of course, rhinos, running in the Australian outback. He laughed and said, 'Let me tell you a story about Kerry.' Tony was referring to the late Kerry Packer, a close friend and mentor, and also Australia's wealthiest man at the time.

In the mid-1980s, Packer asked if Tony had ever done any hunting. It turned out that Packer wanted to bag an elephant. Tony had never hunted but found himself supplied with special boots, hunting outfits and oilskins while Packer brought an armoury. As the pair boarded Kerry's private plane bound for Johannesburg, Tony recalled that they had enough guns and ammunition to supply a small army.

Accompanied by two professional big-game hunters, they set off into the Okavango Delta in Botswana in search of the elephant Packer had paid tens of thousands of dollars to pursue. There are about 140,000 elephants in the Delta, and Botswana issues up to 100 hunting licences a year for trophy elephants. Packer had to find the exact elderly bull nominated on their licence. The elephant remained elusive and on the second-last day of the safari, Packer had had enough and said that he was sick and tired of trying to find this elephant and was prepared to release the right of shooting it to Tony – if he could find it. The good news for the elephant was that they never found it.

In his book *Love, War and Cricket*, Tony's son, Mark, adds a story about the same trip. Packer got the trackers to place a dead crocodile in Tony's tent early one morning. The tracker found a stick and propped open its mouth sufficiently to make it look alive – and threatening. The story goes that Tony saw it just as he got out of bed and then broke the world long-jump record to evade the crocodile. Boys will be boys.

After the trip and emboldened by Packer's obvious joy to be among wild animals, Tony hesitantly suggested that he could use some of his vast pastoral holdings in northern Australia to set up a 'mini-Serengeti' which would be a major tourist attraction. Later, Tony really pressed the point with Kerry who finally relented saying, 'Get it done.'

A year or so later, I mentioned this story to Ken Warriner.

Ken, considered one of the best cattlemen in Australia, had Packer's complete trust. They became good friends in the 1970s spending time bull running and buffalo shooting and Packer especially loved the chance to get away from city business pressures with Ken and mix with the rough-and-tumble bush characters. Over time, Ken managed the entire Packer-owned Consolidated Pastoral Holdings, which some 300,000 cattle on more than 5 million hectares – an area slightly smaller than Belgium. Picking up on Tony Greig's story, Ken said that once Packer had made a decision, he typically wanted action. He committed $50 million to the project to be kept in trust 'so that no bloody politician' could get his hands on it or, in future years, say that it was unaffordable. Things moved fast as they focused on property in the north of Western Australia and discussions commenced with Premier Richard Court's state government about establishing the sanctuary. According to Ken, plans were well advanced with the government very supportive until, as happens, there was an election and Court's Liberal National Party lost power to Labor which saw no merit in the proposal. Sadly, the project simply died.

Not for the first nor for the last time, the politicians had the final say.

*

Lord Alistair McAlpine, best known as chief fundraiser for Margaret Thatcher's Conservative Party, is widely credited as the developer of the world-renowned Western Australia resort town of Broome and the builder of the Cable Beach complex. He also founded the Broome Pearl Coast Zoo. McAlpine first came to Australia in 1959, returning in 1964 to Perth – 'a big farming town' – as a developer, building office blocks and the city's first five-star hotel, the Parmelia. It was the start of a lifelong love affair with Australia. He headed to 'ramshackle' Broome in 1979 with plans to collect seashells, but instead bought a house after he came back from the pub, and went on to sign the deal for the Cable Beach site on the back of a beer coaster. His passion for gardening, especially frangipanis, saw him plant out the city, giving Broome the tropical feel it still enjoys today. He also laid the groundwork for the international reputation Broome pearls now have. McAlpine managed to import a wide variety of animals into his Pearl Coast Zoo including nyala, sitatunga, sable, gemsbok, kudu, eland, nilgai, lechwe, waterbuck, Angolan springbok, Congo and water buffalo, Grevy's zebra, pygmy hippo, and scimitar horned oryx. Significantly for my project, there was not one incident of any of Australia's fauna or flora being contaminated in any way. Good news.

The 1989 Australian pilots' strike and Prime Minister Paul Keating's 'recession we had to have' hammered Broome's fledgling tourism industry and spelt the end of Lord McAlpine's grand plans for the town. Enter one Warren Anderson, a man of grand schemes and sweeping vision, who fell in love with the Northern Territory and bought one of the jewels of the Top End's pastoral belt – the expansive Tipperary cattle station of more than 500,000 acres in lush landscape along the Daly River. It was swiftly redesigned to Warren's blueprint. He transformed Tipperary into a majestic, modern business, equipped to perfection. But it became more than a mere bush outpost; it was also Anderson's private pleasure dome, a parkland conceived on a grand scale and reflecting his own fascinations and tastes. At the time, Kerry Packer and Anderson were Australia's wealthiest men and both exceptionally competitive. To many who were familiar with the station empires of the far north, Anderson's Tipperary could be read as a response to Newcastle Waters, the hub of the outback empire of the Packer-owned Consolidated Pastoral; a remote version of Sans Souci Palace, deliberately constructed to outdo Packer's Versailles. At the time, Anderson's wealth was estimated at $200 million by the *Australian Business Review* and only Kerry Packer was ahead of him. Tipperary was on a different scale from anything, anywhere; it was the wildest venture northern Australia had ever seen. It had its own neat town and post office, an equestrian centre, an indoor tennis court, a sealed runway long and wide enough to take a Boeing 727 and single men's quarters decked out in brass and jarrah wood with a swimming pool and a school.

But the standout feature of Tipperary was the wildlife, roaming pretty much 'free' in 400-hectare paddocks. Anderson loved and prized rare animals and bought all of Lord McAlpine's animals from the bankrupt Broome Pearl Coast Zoo. He collected them and he bred them, and had more than 2200 animals and birds, including zebras, giraffe, several varieties of deer, tropical birds, oryx, two white rhino bulls and, in Warren's pride of place, luxuriating in their dedicated muddy lake, four precious pygmy hippos.

I tracked down Kevin Langham in Cairns. He had arrived from the Mugabe-led Zimbabwe with just $200 in his pocket. A qualified scientist, he did labouring jobs, worked at Western Plains Zoo for a while and then, in 1986, he received a phone call from Warren Anderson which changed his life. Warren wanted Kevin to manage his free-range game park on Tipperary Station, on which he had already spent $100 million. A stipulation was that this was not a tourist venture, this was purely for threatened and endangered species. In Kevin's words,

'Warren was way ahead of his time, not only in a business sense with live cattle export, but also in his views, passion and commitment to conservation. In establishing the Tipperary Sanctuary, Warren had to overcome a raft of "administrative challenges", not unlike those which you have been through, Ray. Tipperary Sanctuary was a project that was on the cusp of making a significant contribution to the conservation of endangered mammals on a regional and international scale.

164

Warren had possibly the largest herd of endangered scimitar horned oryx in the world while the endangered addax, Grevy's zebra, Kafue lechwe and Congo buffalo were all breeding well. CSIRO were working on a research project that had the potential to significantly improve digestion of plant material in cattle, by using rumen microflora from exotic species. A large herd of nilgai antelope was breeding well and showing great potential as a selective browser, controlling broad leaf plants, and the rhino were doing well with plans underway to rapidly increase the number. With just a little more luck, who knows where this would have landed.

'One thing is for certain, Ray, Warren fights hard, he does not entertain failure, or idiots, and from my experience is more interested in "how it can be done" rather than "why it cannot be done" and as you have found out, you need that approach to take on the type of project that you have. Warren demonstrated that it can be done.'

In 2003, Warren got into financial difficulties and was forced to sell Tipperary to Allan Myers QC, in a move that Warren said broke his heart.

With quite some difficulty, I eventually tracked Warren down in Sydney and had a number of really entertaining and interesting meetings with him. Now a very private man, Warren's story was the ultimate rags to riches and back to rags. He left school when he was fourteen, after taking exception to being 'strapped' and giving the teacher 'clip'.

He has been associated with some of Australia's largest developments including the $1 billion-plus Westralia Square skyscraper in Perth; more than seventy Coles supermarkets around country; the Parliament House complex in Darwin, and the redevelopment of the historic Windsor Hotel in Melbourne. At various points in his life, he owned Boomerang, the iconic Sydney waterfront property, and also the heritage-listed Fernhill at Mulgoa.

When he sold Tipperary, Warren sold many of his exotic animals, including the rhino, to Mareeba Wild Animal Park in Queensland, which was opened in 2003. Others went to Mary River Station, which has now become one of Australia's largest game-hunting reserves.

Warren was extremely supportive of what I tried to achieve but was fairly cynical about the future of any such project, believing that the Australian government had little or no interest in conserving endangered species. At the time, I must admit that I thought if Warren Anderson, with all of his financial and political clout could not make a success of protecting the planet's animals in Australia, what hope did I have.

Love him or hate him, and there are plenty of people on both sides, Warren Anderson is certainly one of Australia's most interesting identities. Sadly, his contribution to conservation is unknown and untold.

CHAPTER 14

THREE OF MY HEROES

During my journey as founder of the Australian Rhino Project I met some really interesting people, some of whom were quickly forgotten or avoided, but others who were beacons of hope and light. Three of these were Dame Jane Goodall, Dr Ian Player and Major General Johan Jooste, all of whom became good friends and each made or continue to make an incalculable contribution to endangered species and each, in his or her own special way, is my hero.

I first met Dr Jane Goodall DBE at the World Parks Congress in Sydney thanks to Natalie Houghton, CEO of the Jane Goodall Institute in Australia. Natalie and I got on like a house on fire and it was entirely due to her that I had a private meeting with Jane during her visit. While Jane is tiny, her big heart beats strongly and her smile lights up the room while her eyes flash as she warms to her subject. It is said you know when you are in the presence of greatness and that was exactly my feeling. She is so quiet, so calm, so measured and so personable that initially I was quite unsettled. I'm sure she noticed my nervousness and immediately put me at ease.

While chimps are Jane's first love, she is deeply knowledgeable and concerned about all endangered species. She is a passionate believer in the need for, and power of, education which led her to establish the wildly successful Roots and Shoots program, educating the young across the world.

During Jane's most recent trip to Sydney, I presented her with a framed copy of a poem I wrote for her. She was surprised and deeply moved. The poem can be found in the second Appendix.

In 2019 I again met up with Jane at the Wildlife Conservation Network Conference in San Francisco where she was the keynote speaker. Terry, a friend of our family for fifty years, had long since emigrated to the US and also attended the conference. His two lovely daughters Jenny and Bridget are passionate followers and supporters of Jane and Terry asked if I could possibly arrange for them to meet her. We met in downtown San Francisco and bang on time Jane quietly appeared. Terry is a highly successful businessman and can be a bit of a formal fellow. At his suggestion, prior to Jane joining us, we had a 'dry run' of how we should start the conversation. Now that we were all primed, I did notice that Terry was particularly edgy. I well understood this since it was potentially a once-in-a-lifetime meeting. Having introduced Jenny and Bridget I then turned to Terry who immediately went off script. He blurted out he was a long-time admirer of Jane ever since he had read *Gorillas in the Mist*. There was an awkward silence. I'm sure Jane was biting her lip as she quietly explained, 'That is not me.' It was, of course, the late Dian Fossey who wrote that book. Terry was mortified, as were his daughters. Jane was less than impressed but being the ultimate professional, she managed a wan smile, and we continued the light conversation followed by smiling photographs. I felt dreadful for Terry. He is a dear friend and I think the excitement of the moment simply overwhelmed him.

Jane has an exhausting travel schedule, but when you meet her, you would never guess she is well into her eighties. Margie and I have been fortunate enough to meet her on several occasions and she is always the same. Interested, interesting and inspirational.

*

Dr Ian Player was many things to me. He was the father of rhino conservation, a mentor and an active supporter of the Australian Rhino Project. In short, he was my hero.

Ian was internationally recognised as an environmentalist and a conservationist but he was also a man of many facets and contradictions. Not just a game ranger but a man of culture and the arts, a deep thinker and Jungian. He was an irascible campaigner and a maverick as well as a writer, lecturer and an international diplomat. A man deeply committed to everything and everyone he believed in.

Born in Johannesburg in 1927, he was educated at St John's College then served with the South African Army in Italy during World War II. At war's end he returned home aged nineteen with no idea of what he wanted to do with his life. When he pioneered the 120-kilometre Dusi River Canoe Marathon in Natal in 1951 he expected to see an abundance of wildlife along the riverbank, but to his dismay he saw almost none. Then began an epic personal lifetime journey to fight for nature conservation.

He joined the Natal Parks board in 1952 and established Operation Rhino which succeeded in saving the white rhino from extinction. He also founded the Wilderness Leadership School during the troubled days of apartheid. It was a multi-racial and experiential program that would spawn a global network of conservationists committed to saving wilderness and wildlife throughout the world.

I wrote to Ian soon after the launch of the Australian Rhino Project briefing him on what I was trying to achieve and inviting him to be patron. He immediately agreed and wrote,

> 'I was delighted to see the progress that has been made and you can rely on me to do everything I can to help you make the project a great success. In the 1960s I was trying desperately to get a decent herd of rhino into Australia, but only succeeded in getting a pair to Taronga Zoo. With the situation in this country and the consistent killing of rhino there has been worldwide revulsion so your project could not come at a better time and I am certain that with the right publicity (which you have already started) that you will be inundated with offers of help, including financial help. In South Africa, a great deal of money has been raised, estimated to be over R200m ($AUD20 million), regrettably most has not gone to the rhino.'

If ever there was an endorsement that mattered, this was it. Ian was also particularly proud that someone from his alma mater was working to save the rhino. The reality was that I was standing on his broad shoulders – he had put in the really hard yards. He mentioned he had recently arranged with the Wilderness Leadership School to take a group of young St John's boys on a two-week rites of passage. He said it had done wonders for them, camping in the bush for a fortnight but not without a great deal of squealing; most of them never having had to struggle for anything in their lives let alone going without food for a day. He was a hard man but he loved St John's College.

In a subsequent exchange, Ian mentioned that we had another connection, 'I was very pleased to read that you are a relative of Trevor Dearlove, who worked with me as a ranger in iMfolozi and then went on to do an outstanding job of work in Kruger. He must be delighted that you are involved in this whole exercise which, pray God, will get a decent population established in Australia.' My cousin Trevor conceived the idea of wilderness trails in the Kruger Park in 1978. It was a novelty that appealed to every wildlife enthusiast and satisfied a longing for visitors to be able to walk in the bush among the animals instead of seeing them from inside a hot and cramped motor vehicle.

Recently Trevor dropped me a line saying, 'In Ian's last letter to me, before he passed away, he said your cousin Ray is doing a great job with rhino conservation in Australia.' High praise from one of my all-time heroes.

As Ian's health deteriorated, the tone of his correspondence took on more and more urgency.

'I am glad that you have met the Canberra government officials – all bureaucracies are a nightmare and the only way to get anywhere is to keep on hammering on the door. Let us hope that we can keep this urgent task of moving the rhino to Australia on the road. The poaching has not stopped at all and in fact has got worse and the animal is now under greater threat than ever and it would be a crime if we did not succeed in getting them relocated to a safe haven, like Australia. Hopefully, we can also make this relocation the beginning of sending other African endangered species to Australia as well.'

He went on, 'You have a great missionary task ahead of you in Canberra, Ray, but you must take heart and keep up the fight.'

Ian's comment that the only way to get anywhere is to keep on hammering on the (bureaucrats') door, really resonated with me. I firmly believed this was the only way the import of the rhinos into Australia would happen. It was also one of the reasons I fell out with the three directors of the board. They believed we should go softly. Ride with the tide and go with the flow is not my style.

Ian finished his letter on a sobering note, 'I regret to say that my decrepitude is getting progressively worse and the old rhino capture injuries, as well as the onset of muscular dystrophy, places more and more restrictions on any movement. It is unbelievably frustrating, but if the situation ever demands it, I will get into a wheelchair and travel with you to beard the bureaucrats. I know only too well how their minds work and there are ways of dealing with them.' Here was a man who had travelled this road and just could not believe it was happening all over again.

What is not widely known is Ian and Gary Player are brothers. The Black Knight, as Gary came to be known, accumulated nine major golf championships including a golf grand slam and won 165 tournaments on six continents over six decades. An extraordinary achievement and a talented family by any measure.

Margie and I visited Ian and Ann Player at their farm near Howick in Kwa Zulu Natal in October 2014. Ian's eyes were misty but alert and his handshake strong although he was not at all mobile. I had written a poem for him which he asked me to read. I found doing so was tough and emotional. I called the poem 'For Dr Ian Player – the Father of Rhino Conservation'. Ian had tears in his eyes giving Margie and me a big hug. The poem can be found in the second Appendix.

The day we met Ian and Ann, there was a delegation of game rangers from Northwest Parks who had travelled 1600 kilometres to pay their respects. In an incredibly moving show of love and admiration each one of these men, young and old, knelt in front of the seated Ian, took his hand and briefly held it.

Just a month later Ian had a severe stroke signalling the beginning of the end. Good friend, Sheila Berry, penned this beautiful note on behalf of the Player family,

'A week ago today, Ian cast his canoe on to the river that would take him across to the other side. He is a strong man but there are signs he is approaching his destination. His pulse is regular and his grip is firm but not as sustained as it has been. It is more like a comforting squeeze, as if to assure those he loves, he is still here. And so, he is being caring, considerate, generous and thoughtful of the needs of others to the end.'

When Ian died there were tributes from all over the world. I wrote to Ian's family, *'Although expected, this news is crushing. Ian's contribution to conservation has been immense. When I first started out on the Australian Rhino Project, Ian was intensely supportive, insisting that spreading the risk – as he had done before – was vital in the attempt to preserve the species. Ian has been our greatest supporter and my wife Margie and I were blessed to meet with him and Ann a few short weeks ago. He was resolute in supporting our project and we will do everything that we can to play our small part in keeping Ian's dream and passion alive. The words of the poet Maya Angelou seem appropriate – I have taken the liberty of including rhinos in the poem.'*

> *When great trees fall,*
> *Rocks on distant hills shudder,*
> *Lions hunker down in tall grasses,*
> *And even elephants (and rhinos)*
> *Lumber after safety.*

Sandile Masondo is a young Zulu man who had joined an Ian Player Wilderness Trail a few years before. He is from a humble township in Howick about 25 kilometres from Ian's farm. He arrived at the farm the morning after Ian's death. Sandile leads a deceptively simple life while actually being extraordinary. After the wilderness trail, Sandile climbed Kilimanjaro with the South African Rhino team to draw attention to the plight of rhinos and to encourage South African youth to become involved in trying to stop the slaughter of these magnificent animals which are traditionally considered royal to the Zulu people. In 2015, Sandile walked 3500 kilometres to promote the Zulu language and culture. He strongly believed African people who had lost contact with their traditional roots have no moral or spiritual compass to guide their lives.

Sandile explained the purpose of his visit to the Player

173

homestead. According to Zulu tradition one's burial place is one's final house. Sandile had come to ask if he could be given the honour of digging Ian's grave, he wanted to prepare a comfortable last room for Ian's body. Sandile's wish was granted. He was grateful to be able to assuage his pain and shed his tears through the sweat of his body as he dug the grave for this giant of a man whom he deeply revered, respected and loved. And so, very early before any rays of sunlight touched the eastern horizon, Sandile was waiting at the little church where Ian's family and closest friends were gathered to bury Ian's mortal remains.

In many ways I am pleased Ian was not here when I left the Rhino Project. I would have hated to explain to him the Australian government delays and internal politics had destroyed his and my dreams.

I am truly blessed to have had Ian Player in my life.

*

I first met Major General Johan Jooste in 2013 when I travelled to South Africa to try and get a first-hand feel for the rhino poaching situation and to assess the likelihood of sourcing rhinos for our project. Without doubt he is one of the most impressive men I have ever had the pleasure of meeting.

In 2012, South African National Parks (SANParks) Management decided to form a special department to deal with the increase in wildlife crime, in particular rhino poaching, in the Kruger National Park. General Jooste was approached to head this group. His brief was to put in place para-military strategies, structures and systems that would enable SANParks to respond to the increasing threat and constantly changing tactics of poachers. It was clear that counter-poaching measures conducted within the boundaries of the national parks alone would not be sufficient. The term 'clearing the park from the outside' was coined by the General.

Johan had retired from the army in 2006 after thirty-five years of active service. He served the last part of his military career in the army's general staff in various capacities but was always involved with strategy, leadership development and knowledge management. An articulate man he is highly qualified with an MBA in military and strategic leadership. He was appointed by SANParks CEO David Mabunda, who said, 'We know that we will not be able to put a ranger behind every rhino … we need to develop innovative, modern ways of protecting the rhino in the wake of this well-organised onslaught.'

In the same statement, Jooste said, 'I am not a messiah, but I will do my best to bring acceptable results … this fight against poaching is not about an individual, and success depends on the collective collaboration and commitment from the men and women tasked with the responsibility of conserving our heritage.'

I next met the General a year later in his office in Skukuza. That and every subsequent time I met with him he was completely open about the sordid detail around poaching and the challenges he faced at almost every turn. I will never betray that trust. He started this discussion with the comment, 'The world has rhino fever.' We agreed this was a good thing in that at last the world was sitting up and taking notice of the wildlife crime occurring right across the globe. Having just arrived from Sydney, I was heavily jet-lagged and as we were talking the General mentioned the name Buffett. He must have seen the look of surprise on my face as my mind played back what he had said. Did he just say *Buffett?*

'Ja, ja,' he said, 'I was having dinner in Joburg with Mr Howard Buffett, son of Warren,' typical General, always so formal, and respectful, '… and he asked me how much money I needed to fix the poaching problem.'

The General responded he thought about $US10 million should do the job. Buffett didn't blink and asked him to check and confirm the amount required. The General smiled at me, 'Ray, I walked back to my hotel and my legs were shaking.' He reviewed the numbers and somewhat apologetically told Howard Buffett he actually needed $US13 million. Buffett then went through the list item by item and once he had finished, he said, 'What about the helicopter, you said you needed a helicopter?' The General mumbled a response and Buffett told him to include it, adding another $US6 million. 'Now what about that eye in the sky thing that you said you needed?' Buffett was referring to the Tethered Aerostat Radar System used for surveillance. Again, the General mumbled they were unsure about the effectiveness of the technology. 'Add it in,' Buffett said. Another $US6 million. Howard Buffett smiled at the General and they shook hands on a $US25 million donation. The General beamed, 'This is an absolute game changer, Ray.'

I recalled this conversation recently when the news broke that the Walton Foundation had donated $US100 million to African Parks. This will bolster the Parks' efforts to meet its target of protecting 30 per cent of the African continent for the benefit of people and wildlife by scaling effective park management. The poaching rate has certainly slowed only because there are fewer rhinos.

On a worrying note, the General observed I had undertaken a very big and very important project which he was certain would require the South African cabinet approval. I shuddered. Additional government involvement was less than ideal. One aspect he really liked was our goal to get the rhinos to breed faster which required good habitat and good security. This was April 2014, and he saw the tipping point for rhinos as being about twenty-four months away. Others believed that point had already been reached.

After the meeting, I wrote to thank the General and he thanked me for making time to consult. 'I have no doubt that you are a real "friend of rhinos" and I appreciate and respect your ambitious project. I wish you well – please keep us posted. The danger of the Rhino War is "too little too late" and I hope somewhere you get the attention you deserve.'

I treasured this message and would often refer to it as I did with another piece of advice from Margie, 'Be careful that the emotion doesn't take over from the reality. You will have to have a steely centre to get it through the crap of the political expedience. Some people will not look beyond how it can help or hinder their careers. The ultimate outcome won't mean anything to them. They are only looking at the immediate benefit.' My wonderfully perceptive wife always keeps me grounded.

Soon after my visit, I sent the General a copy of my poem, 'For the Rhino'. He really liked it and a while later I sent him another poem which I called 'The Game Ranger'. It tells how the roles of rangers have changed from being conservationists to armed protectors of rhino, placing both rangers and rhinos solidly in the firing line. The General loved the poems and invited me to attend International Rangers Day in Kruger. Unfortunately, I couldn't make it, but my cousin Robbie Robertson represented me. Both poems featured in the official program, and were read out at the celebration of all South African Game Rangers. Even though I wasn't there it was one of the proudest days of my life.

On my next visit, I presented the General with a framed copy of a poem that I had written for him which can be found in the second Appendix. Not one to show much emotion, he was visibly moved.

In another conversation, he told me, 'We are fighting a war', as he detailed what he and his team of rangers were doing to protect the rhinos. He said approximately 80 per cent of poaching was done by Mozambique nationals who infiltrated the park south of the Olifants River usually at night, and walked up to 25 kilometres to kill. Of concern now that his teams had put pressure on the east, poaching from the west of Kruger, the South African side, had increased. According to the General, conservatively up to a dozen groups of three poachers were in Kruger at any one time. Meaning a total of thirty-six to forty poachers entering and exiting the park every single day.

The General explained, 'Sometimes during the full moon period, they will concentrate in one area, knowing that the rules of engagement favour them, and this puts us on the back foot. We have to arrest them; we're not allowed to kill them. They know this, so their theory is "let them chase us", and they will come into the park in such numbers that we just cannot plug all the holes.'

I asked him to describe a 'typical' poacher and he said,

'They are young men usually in their twenties recruited from poverty, uneducated with very little hope of getting a job. The shooters, however, are specifically selected because their .458 and .375 rifles are high-value assets. The navigator is important because he's the guy who knows the park who has been in before and can guide them at night. The navigator will typically carry a GPS device and a couple of mobile phones. The third guy carries the knives and axe, food and water. A self-sufficient poaching group could spend up to four or five days in the park.

'As much as I despise them, the poachers can survive well in the bush, and their bushcraft is remarkable. They walk extraordinary distances at night to find their target and be back in Mozambique before daybreak. Their tracking is good, and they are a formidable opponent. With no rules. If you've grown up in poverty, one successful poaching expedition changes your life. The communities adjacent to the game reserves don't have any ownership, so they ask: What do I get from that park? A few of my community work there, but most of us, what do we get? The growth in poaching is slowing, but poaching is not decreasing. To bring the numbers down will require a national, regional and global solution, of which demand reduction is critical.'

Technology is critical to the success of any anti-poaching efforts and the General's plan was to use an array of sensors to give early detection of the poachers. I asked if by default, the rhinos outside of the Intensive Protection Zone would be 'written off'. The General bristled at the question saying they were not neglecting the rest of the park's rhinos but given their scarce resources they just had to prioritise. This must have been an extremely difficult decision.

'We must create a safe haven, a bastion, a fortress to make sure that we safeguard this core rhino population. If poachers get in here in numbers, they will kill as many as they can. If we lose Kruger, it is all over for the rhinos.'

More and more, the General was placing a great deal of emphasis on dogs for anti-poaching. 'We've expanded the dog teams – known as K9 units – and we're aiming to place dogs at all the gates. One of the dogs is an explosives detector, so he can pick up ammunition or weaponry, while the other is a natural asset detector, trained to pick up animal products, specifically rhino horn. In 2018, all 102 contacts with poachers involving dogs resulted in arrests.'

On a recent trip to South Africa, I was honoured to meet Bruce Leslie, head of special operations in the Kruger National Park. I presented him with a framed copy of my poem, 'Killer, the legendary anti-poaching dog'.

On the shoot-to-kill policy, the General said, 'Shooting to kill will improve our success rate and it will be a deterrent but it won't stop the poaching in this park which is 20,000 square kilometres of thick bushveld. It is too difficult to detect people so the risk is low and poachers know this.'

It reminded me of an incident related to me a year or two later. A poacher had been killed while on a mission inside Kruger and his funeral was taking place in a bordering Mozambican village. After the funeral as the mourners drifted away a man who had been watching from a distance approached the distraught widow still grieving at the graveside. He commiserated with her, offered his condolences and then pulled an envelope from his pocket saying her husband had been a good man and here was a bonus. As he walked away and through her tears, she called out to him asking him to wait. She wished to introduce him to her son who wanted to take his late father's place as a poacher. A truly desperate situation.

A major dilemma for the General is that the park is an international tourist destination, not an army base. He constantly questioned himself whether he really wanted a large number of enforcement staff within the park. As he pointed out, with all those extra people comes additional risk because there will be far more people entering and leaving the park.

His strong belief was he must clear the park from the outside. Chasing poachers is one thing but frustratingly, this is usually after a rhino has been killed and the horn removed.

'We know many of the "level 2" poaching bosses live just across the Mozambique border in Massingir and, in truth, 80 per cent of the solution probably lies in taking these guys out. Trust me, Ray, it's enormously tempting for my teams to go across the border and bring them back here, but we can't do that. It's politically unacceptable so these middlemen see themselves as untouchable. We are fighting a war. Mozambicans are making armed, illegal incursions into my country, plundering and exiting with our resources. We have armed incursions by poachers every day, about 150 per month. To me, that's an act of war. To win this war, there are only two long-term solutions. Giving ownership of Africa's parks to surrounding communities, so they take responsibility for their wildlife and feel a strong sense of ownership in the wellbeing of their wildlife. And second, we have to reduce demand in Vietnam, Thailand and China.'

The world will watch and wait and hope but, in the meantime,

I introduced Tony Park, a prolific author and a great supporter of mine, to the General and, as a result of that introduction, I am proud to say that their co-authored book, *Rhino War*, was published in June 2022 and made it to the top of the non-fiction bestseller list in South Africa. This is an excerpt from the book.

> 'Ray Dearlove, a South African businessman who had moved to Australia, had set up a charity called the Australian Rhino Project, with the aim of relocating eighty rhinos to the Western Plains Zoo in Dubbo, New South Wales. Ray was, and still is, passionate about saving rhinos.
>
> 'The idea was that in a worst-cast scenario we would have a rump population of South African rhino safe outside of the continent. Already, there was another NGO relocating some animals, such as roan antelope and the last surviving northern white rhino from overseas zoos back to Africa. There was a precedent for moving rhinos to Australia – the media tycoon Kerry Packer had bankrolled the translocation of endangered black rhinos from Zimbabwe to the Western Plains Zoo in the early 1990s. Some had died of disease and other complications related to their diet, but valuable lessons had been learned and 10 calves had been born in captivity.
>
> 'Ray's project was meticulously planned and well-resourced and he devoted a good deal of his own time and effort to it. Unfortunately, politics and personalities prevented the relocation of rhinos to Australia. This was a great pity and I often wished I could do more to help him. The whole story is related in Ray's book, *The Crash of Rhinos*.'

The General deserves all the recognition and support possible. I will always cherish his friendship.

*

A few years ago, I met with the South African High Commissioner to Australia, Her Excellency Koleka Anita Mqulwana. The purpose of the meeting was to brief her on what I was trying to achieve and why. She made an interesting observation, saying, 'Ray, it is vital that you understand that the communities in South Africa have no connection to wildlife. They see no value in it. It is the same with trees. My people have no connection with trees, they see them solely as sources of light, of warmth and for cooking. So, they cut down the forests.'

In our conversation, she used the word 'connection' several times. It was an awkward discussion. Her Excellency clearly held the 'apartheid' regime responsible for the onslaught on species such as rhinos and elephants and by definition, as a white sixty-something who spent the first forty years of his life in South Africa, I was part of that collective. My role apart, without going into the whys and wherefores, she is absolutely right. For decades black communities were barred from national parks and the benefits and healing solitude of the wilderness. I can clearly remember when Balule Camp in the Kruger National Park was reserved for 'non-whites' only. It was the only accommodation in Kruger available for people of colour and it could best be described as rustic without the excellent facilities available at the other rest camps.

Her Excellency is spot on. The only way to reduce the poaching rate is to engage and educate communities to understand that animals such as rhinos and elephants are worth more alive than dead. This is a huge task and unfortunately, it will take a generation or more to achieve.

In my opinion, that will be too late.

CHAPTER 15

GOLF

In 1998 I was working with the global data storage company EMC in Sydney. I was one of two sales managers and my area of responsibility was the northern district My counterpart who ran the southern district lived in Melbourne. Our managing director, Mike Foster, definitely the best executive I have ever worked for, was underwhelmed with my colleague's performance and asked me to step in on an interim basis. It meant spending the last quarter of 1998 in Melbourne looking after both districts and even though it involved a weekly commute I jumped at the chance. Since arriving in Australia, I had not spent any time in Melbourne and what do you know, the inaugural golf Presidents Cup was due to take place at Royal Melbourne in December. EMC was a tier-two sponsor and the company planned to have a hospitality marquee right on the golf course. Inviting customers or prospects to events can often be difficult; how things have changed since the 70s and 80s when customers would gladly accept invitations to major events. This event was a pleasure however, since the invitations were for couples, not singles.

Despite the tournament being on a weekend the opportunity to see some of the best golfers in the world at close range was not to be missed. I was asked to host the event on behalf of EMC and I had a ball. Margie came down from Sydney and we saw some wonderful golf and met some terrific people. The clients loved it.

The international team got off to a cracking start on the Saturday under a hot sun. Seeing players like Phil Mickelson, Fred Couples and a very young Tiger Woods on the US team and international stars such as Greg Norman, Ernie Els, Nick Price and VJ Singh was a once-in-a-lifetime experience. Two legends of the game – Jack Nicklaus and Peter Thomson – captained the sides.

Melbourne's erratic weather was on display for everyone to see as the Sunday turned freezing cold. This was December, the middle of summer. To the locals' delight the international team prevailed winning 20.5 to 11.5, the only time the international team has won this biennial contest.

As part of the EMC sponsorship Ian Baker-Finch, universally known as IBF and winner of the 1991 British Open, was contracted to join our guests. He was in the marquee before play started, at lunchtime and after the day's play to discuss each player's performance and strategies. He pointed out which players we should watch, the best vantage points on this wonderful golf course and gave us personal titbits about many of the players. Ian did an outstanding job.

For quite some time I had been considering holding a customer golf day in Sydney. Golf was in EMC's DNA and many of our customer executives played the game. I had a clear concept in my mind: I would invite nine senior customers to play at a quality golf course starting with an early breakfast and have three or four EMC executives join the customers accompanied by a professional golfer. We would finish with a light lunch and the customers could be back at their desks by 2 pm, if they wanted to.

I approached IBF and asked him if he would be interested. He was but when he mentioned his fee, I knew I would never get approval to spend that kind of money. Somewhat cheekily perhaps, I asked if he would recommend any other top Australian golfers. He suggested Peter Senior or Craig Parry.

I had always admired the way Peter Senior went about his business having secured thirty-four PGA wins with a no-nonsense approach and an ever-present smile on his face. I gave Peter a call and he said he would love to be involved – and at a very reasonable rate. I approached the EMC executives and they saw significant benefit in the idea and signed it off.

So, for the next six years Peter would arrive at Pennant Hills Golf Club early in the morning, play with our customers and then regale them with stories of the various tours he had played on. A regular question in the Q and A was, 'What's it like to play with Tiger?' Peter is not a tall man and he would never describe himself as 'athletic', but when he drove the ball, he gave it everything he had. Leaving nothing in the tank he would wallop the ball down the fairway, but to his annoyance and frustration Tiger would hit the ball with apparent ease. He'd then nonchalantly walk past Peter's ball without a word and about 60 metres ahead turn around, lean on his bag, look at Peter, and give him a big smile and a thumbs up.

Over time, I became very friendly with Peter. He has a wonderful family and is as kind and generous a man as you would find.

*

About fifteen years ago a group of us attended old friend Reg Mundell's 'significant' birthday celebration and someone observed the only time we seemed to get together was at funerals and birthdays. Most of us were from South Africa and had known each other for a long time and we all played golf, some better than others. I offered to arrange a regular game and that's how the Baby Boomers was born. The group has grown to more than twenty couples and we try to play a different Sydney course every month or so. It has been a very successful initiative and after the golf the non-playing partners join for dinner. My view is that, as we grow older, such friendships and relationships are so important. Marriages aside, many of the group have known each other for half a century and more. One of the founding members, Pete Walker, commented several years ago that the Boomers would become increasingly important as time wore on and we started losing members through death or illness. He was spot on.

Tony Gresham AM is arguably one of Australia's best golfers but because he never turned pro his extraordinary record is not widely known. He represented Australia in seven Eisenhower Cup teams and in one of those he was crowned World Amateur Golfer Champion. In 2020, Margie came up with the idea that the Pennant Hills Golf Club where Tony had played for fifty years should honour his achievements at a special tribute dinner.

The concept was eagerly supported by the board and planning was set in motion. In his long career Tony had played with or against the best players in the world including the Golden Bear Jack Nicklaus and the Black Knight Gary Player. I decided to try and obtain personal video messages to Tony from both Jack and Gary. Other than Margie, nobody knew this was happening behind the scenes. I believe in under-promising and over-delivering.

This was not easy and from previous experience I knew getting to these golf legends would be difficult since they, like many other celebrities, value their privacy. Given that, the internet is a wonderful thing and Mr Google certainly does help. After several weeks of searching and researching, I was able to speak directly to Marlene, Jack Nicklaus's executive assistant. In parallel, I managed to track down Ciska, Gary's client service and communication executive. Well, within a fortnight I had video clips from two of the all-time greats of golf, as well as from Australian aces, Peter Senior and Peter O'Malley. Both Jack's and Gary's messages were very personal and each recalled playing with Tony. Gary also alluded to the fact he had won seven Australian Opens, 'pipping Jack, who only won six!'

Any number of people asked me how I had secured these messages and the answer is simple. There is no magic, it is simply a question of persisting and doing the hard yards. Without being arrogant, it's what I do.

Tony gasped when the clips were shown at the tribute dinner and he had tears in his eyes. He just could not believe it.

*

My golf game has been in steady decline since finishing runner-up in the Natal Schools Golf Championships when I was eighteen, noting the tournament was split into handicap divisions. Several years ago, when Tim Ebbeck was Australia and New Zealand managing director of the global IT giant SAP, he would arrange client golf days with one or more of the international SAP sports ambassadors in attendance. Because of the sponsorship and strong association with Sydney University Rugby, he invited me along, mentioning in passing that SAP ambassador David Leadbetter, who is acknowledged as one of the best golf teachers of all time, would be in attendance. I grabbed the opportunity before Tim changed his mind but knowing my game was at best rusty, I was a bit nervous. We were asked to arrive by 10 am to participate in a teaching clinic and as I topped a few balls on the driving range I noticed that David, accompanied by Tim, was making his way down the line of players offering tips and advice.

As David introduced himself, Tim commented, 'David, I wouldn't spend much time with Ray, his golf needs major surgery and, in truth, is a bit of a lost cause.' I blushed; Tim guffawed while David smiled ever so politely. We then made our way to the first tee at the magnificent New South Wales course, where I shanked my first of many shots. Are you surprised?

*

In 2005, our son Paul was playing professional rugby in Scotland when Tom, one of his closest friends from Sydney, visited him in Glasgow. The British Open was being played down the road at St Andrews and they decided to try their luck and watch some of the play. There was no accommodation within miles of the golf course and they didn't have tickets for the tournament, but undeterred after a good few beverages at a local establishment and without any hint of a plan, they decided to chance their arm by climbing the fence into the golf course.

The St Andrews course is renowned for the depth and size of the bunkers so the lads figured these would be perfect for sleeping. With the sand still warm from the day's sunshine they hunkered down. Probably thanks to the number of beers consumed, sleep came easily until dawn broke with the voice of the startled Scottish greenkeeper peering into the bunker, 'Bejesus Jummy, are they deid?'

Fortunately, he saw the funny side of these two innovative young Aussies and gave them prime viewing position outside the rope. He didn't even mention the rapidly dying fairway patches from the midnight piddles.

CHAPTER 16

THE REAL ESTATE INDUSTRY

I spent thirty-four years of my life working for IBM, EMC and NetApp, all US-headquartered information technology companies. By and large they were good years and I enjoyed my time with these global organisations. If you worked hard and performed you were recognised, both financially and in advancement. What all these highly successful companies had in common was to relentlessly drive sales of their products, and in the 1990s and into the new millennium there was ever-increasing pressure on sales teams for accurate sales forecasting to meet aggressive targets.

Mostly driven by the stock market, quarterly forecasts became monthly, then weekly and then as one approached quarter-end, there was a requirement for daily updates of major deals. As a sales manager, I had always employed the strategy of low-balling the forecasts and then wherever possible, over-performing. As sales targets increased this strategy became unworkable and my peers and I were required to up the forecasts, however unlikely it was we would achieve 'the number'. EMC in particular had a fairly ruthless approach. If you missed your quarterly forecast twice or more you were likely headed for the door. Brutal it may seem but it certainly ensured that the sales team was focused and it also gave management the opportunity to refresh and renew the selling skills and capability of their teams. Fortunately for me, both EMC and NetApp were fast-growing companies with outstanding technology. Both firms attracted some of the best and brightest sales and technical talent in Australia. We were well paid and it was a positive and often exciting environment in which to work. With success came rewards. Margie and I had several 'recognition' trips to glamourous destination such as Maui, Whistler and San Francisco. Working at EMC were some of the best years of my life and it was thanks to good friend Reg Mundell that I scored an interview and I met great leaders like Mike Burnie and Mike Foster.

By 2004, as I approached sixty, I thought it was time for a change. In 2001 after a particularly successful sales year, we had bought a lovely holiday home at Copacabana on the New South Wales Central Coast, about 60 kilometres north of Sydney. The plan was to retire there at some future point and since I had always wanted to run my own business this seemed to be as good a time as any. I left NetApp and we bought a real estate agency in Ettalong Beach, close to Copacabana.

With the benefit of hindsight my research and due diligence were weak. I had the naïve view that if I could sell computers, and I had been quite good at that, I could sell anything. Little did I realise how tough the real estate business actually is. It is a cutthroat industry and only the good sales teams and management survive and thrive. We bought a franchise which was almost solely a Sydney-centric group and hence we were the odd one out in terms of brand awareness.

The local family we bought the business from also owned the commercial premises in which the business was housed. For reasons we did not and still don't understand, the next five years were exceptionally difficult. We wondered at times if the family regretted selling the business despite banking a tidy sum from the sale. More on that later.

Margie, Kevin and I had a steep learning curve. Kevin had some previous experience working for a real estate company in Sydney but that was all. We inherited one of the previous owner's family as an employee and as the nominated licensee of our office he had a certain amount of power which he exercised, and it seemed to be seldom in our favour. To protect our business, I quickly rectified this difficult situation by doing the required certification to become a licensed real estate agent in record time. At least we were then masters of our own destiny.

My second major error was that we were given undertakings we were buying a 'going concern' and the financials presented to us seemed to reflect this. Sadly, this was not exactly the case. The cupboard was bare in terms of existing listings and the business had a relatively weak reputation in the area.

Much of my previous success had come about by building a strong sales team and as hard as I tried, it became increasingly obvious that the talent pool of quality real estate agents on the Central Coast was very shallow indeed. While most agents in Sydney were on a commission-only payment structure, many of the Central Coast agents were paid a base salary in accordance with the real estate award rate. While not a large sum, most agents seemed able to live on the wage and occasional house sales were seen as a bonus. This resulted in a low energy approach to making any form of contribution or effort which went against everything that Kevin, Margie and I believed in and stood for.

We had to shell out a weekly wage bill with limited sales income and a diminishing yield from the rent roll. Sadly, the property managers we had also 'inherited' were steeped in their old ways and reluctant to embrace change particularly in terms of process, technology and most importantly, customer service. Equally sadly, the word 'loyalty' seemed not to be in their vocabularies. It wasn't long before we moved them on. In our six years in the business, they worked for five different real estate firms in the same town. Their modus operandi seemed to encourage property owners to follow them to the new organisation. This is considered one of the cardinal sins of property management in that the rent roll is the only true asset of a real estate business. While they saw this as part of their value it was not at all well received by any of the principals of the businesses who were caught short. As we were.

Our assigned territory included Ettalong, Umina, Bensville and Woy Woy. Spike Milligan, whose parents retired to Woy Woy, famously referred to the small town as 'the largest above ground cemetery in the world' and 'God's waiting room'. He was also fond of saying, 'If you plugged your electric toothbrush into the socket in Woy Woy all the town lights would dim.'

In terms of physical beauty Ettalong Beach is located along one of the most beautiful stretches of the long New South Wales coastline and yet it is one of the best kept secrets as a holiday destination. Early on I decided to try and improve this situation by doing my little bit to put Ettalong on the map.

With strong support from Gosford Council, I established the Ettalong Beach Business Group (EBBGI), an incorporated legal entity. Our goal was to publicise as widely as possible that Ettalong was a safe, beautiful village situated just an hour's drive from Sydney's 5 million residents. Local businesses bought strongly into the plan. Most were sole traders or family businesses and typically in a town of this size there were plenty (too many) hairdressing salons and real estate agencies and all had low entry points in terms of employee qualifications.

One critical success factor in growing and developing Ettalong and the Central Coast was physical access. If there were fires or a major accident between Sydney and the Central Coast, the M1 highway could be closed for hours or even days. The same applied to the railway line. Many people like Alf Salter had spent countless hours trying to convince local, state and federal governments to support the introduction of a fast ferry service between Ettalong and Circular Quay at Sydney Harbour. To Alf and me, it was a no-brainer; think the ferries between Auckland and Waiheke Island, or Hong Kong to Macau and their outlying islands. We did all the hydrological work and costing in presenting the case to government but they just did not have an appetite for it. (I am very pleased to say that I met with Rowan Lund, chief executive of the NRMA which acquired Manly Ferries, and who has definite plans to introduce such a ferry service between Circular Quay and the Central Coast. This will be a game changer for the region.)

Gosford Council approved our promotional plan and granted us some serious seed money. The Ettalong community then got to work. We had working bees, we built on events such as the Oyster Festival, we reduced litter and we eliminated graffiti and in a very short time we managed to galvanise a very willing group of residents and business owners to participate. The ocean and beach were hidden by weeds and bushes and a foul toilet block which was rapidly demolished and some of the bushes cleared revealing the long-hidden beauty of the view. Gosford Council, led by Kim Radford, and the local community teamed with us to beautify the foreshore to what it is today with strong support from local politicians, Lucy Wicks and Chris Holstein. It was a fun time with tangible and visual results.

On the other hand, there were some events that were less memorable. I suppose our children had a somewhat sheltered upbringing, attending private schools and then residential colleges at the University of Sydney. Kevin's time with us at Ettalong changed all that. We saw the best and the worst of humanity. There were some harsh lessons for us all.

The Central Coast peninsula of which Ettalong is major part is a diverse area. There are some extremely wealthy pockets but there is also high unemployment, single parenting and domestic violence. We regularly saw the results of the latter and it was very uncomfortable. On one occasion I was called to inspect the home of one of our tenants who had not been seen for a while. I was accompanied by Barbara, one of our property managers. Upon arrival, I unlocked the gate into the well-kept garden. As I opened the screen door, I saw this chap hanging from the ceiling in the kitchen, a broken chair a few feet away. I screamed as I pushed Barbara away. What drives people to that absolute level of despair? The police and ambulance arrived and we left feeling dreadful but full of admiration for these uniformed men and women who face awful and confronting scenes like this on too regular a basis. As hard as we tried, we were unable to track the tenant's next of kin and to paraphrase the Beatles' song, 'Eleanor Rigby', '… he was buried along with his name'.

Building a strong, cohesive and motivated team was a real challenge. One of our sales team had a drinking problem. When he was sober, he was wonderful, compassionate and diligent. Give him a few drinks and he was a changed man, prone to violence and confrontation. It was from him I first heard the expression, 'One drink is too many, ninety-nine is not enough'. Last I heard, he had been dry for several years. Well done to him in conquering his demons, at heart he is a good and kind man.

Gail was the rock of our sales team, she worked hard, is as honest as the day is long and was a pleasure to work with. Her brother Peter too is a lovely man and always looked out for his sister. He is the quintessential strong and silent type.

In 2008 our lease was about to expire and there was no doubt in our minds that our landlords would not renew it. In fact, the word was out they were going to open their own real estate business next door in direct competition to us. Not quite cricket as they say. In any event, we couldn't wait to vacate their offices and sever ties.

At the same time, we had been engaged to sell some commercial premises in Ettalong. The location was excellent and the property was valued at well over a million dollars. The sales campaign was going well and then the Global Financial Crisis (GFC) struck. Overnight, property values slumped. The property was a deceased estate so there was a degree of urgency on behalf of the solicitors who were acting for the estate and they were proving to be tough negotiators. By now Margie was sick of the constant nonsense and she suggested we buy the property. This made sense. We could then move our business to those premises and be in control of our future. A local businessman whom we knew quite well and who owned a lot of property in the area then approached me with an offer to partner with us in the purchase. I wasn't that keen but in truth, the quantum was a bit of a stretch for us and I accepted. He duly paid his 50 per cent of the deposit and we prepared for settlement. A few days before we were due to settle, he pulled out saying he was unable to raise the balance of the purchase price. This left us in a real pickle. We scrambled to raise the difference and our accountant came through by arranging a loan. It was not cheap money.

The purchase was made, we refunded the other fellow's share of the deposit and that was that. Or so we thought. The saga went on and on and eventually became quite unpleasant.

A week or two later he turned up in the office wanting to see me. He told me he wanted his share of the commission of the sale. Initially, I thought he was joking. We had a good relationship and I laughed. He told me it was far from funny and when could I pay him? I tried to explain we had not earned any commission on the sale because we were the buyers.

We eventually paid him off. When we met with our tax accountant, he questioned the reason for these not inconsequential payments. I felt ashamed and embarrassed telling him the story. Well, he just stared at me and flicked through his Kardex filing system, 'Don't ever do that again, Ray ... Just give me a call and I'll put you in touch with Big George.' He pulled out 'Big George's' business card which reflected his title, 'Negotiator'. I still have the card but hope and pray there will never be a need for it in the future.

CHAPTER 17

THE BRUMBIES

Our son Paul had always wanted to be a professional rugby player. Both he and younger brother Kevin represented Australia at junior rugby levels, Kevin at outside centre for the Australian Schoolboys and Paul at number eight for the Australian under-20 side. Kevin's flair and speed made him a very good player but his body was possibly more suited to the Australian Rules game than the increasingly physical demands of rugby. After multiple injuries he retired early. Paul's achievements were characterised by dogged determination, toughness, focus and commitment.

We were having a family holiday in South Africa in 2002 and through Tim Lane, then Australian coach of the Lions Super Rugby team, I was introduced to Jake White. Jake was living in Cape Town and coaching the South African shadow Super Rugby team.

Paul and I met with Jake and we were immediately impressed. He was enthusiastic, good company and certainly knew his rugby. He kindly put Paul in touch with the Natal Sharks rugby team for a trial and we agreed to remain in touch.

Jake's career really took off in 2004 when he was appointed as coach of the Springboks. Each year thereafter when the Springboks toured Australia for the Tri-Nations tournament, I would invite him to be either a guest or a keynote speaker at various fundraisers and through this we got to know each other quite well. When the Springboks won the Rugby World Cup in Paris in 2007, he was an instant hero in South Africa. To most people's surprise he was not reappointed as coach and spent the next few years working with the International Rugby Board. Not ideal for a man with his track record or ambition.

He called me in early 2012 saying he had been approached to coach the Brumbies, the most successful of the Australian Super Rugby franchises. I was really pleased since not only was he a good friend but he was without peer as a rugby coach. As a real estate agent, I also undertook to help him find a house when he and his wife Lindy arrived in Canberra. One Friday evening Margie and I were having dinner at a restaurant in Beecroft when my phone rang. It was Jake and as he can be, was quite animated. He had been in Canberra for two weeks and said, 'Can you believe it, Ray, I still don't have any Brumbies kit, I'm still wearing my Bok gear and I feel like a real doos. These guys are so unprofessional.'

This was an easy fix. I knew the Brumbies apparel supplier was Kooga which was owned by good friends, Gold Coast-based South Africans Kim and his son Tyron Brant. I immediately called Tyron and explained the problem. By Tuesday morning, Tyron delivered. Jake had a full set of Brumbies gear. He was impressed with Kooga (and with me).

A week or so later Jake called again. This time he was really annoyed he could not get anything done at the pace he was used to. Out of the blue he invited me to take on the role of team director. It is worth pointing out that Jake had coached at the highest level and was considered the best rugby coach in the world. He was known to set very high standards and he expected everyone else to meet those standards. Patience is not one of his strong points.

I thanked him for his confidence in me and said I would call him back. Margie had heard the conversation and after I put down the phone, she looked at me quizzically. I started to laugh. Here I was aged sixty-four and a rugby tragic. All at once I was amused, flattered, nervous but most of all, excited. What an opportunity for an old fart to work with the best rugby coach in the world and with the best rugby team in Australia. I thought I had died and gone to heaven. Margie had that Mona Lisa smile.

I called Jake the following day and said I would love to take the role. An early lesson for me; Jake makes quick decisions and often needs someone to sweep up the broken glass behind him and the thought did occur to me – was this just a thought bubble? I was working with Sydney University Rugby at that time and club president David Mortimer was understanding, as always. Later that week I drove down to meet with Jake in Canberra. The team director's responsibility was, 'to handle all off the field team and rugby related matters to enable the head coach to focus on coaching and to enable him and the coaching team to operate at the highest possible level to ensure the team's success. He is also responsible for building on the strong culture and tradition of the Brumbies.' Even so, it became patently obvious to me that Jake was also looking for a man Friday whom he could trust. As a fellow South African, he was comfortable with me.

At considerable expense I leased and furnished a one-bedroom apartment in Canberra with the plan that Margie would join me in due course.

The first few months were great. Jake's coaching skills and technique were cutting edge. At the first team meeting all the players turned up with their notepads, not iPads. Jake immediately set them straight telling them there would be no playbooks which was then a standard coaching requirement among professional rugby teams. At Jake's Brumbies, the players would practise, practise, and practise until they could do the moves 'in their sleep'. Judging by the looks on their faces this was a very different approach.

In truth, the Canberra training facilities for a quality, successful professional rugby club like the Brumbies were well below par. Jake and Lindy had spent hours and hours in the off-season cleaning, painting, scraping and polishing the old lawn bowls clubhouse to improve it and give it a professional look.

Jake also introduced a radical change to the players' training schedule. He commissioned a full industrial-scale kitchen to be built in the clubhouse and hired a highly qualified chef who also conveniently happened to be a rugby tragic. The players were expected to turn up for training by 7 am when they would be served a full breakfast of cereal, fruit, eggs, bacon, sausages and toast – as much as they wanted or, in the case of the front row, could eat. The same happened at lunchtime. Jake's theory being, if he could manage and control what the players ate for two out of three meals a day, there was virtually no chance of them binging on fast food or other rubbish. He and Lindy had also begged, borrowed or, as a last resort, bought bunk beds for the players in a darkened room to have a nap during the day. Revolutionary thinking.

There was a buzz around the club. Jake had inherited a young side with limited professional rugby experience with the only Wallabies in the squad being Ben Alexander, Stephen Moore and Stephen Hoiles. Jake had the knack of showing the uncapped players a clear pathway to represent their country. As an example, he would say to the halfbacks, 'Consider this, there will always be two halfbacks, maybe three in the Wallaby squad and there are only three other franchises that you will be competing with. Two injuries in a season and you are in the frame.' It was compelling for these young men who could immediately see the road to success if they did their bit and put in the effort, with the added confidence Jake would back them all the way. And he did.

I particularly enjoyed working with the Polynesian players, men like Tevita Kuridrani, Henry Speight, Scott Sio, Christian Leiliifano and Joe Tomane. It was Joe who gave me the nickname of 'Razor' which has stuck with the Brumbies players of that time.

It was at Jake's encouragement that Tevita went through the process of qualifying for the Wallabies rather than for Fiji. A major decision for a man who is extremely proud of his heritage and culture. He went on to represent Australia on sixty-one occasions. Jake was also a great judge of talent. Michael Hooper had joined the Brumbies as an unknown breakaway, with Colby Fainga'a the incumbent. Before the first match of the season I asked Jake who was likely to take the number seven spot and he said Hooper would and that he had a great future. Hooper now captains the Wallabies and has played more than a hundred tests.

One of the less pleasant aspects of being the team director was the need to liaise with player managers or agents. Admittedly, my personal experience had probably clouded my opinion. In 2000, our son Paul represented the Australian under-20 rugby team in the Junior World Cup in New Zealand. He had a good tournament and during the last match against Wales in Auckland, a fellow who had been glancing at me sidled over and asked if Margie and I were Paul's parents. He introduced himself as a player agent and asked if he could have a chat. Naturally, as a parent your mind races and you picture your son as a Wallaby, so we enthusiastically agreed. Paul had set his mind on becoming a professional rugby player with the goal of playing for the Wallabies so this seemed to be a giant step in that direction. He was excited and we supported his decision to sign up. Incidentally, Paul qualified to play for four countries, South Africa through me, France because it was his birthplace, Scotland because of his maternal grandmother and of course Australia. Our expectations were high, but the agent's strategy seemed to be to sign up a lot of promising young players, sift out the best and focus on the chosen few. Unfortunately, Paul was perceived by him as being in the second tier and there was very little communication. I eventually intervened and contacted the Glasgow Warriors Club in Scotland directly and negotiated a contract on Paul's behalf. Paul eventually played professional rugby for twelve years in Scotland and France and represented Scotland on their tour of Australia.

I subsequently applied to the Rugby Union Players Association (RUPA) and became an accredited player agent and through this, I met a number of agents at different seminars. They are certainly a different breed and, in my opinion, in general are far more interested in their own commission than doing anything positive for their clients, most of whom are young and naïve athletes with stars in their eyes and trusting and equally naïve parents.

My experience with the agents representing Brumbies players was no different. Jake shared my view but as he rightly pointed out, they are a necessary evil. As far as I could tell very few, if any, agents took much interest in the player's post-rugby career. This contrasted starkly with the Sydney University Rugby Club's mentoring program which is unquestionably best practice in rugby in Australia. What was also interesting and probably also understandable was that over time some of the older and more experienced players took to representing themselves rather than working through a third party.

The dynamics among and within the Brumbies coaching and administration staff were at best interesting and on occasions, fairly volatile. Laurie Fisher, he of the flowing locks, was and still is the best forwards coach in the country. I found him a complex man who held the view Ray Dearlove could add minimum value to the Brumbies, which are a strong part of his life. The great

Stephen 'Bernie' Larkham is a quiet, sensitive man who was at his best when he was demonstrating moves, strategy and tactics on the pitch. He didn't say much but when he did everyone listened. He was always calm and totally professional. Hindsight is a wonderful thing but his and Michael Cheika's personalities were never going to gel while coaching the Wallabies.

Andrew Fagan was CEO at the time. He was not particularly popular with the Canberra rugby community mainly because of the way he had allegedly terminated Andy Friend's tenure as coach of the Brumbies. Andy had been enormously popular with the Brumbies faithful but, being fair, Fages was grudgingly praised for securing Jake's services.

Andrew and Jake had a day-to-day relationship. Fagan knew his job was on the line if the Brumbies had a poor season under Jake's expensive tutelage but both seemed to have an 'us and them' attitude between the players and the administration. It was difficult for me since I was often the meat in the sandwich. I had a dual reporting line where both were my boss depending on the situation. Jake would send me to ask Andrew for funding for say gym equipment. Andrew would refuse, quoting budget issues. I would tell Jake who generally would react with 'well, bugger that'. The next week Andrew would ask me to get Jake to appear at a sponsors' function and Jake would decline citing another appointment, and so on it went. I can probably count on one hand the number of times Fages ventured into the players area while I was there. Not ideal but perhaps not surprising given the strength of the two personalities and they were joined at the hip with the exact same goal to win the Super Rugby competition.

Jake was a master not only for recognising talent but also in building the best possible support team around him. In addition to Fisher and Larkham, Jake brought in Dave Wessels from South Africa as defence consultant. Dave had significant success with the Brumbies conceding the fewest points in the Australian

Conference and the second least in the total Super Rugby competition. Until recently Dave was the head coach for the Melbourne Rebels and in my humble view he will have a stellar career in rugby coaching.

Jake also engaged Dr Sherylle Calder, sports scientist and performance coach, and one of the most interesting people I have ever met. A former South African hockey international, Sherylle has transformed the training of individuals and teams with her revolutionary work at her company EyeGym. Some quotes from her include, 'Our eyes and our brain can be trained impacting motor response and decision making' and, 'Using mobile phones has destroyed some of the skills, such as peripheral vision, which we think are effective in being productive in business and sport'.

Sherylle has worked with and had astonishing success with individuals like Ernie Els and teams like the All Blacks, the England Rugby XV and the Australian cricket team. Her effect on the Brumbies was immediate and lasting.

Jake White was an enigma in so many ways. As Sibusiso Mjikeliso wrote in a *Sport24* article, 'There are few people on the planet that White is enamoured with and he certainly has his critics, but ultimately, he has been successful with every team he has coached.'

As a Rugby World Cup winner, Jake was definitely not short on ego but equally, he would do anything for his players. He was focused on professionalism and highly respectful of tradition. He and Lindy made an excellent team and she clearly adored him. Despite being fiercely patriotic he felt he had been poorly treated by the South Africa rugby hierarchy and he never gave up hope of once again coaching a first-tier international side. To date, this ambition has not been fulfilled but his desire has never wavered.

In late 2011, a few months after Jake had been appointed as Brumbies coach for a contracted period of four years, England rugby was looking to replace Martin Johnson as coach of the national side. Jake and I were usually first in the office in the mornings and we would chat about everything under the sun. One day I asked him if he would have been interested in the England job. He just smiled and walked away. A few days later I asked him again. He closed the door and said he was and he was having a Skype interview with the England selection board the following day, saying that he wanted to coach an international side and the England job with all of its resources was first prize. He believed the Brumbies would understand.

I had my doubts about that. I had seen Jake's contract and the Brumbies were paying him a serious amount of money. The next day Jake was approached by the media on the topic. He denied any interest but very soon after he changed his position saying he had been approached but had turned down the offer. A BBC article took up the story, 'Jake White said the RFU had approached him about coaching England but while he had used the phrase "turning down" the opportunity, he had not actually been offered the job.' As I write this, Wallaby coach Eddie Jones is under fire for allegedly being in contact with the Japanese Rugby Union before one of the most critical matches – for the Wallabies – at the 2023 Rugby World Cup.

In 2013, the Australian Rugby Union (ARU) was once again in turmoil. Bill Pulver had been appointed in January to succeed CEO John O'Neill and when he was appointed, he said of the then Wallabies coach Robbie Deans, 'Robbie will be coaching the Wallabies right through 2013, and then at that point we will consider the coaching positions to take us to the Rugby World Cup in 2015'. And yet, by the time the second test against the British and Irish Lions came around the ARU were searching for a replacement for Robbie, who had been sacked six months before the end of his contract. One of the candidates was Jake and to this day Jake will attest he was 'tapped on the shoulder' and told the job was his. I believe him. A few short weeks later the ARU announced Ewen McKenzie would take over from Robbie.

Jake was quoted as saying it wasn't just a perception McKenzie got the nod over him because of his Australian heritage, 'It's not a perception, it's a fact. It just happened. The Australian Cricket Board fired the South African cricket coach (Mickey Arthur), put an Aussie in, fired the Kiwi rugby coach and put an Aussie in. South Africa pick a South African, Kiwis pick Kiwis, England rugby pick English people to coach the team. Australian sport has tried foreigners and I appreciate that … that doesn't mean that I have to agree or disagree with it. That's the nature of the game we're in.'

Interestingly, as I write this, in Australia there are South Africans heading up Tennis Australia, Craig Tiley; Australia Rugby, Andy Marinos; the NRL, Andrew Abdo; and until recently the Melbourne Rebels rugby team, Dave Wessels, who has now been replaced by another South African, Kevin Foote. *Plus ça change, plus c'est la même chose.*

Jake was deeply disappointed he had missed a chance to lead the Wallabies to the 2015 World Cup. The Brumbies were on record of being supportive if he was appointed the Wallabies coach, but he said he was committed to remaining in Canberra until the end of his four-year stint.

A year later, Jake broke his four-year contract with the Brumbies while on holiday in South Africa, a decision he now regrets. A few years later his contract with French Pro14 club Montpellier was not renewed and he is presently successfully coaching the powerful Blue Bulls Super Franchise in Pretoria. International rugby has not heard the last of Jake White.

*

Off the field there were some interesting moments. At the end of 2011 the Brumbies lost the major sponsorship of long-time partner Computer Associates and the hunt was on for a replacement.

In December 2012, Andrew Fagan announced Huawei as the Brumbies main sponsor. Very soon after, Wayne Smith wrote in *The Australian* newspaper,

> 'Brumbies chief executive Andrew Fagan declined to comment, but it is known he was alerted that Huawei, China's largest privately owned company and one of the world's leading manufacturers of telecommunications equipment, was backing out of a deal he believed was as good as done. Indeed, it is understood the China-based board of the company had actually signed off on the Brumbies deal and had even approved jersey designs incorporating the company logo when Huawei's satellite board in Australia encountered a massive problem unconnected to the club and withdrew its lucrative sponsorship. That has given rise to speculation that Huawei had been told it would be allocated no part of the Australia wide National Broadband Network rollout.'

Andrew phoned me and asked if I could help by calling some of the people I knew well to take on the primary sponsorship. I called Gary Edstein of existing sponsor DHL who declined to upgrade. I also called Cameron Clyne, then CEO of the National Australia Bank, who was keen but unable to help. Fages eventually signed a long-term sponsorship agreement with the University of Canberra which has been beneficial to both parties.

Professional sportsmen and women can often get caught up in their own little bubble and their chosen profession can be both false and fickle. At the end of the day, they are usually young men and women who have a specific talent and are doing their best to reach the top and stay there. In the Brumbies' case, the players lived and breathed rugby and in both Jake's and Fages' cases they strove to provide every player with the best possible environment to ensure their and, as a result, the Brumbies' success.

Pre-season training for all sports people is long, hard and can be tedious. During the 2012 pre-season I asked players and staff to pop a gift under the Christmas tree for the children in the cancer ward of the Canberra Hospital. Their response was excellent and several players accompanied me to hand out gifts. It was a sobering experience for these tough young men who were generous to a fault and who reluctantly left the ward, all quiet and thoughtful. Andrew Fagan commented, 'This is a great gesture, good for the kids and for our players.'

Jake was always looking for innovation and that 'edge'. When I suggested all Brumbies players be honoured with a specially designed numbered cap, he was all over it. Soon the caps arrived and the first ever Brumbies, Patricio Noriega, Marco Caputo, Ewen McKenzie and David Giffin, were presented with their individually numbered memorial caps. The tradition continues today as a highly successful and popular program and recognition for those who have proudly worn the rearing Brumbies strip.

After six months in the role of team manager, I realised professional sport was not for me. I had played or been involved in sport for most of my life and loved it but professional sport is a whole different world. It is a complex and politically charged environment and, in many ways, false and artificial.

My expectation when I arrived at the Brumbies was that everyone would be excited to be paid to be involved in rugby and they would be making the most of 'living the dream'. In reality for a few it seemed to be just another job and sometimes all a bit of a chore. The tribalism and fierce loyalty I had experienced in the amateur game was replaced by some looking to maximise their earnings potential during their relatively short careers. There were the few who suggested it was 'my brand' before 'my team'. It surprised me that anyone actually complained about their job. With hindsight, I suppose this was normal, people have always complained about their jobs but having come from an amateur game where if you didn't want to be there you didn't have to be, I had expected a similar attitude among professionals. This annoyed me and I avoided these people. In amateur rugby I saw young men finish a day of labouring in the wind and winter rain then jump in the car, catch a bus or hitch a lift for forty-five minutes to be on time for training. They didn't have to be there and most would have done anything to get an opportunity to play professional rugby. As recently as 2020 there were three Queensland players, one a Wallaby, refusing to take a pay cut alongside the rest of the Rugby Australia contracted players affected by COVID-19. They really were a long way from reality and don't know how good they have it by flying business class and staying in five-star hotels all over the world. I remember being in the business-class cabin with the New Zealand Highlanders team travelling to South Africa and there were a few younger members who were very obviously on their first international flight. They were like kids in a lolly shop, taking selfies and immediately donning the Qantas pyjamas.

In order to obtain another independent view, I asked our son Paul, who played professional rugby for ten years in Scotland and France, for his perspective. He wrote,

> 'The side of being a professional athlete that caught me by surprise was the attitude of the clubs to the players. In the eyes of a club, a player is a commodity and, if that commodity isn't delivering results or he gets injured, it is likely he will be replaced by another commodity. In today's world, you hear a lot of business leaders talk about the value of their people and how they are the most important resource. This often isn't the case in professional rugby. If you are playing well, you're a star and handsomely rewarded. If you're injured or out of form, you are no longer adding value and are likely to be discarded. I saw players treated extremely poorly by their club and, in many ways, this likely contributed to the often-mercenary attitude of players.
>
> 'The lifestyle of the players and management team is also drastically overrated. If you are in your early twenties it is

probably considered exciting but, if you have a family, the long hours, constant travel and fickle media coverage take their toll. The playing group also never really matures as there is a constant turnover of older players (into their thirties if they're lucky) leaving and younger players replacing them. This leads to many of the usual challenges with managing testosterone charged young men, with significant disposable income, in a world with cameras in every phone and with social media allowing poor decisions to spread like wildfire in the matter of hours. Overall, professional rugby, when the cover is lifted, has a less than pristine underbelly. I was happy to return to the amateur game. There was much more loyalty, passion and fun.'

As Paul describes, I was probably just a commodity in Jake's eyes and once I had outlived my usefulness, this commodity was free to go. And so, after six months I left Canberra and returned to Sydney. Not exactly with my tail between my legs, but not far off it. Out of pocket yes but nonetheless certainly wiser. I'm not sure such a role is suited for someone in his mid-sixties. It is a young person's game. Did it hurt? Of course it did.

As Craig Ray wrote in the *Daily Maverick*, 'It's that attention to detail and that unflinching belief in building a foundation that has made [Jake] White such a successful coach across the world.

'That hard-headedness has also led to clashes with people. It's part of the business where the only currency is winning. But it's the only way he knows how. It's his way or the highway. And almost always, his way is the right way.'

I was privileged to work with one of the best rugby coaches of all time.

CHAPTER 18

RUGBY UNION AND RUGBY LEAGUE

As a sport, rugby league is virtually unknown in South Africa. I was once asked the difference between the two and a definition as good as any is that the aim of rugby league is to run *into* people, while in union the goal is to run *around* people.

Margie's family were enthusiastic rugby league followers and with me being something of a union fanatic our conversations were often at cross purposes and occasionally quite heated. One of my favourite stories which I occasionally referred to in such conversations featured the great David Campese. In 2003, someone at the Australian Rugby Union came up with the divisive plan to pay a great deal of money to rugby league players Lote Tuqiri, Wendell Sailor and Matt Rogers to switch codes. Soon after in an interview, Campo was asked what he thought these three had actually brought to rugby. He thought for a while and then responded, 'Tattoos, mate.' Epic.

Several years ago, when I was general manager of the Sydney

University Rugby Club, the club president, David Mortimer, met up with Academy Award winning actor Russell Crowe in a private box at the Australian Tennis Open. Russell is co-owner of the South Sydney Rugby League Club – the Rabbitohs – one of the most consistently successful teams in the national competition.

They discussed that since both clubs were in the same geographic area with very similar goals, they should explore ways of working together. The Rabbitohs is a professional club while Sydney University Rugby aspired to be the most professional club in an amateur competition. David asked me to reach out to the Rabbitohs CEO Shane Richardson and the Gladiator similarly asked Richo to contact me. I was the first to move and called Richo who somewhat warily agreed to meet.

It was like a blind date when we met, trying to find some common ground while grumbling it was all very well sitting in a centre court catered box sipping champers and nibbling on tasty hors d'oeuvres dreaming up grand ideas. We agreed to make a start by getting the two sets of coaches together to share strategies and plans. I was enthusiastic about this, feeling we could learn a lot from fully professional coaches. It was a unique opportunity; the ball was in our court but for some reason our coaches didn't seem to grasp the offer to build a relationship. This failure caused considerable embarrassment to both Richo and me.

Another area of potential collaboration was in sports medicine since (obviously) the injuries players from both codes suffer are similar. This initiative had immediate benefits thanks mostly to our club doctor, Katherine Rae.

By far and away the best idea we came up with was to have a 'hybrid' match between the two clubs. One half would be played according to league's rules and the second half with union rules. The game would be played on a Friday night at Redfern Oval, home of the Rabbitohs right in the middle of their supporter base which has a strong Indigenous population. There would be no entrance fee but we would ask for a gold coin donation which would go to a nominated charity. We agreed that an under-20 game would best showcase the speed and skill of the players. We would have two referees, one from union and one from league, who would each control their half of the field. It was an exciting concept.

Richo and I knew we'd need approval from our national controlling bodies to stage the match. Given it was a 'colts' game, that there was no entrance fee and that charities would benefit, it was a good news story all round. Richo had strong relationships within the NRL and from our side the University of Sydney was seen as the most successful and progressive club in the competition with strong relationships with the governing body. Richo spoke to David Gallop, CEO of the NRL, who endorsed it as a really good idea. I then contacted Matt Carroll, deputy CEO of the Australian Rugby Union, to get his approval which I really thought would be a simple formality. His reply ruined my day, 'We have discussed your request to sanction a "hybrid" match between teams representing the University of Sydney and South Sydney Leagues. The policy of ARU is not to approve such matches and while I appreciate that this is a low-level promotion, we are not prepared to grant an exception in this case.'

I was stunned and even more so when Matt added a 'by the way', David Gallop had not approved the match. Richo's reaction was unprintable. We both had the letter from Gallop approving the match as a one-off. I sent Matt a copy the letter but to no avail. He would not budge. Both codes, but more particularly rugby union, needed any and every bit of positive promotion. This would have been a grand showpiece for both.

As time passed Richo and I became good friends. He would attend the Sydney University Rugby fundraisers and he opened his office systems and procedures to us. This was really useful since the Rabbitohs have the biggest paid memberships of any

NRL club and are one of the very few to make a profit.

Greg Inglis is one of the greats of rugby league and would have been a sensation in union. In August 2011, the media picked up that he was planning a move from his club the Melbourne Storm to either the Brisbane Broncos or the Rabbitohs. I was in hospital recovering from surgery and the newspapers were full of 'Where will GI play next season?' I called Richo and asked where negotiations were up to and when he responded, 'It's done, mate, he is about to become a Rabbitoh', I then hit him with an idea. The University of Sydney offered a master's degree for elite sportsmen and women which was tailored to enable them to study more or less at their own pace while in Sydney and when they were away on tour. I suggested Greg Inglis would seem to be an ideal candidate for such a program. Nationally and internationally, he was seen as an excellent role model and with his Indigenous heritage he could make a lasting positive impact on his community across the land.

Richo clearly saw the benefits to GI and to the Indigenous community and was out of the blocks and ready to set the wheels in motion, but when I said it was just a germ of an idea, he agreed to let me first consult the academics at the university. I called Professor Nick Wailes who was MBA director of the University of Sydney Business School and being a keen rugby man, his reaction was the same as Richo's, 'let's do it'. I then arranged a lunch at the University Grandstand restaurant with Professor John Shields, head of human resource management, Richo, Nick and I, all dressed in our suits and ties. In strode Greg Inglis in shorts, thongs and the ubiquitous baseball cap. Actually, he seemed to glide in – he is the ultimate athlete – a big man, his handshake was firm and all-enveloping.

My briefing of John and Nick had stressed that we needed to be measured and calm with GI since it was likely tertiary education would be foreign to him. We had a good chat and John and Nick assured GI he would get every support possible from the university to ensure his success. He was keen but the timing was not ideal since he and wife Sally were in the process of moving from Melbourne to Sydney and he also needed surgery on his shoulder. We all agreed to keep in touch and meet again when he was ready.

I was happy the seed had been planted and I continued to try and get something concrete happening between the university and the Rabbitohs. Richo was receptive but in truth there was no progress. Finally, I took matters into my own hands and wrote directly to the university's Vice Chancellor, Michael Spence, expressing my frustration. The university talked a good game when it came to upliftment of the Indigenous community but that was about all. I outlined to the VC everything the rugby club and I had done with the Rabbitohs which had a strong Indigenous playing and supporter base. I (politely) suggested it was a classic case of the tail wagging the dog.

I didn't expect much from my note so I was pleasantly surprised when the VC wrote back complimenting me on our efforts and agreeing the university had dropped the ball. He ended by saying he had appointed Dr Shane Houston of Aboriginal descent as a deputy vice chancellor to address this issue campus wide. He asked me to meet with Shane in the first week of his appointment.

I duly met with Shane who was really excited at what we had achieved to date. He said he loved the Rabbitohs and that he had 'one red and one green eye', the Rabbitoh's colours, adding that he would support us in any way he could. I mentioned that thanks to Bruce Corlett and John Atkin I had secured a $30,000 scholarship to be used for assisting an Indigenous student who played rugby to enrol at the university. In some ways this was a departure from the norm in that scholarships were usually awarded to promising rugby players, not the other way round.

While I beavered away trying to find a suitable applicant for the scholarship, the word came down that Shane had convinced the Trust Company that he was better placed to find a suitable candidate than I or the rugby club. I was less than impressed, in fact I was bloody angry. Still, I continued trying to identify an Aboriginal lad who had the aptitude to complete a university degree course, it being a plus if he played rugby.

A few months later I was surprised by a call from Richo thanking me for my part in the development of the Memorandum of Understanding (MoU) between the university and the Rabbitohs. The MoU was centred around Greg Inglis commencing study in 2013. Shane Houston had been busy. The signing ceremony, which I attended only thanks to Richo, was a major media event. Everyone was delighted including VC Michael Spence. Greg Inglis was quoted as saying, 'As long as it takes me, I just want to walk away with something at the end of my career.'

I wish I could say that this story had a happy ending. Shortly afterwards I left Sydney University Rugby and joined the Brumbies so lost touch with both the Rabbitohs and the Business School. In December 2013, I was invited to a Business School end-of-year function and asked John Shields how Greg Inglis was getting on. Turns out he had failed the year through 'non-attendance'. After all the work we had done this was a real shock and a very disappointing turn of events. John, for whom I have the highest regard, was equally annoyed and embarrassed. I asked him if he minded if I try to get this unique opportunity back on the rails. He agreed.

I was not close to GI. I had met him a few times and that was all. After the signing of the MoU I had felt confident it would be an excellent partnership and GI, being a highly competitive man, would thrive. So, I reached out and met with him and Sally at a café in Coogee. We had a long chat about what had gone right and what had gone wrong. GI said he had time pressures but Sally intervened and explained how it really was. The whole experience was altogether way too daunting. Clearly, the university had dropped the ball. As I wrote to Michael Spence, 'When I first conceived this project, we all agreed that it should not be allowed to fail. It has, albeit temporarily.'

Michael responded, 'Thank you for your work with Greg. I was dismayed to learn from you of the difficulties that Greg had encountered and pleased that things seem to be back on track. I am very happy just to let you and John get on with the business of supporting Greg through this degree.'

GI's athletic prowess had been recognised early in his life and this took precedence over everything else. As a result, his schooling suffered and quite understandably he found the challenges of starting a whole new studying experience intimidating, and who wouldn't? Despite all the assurances, the university had not provided any safety net. Everyone involved felt sick about the experience but for me it was particularly galling that nobody had raised any red flags. We had failed GI. We had also failed Sally, who seemed to be a tower of strength.

I believed strongly in the opportunity and believed equally strongly in Greg and I undertook to do whatever I could to ensure he obtained that degree. When we met, he agreed to re-enrol and was committed to completing the course. Unfortunately, this did not transpire. He is an impressive and generous individual who is often conflicted between his football career, his family obligations and his fame.

Knowing what I now know, this was truly one of those situations where I wished I could have the time again to help craft a different result. Greg Inglis had not failed us; we had failed him.

Teddy Roosevelt's quote was cold comfort, 'It is hard to fail, but it is worse never to have tried to succeed.'

*

In 2014, I managed to secure a substantial scholarship from

Sydney University Rugby sponsor Concierge Travel through founder Don Ferguson. The scholarship was specific in that it would only be awarded to an Indigenous lad who could play rugby to enter the university. One would think this would be a relatively straightforward task, given there are 189 Indigenous players in the AFL, representing 10 per cent of all players, and 12 per cent of all Rugby League players are Indigenous. In rugby, just fourteen Indigenous players have represented their country out of a total of 944 Wallabies. A damning statistic given these men and women are natural ball players.

Well, I attacked this opportunity with enthusiasm. What an opportunity for a young Indigenous man to attend Australia's oldest and most prestigious university. I wrote to the principal of every single school on the Australian Schools Rugby database. All 641 of them. My letter outlined the details of the scholarship. 'It will assist the successful candidate with the costs of tuition as well as accommodation in one of the residential colleges of the university. We see this as a significant opportunity for rugby players of Aboriginal and Torres Strait Islander origin and I would encourage you to make eligible candidates aware of this opportunity.'

The response to my letter was deeply disappointing. Journalist friend Peter FitzSimons gave things a kick along in his weekly *Sydney Morning Herald* column 'The Fitz Files' but despite everyone praising the initiative candidates were few and far between.

Sorting through a handful of candidates, we finally settled on a young man whom we will call Kobi. He was in his final year of study at St Joseph's College, one of Australia's great rugby nurseries. He came from the town of Walgett in north-west New South Wales, where Aboriginal and Torres Strait Islander people made up almost 30 per cent of the population. According to the 2015 *Dropping Off the Edge* report, the town was listed as one of the most socially disadvantaged areas in the state. It is a tough place.

This was not a random selection. We did as much due diligence as we possibly could. Kobi boarded at St Joseph's and lived with his single mother when in Walgett. He represented his school's first team in both rugby and cricket which is no mean feat since it is a very strong sporting school. We were also advised his grades were average. All of this was fine with us and he seemed like a good all-round fit. During the school holidays I arranged for Kobi to fly from Dubbo to Sydney to meet some key university people and to have a look at the facilities. He was a well-presented, quiet young man and I sensed he was a bit overwhelmed by this historic, 160-year-old sandstone institute of learning. Having said that he was also clearly excited as he was shown around the campus training facilities and the St John's residential college.

Kobi returned to Walgett and that's when the trouble started. He didn't use a mobile phone or email and I'm not even sure he had an internet service at his home. He literally went off the radar; I was unable to contact him, his mother or his grandfather. I persevered until I was eventually told he was in hospital. Allegedly, upon his return from Sydney, he had been hammered by some locals who took exception to him flying to Sydney and the fact that 'he was going to the University of Sydney'. After this, I and others did everything possible to reach out to him, but to no avail. We then had two further shocks. We were advised his matriculation results were in the lowest possible band which would eliminate any possibility of him entering the university. A few weeks later we learned his girlfriend was pregnant, and he would be a father in three months. To be honest, we were devastated. I wrote to Kobi and wished him every success in the future. He did not respond.

The most recent review of government expenditure on Aboriginal and Torres Strait Islanders is staggering. It estimates direct expenditure was $33.4 billion, an increase of around 23.7 per cent since the first report in 2008–09 taking inflation into account. This equates to $44,886 per Aboriginal and Torres Strait Islander, almost exactly twice the amount of direct government expenditure per person on the rest of the Australian population.

We continued the search but eighteen months after the Concierge Travel scholarship was announced, we were still not able to identify a suitable candidate. As I wrote to Mike Hawker, chairman of the Australian Rugby Union at the time, 'It is really disappointing that rugby has not been able to provide a suitable candidate for this golden opportunity.'

It is such a complex situation and there are no simple answers. Sadly, young people like Kobi become unintended victims of their own circumstance.

*

In the past three years in Australia probably more words have been written about Joseph Suaalii than any other sporting identity. Variously described as, 'The most sought-after teenager of his generation ... a teenage sensation ... a rare talent, and, the next rugby league great', Joseph first caught the eye while playing rugby for the King's School, another of Australia's leading rugby nurseries, with his speed, his athleticism and his skills. Everyone agreed he was something special. His school fees were covered by a scholarship funded by one of the highest profile rugby league clubs but sadly for lovers of rugby union these skills were not on display in his last two years at school because playing would have conflicted with the conditions of his league club contract. Nevertheless, he was a hero at school idolised by those younger and respected by his peers and teachers alike.

I met him briefly while watching my grandson Leo compete in the annual school athletics carnival and was impressed by his poise and manner. Later, after reading yet another puerile article purporting to give him some spurious advice, I decided to write him a letter. Those who know me will attest that is the type of thing I do. I told him a little about my family's story, how we left a comfortable life in Johannesburg for whatever lay before us in Sydney, that we had taken the decision to give our children a secure and safe future and because of this when we arrived, we chose to sacrifice everything to provide them with the best possible education. We were extremely fortunate to enrol the boys at King's and Hayley at Loreto in Normanhurst. I described how we scrimped and scraped to afford the school fees and were careful with our money, how we persevered and how encouraged we were by the fact that all three children were happy at their schools. I went on to write, 'The reason I am telling you this is that both Kevin and Paul made life-long friendships at TKS. They respected the traditions of the school and the excellent academic and sporting support that the school provided. It is a tribal system and the bonds are strong and for life and the school provides excellent safety nets if required.'

I noted everyone wanted to leave a mark and quoted Bob Teague, 'We all leave footprints as we journey through life – make sure yours are worth following.'

I finished, 'Do not waste a day at the King's School. Set yourself goals which will ensure that you are well liked, well respected and build friendships, they will be gold in years to come but, most importantly, live in the now and be your own man. Ignore all the noise around you and embrace the opportunities that the King's School offers you. With lifelong friends who will stick with you through thick and thin. With no regrets.'

This will probably seem presumptuous but everywhere where sport was discussed or written, this young man of seventeen was being peppered with 'advice'. I thought I could at least offer some honest suggestions which were about him as a person, Joseph Suaalii.

In a remarkable coincidence I had just finished writing the letter and was pondering how I could get it to Joseph when my phone rang. It was Jimmy Hilgendorf, a close friend of my son Kevin and the coach of the King's School First XV. Jimmy and I had previously discussed employment opportunities and I had told him of my involvement with the Friends of Sydney University Rugby's mentoring program. Jimmy shared the career information with Joseph who asked if he could possibly have a chat to me about his future. I was surprised but delighted to agree and a few weeks later we caught up at Gowan Brae where Joseph was the house monitor looking after the first year boys.

First impressions are always revealing. I had read a great deal about Joe, but was pleasantly surprised by his calm, confident and respectful manner. Given his age he seemed so mature. By the time we met, he had signed a lucrative, long-term contract with the Sydney Roosters. We spoke about his future aspirations and I told him about the letter that I was about to send to him which I never posted.

When I suggested that given 2022 was likely to be a very busy year cementing his place at the Roosters and that he should consider taking a year off, he categorically rejected this option and was adamant he wanted to continue studying and that football was a part of his life, but not his whole life. He well understood the need to have choices. We did not discuss the ever-present spectre of a possible career-ending injury.

I left that meeting impressed but also motivated to assist this talented young man to achieve his goals off the field. I was determined there would be no repeat of the Greg Inglis saga when he had been let down by the system.

Over the next few weeks, I introduced Joe to Wayne Erickson and Leonie Lum. Wayne, known to most as Gus, is a former international rugby referee and is principal of St Andrew's, one of the University of Sydney residential colleges. He is a generous and caring man who has responsibility for the wellbeing and development of more than 300 young men and women. Leonie is head of sport at the University of Sydney and her responsibilities include the recruitment and management of elite athletes. In her fifteen years at the university Leonie would have interviewed thousands of aspirational young men and women. After meeting Joe, she commented he was one of the most impressive young athletes she had ever met. High praise indeed.

Our meetings were clandestine. Joe is a very private person with a tight, supportive family of Samoan and Cambodian heritage who do their very best to shield him from the media frenzy that accompanies his every move.

Despite being a full-time professional footballer, I was really impressed how seriously he took his studies. He was determined to obtain the best possible score in his matriculation. He fully understood that, rightly or wrongly, it would either open or close doors in his immediate future. The King's School supported him all the way. Three times a week Joe would leave school at 5.30 am and drive into Roosters headquarters in the city. From 6.30 am to 8.30 am, he would do his schoolwork under the watchful eye of a tutor paid for by the club. Not once did he miss a session. He is a highly focused individual with remarkable discipline.

As I write, Joe is having a great season and he has been accepted to do a degree at the Australian Catholic University. Whichever way, Joe Suaalii has a bright future.

*

Early in 2022, an outstanding young golfer at my golf club, Andy Richards, mentioned that he intended to turn professional as soon as he could. Andy played off a handicap of +5 and is a very determined young man. His focus and commitment appealed to me and I offered to help him raise some money to give him a running start to his professional golfing career. In the past, I had many discussions with Peter Senior about how difficult it was to succeed as a pro; talking about sleeping in cars, staying at cheap motels and the like. Andy seemed willing to endure the hardships to make his dreams come true.

At our first meeting, we agreed that raising between $15,000 to $20,000 would be a good result and off I went. I reached out to all my sporting and other contacts and explained how focused Andy was. I organised a golf day, a raffle and a dinner where Susie Burrell, Australia's leading nutrition and dietician, was our guest speaker. Once the short, sharp campaign was over we were able to present Andy with a cheque for $55,000 – an extraordinary result by any measure. This confirmed to me, once again, the generosity of people who believe in 'the cause' and are willing to support it. We will all watch Andy's progress with a great deal of interest. He certainly has the ability and the drive to make his mark on the professional circuit.

Above: Meredith Burgmann (being dragged) and her sister Verity on their way to getting arrested on 6 July 1971 at the Springboks' game in Sydney.

Above: 'Barbed wire and bloody mayhem' during the 1971 Springbok tour of Australia.

Left: Kevin, Paul and Leo – all winners of the best under 13 athlete at the King's School.

Above: Lifestart's Kayak for Kids on Sydney Harbour.

Above: Jonathan Wilson-Fuller, 'the boy in the bubble'.

Jonathan Wilson-Fuller,
9 Keith Place,
Baulkham Hills, 2153.

December, 1993.

Dear Ray,

Just a note to wish you the blessings of Christmas and a healthy and happy New Year.

This year has been very difficult for me: My health has deteriorated owing to the actions of new neighbours on both sides – they are chemically very irresponsible. Also my Grandfather died at the end of September. However, there is always good news, I have been accepted to study for my B.Sc by correspondence from the University of New England (Armidale, NSW) with exemptions having been granted with regards to practical work and residential schools.

I am looking forward to the New Year with faith and trust that it will be better than this one.

Thank you for all the kindness you have shown me.

Bye for now, with my many wishes for your health and happiness, and an especially wonderful Christmas.

Jonathan.

Above: Letter from Jonathan Wilson-Fuller.

Right: Sons Paul and Kevin with Alyson Annan OAM at the partially completed Olympic hockey fields.

Left: Johnny Depp and Amber Heard's dogs, Pistol and Boo (or maybe Boo and Pistol).

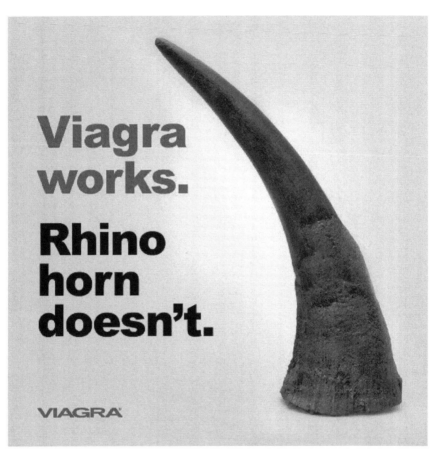

Above: Graphic by Julie Furlong of D+M Pty Limited.

Above: The cover of Joachim Schmeisser's book *Last of their Kind*.

Above: Nick McCardle, Murray Mexted, David Mortimer AO, the author.

Above: Tony and Wendy Gresham, John Eales AM, Ray
and Margie Dearlove and Michael Rowan.

Right: The author in
the isolation ward with
Scarlet Fever.

Above: Professor Michael Kidd AM.

Above: The author with the South African High Commissioner to Australia – His Excellency Marthinus van Schalkwyk.

Above: COVID-19 social distancing in the wilds of Africa.

Above: Professional rugby league footballer Joseph Suaalii with the author.

Above: Craig Spencer, founder of the Black Mambas with the author.

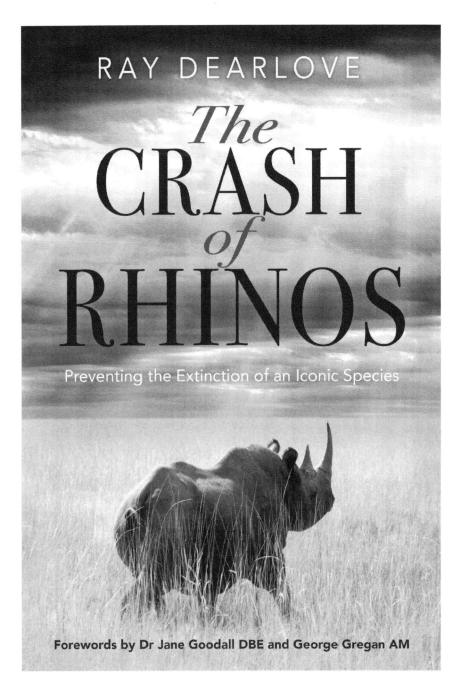

Above: The cover of my first book designed by David Henley.

Above: The author resplendent in a pith helmet with Franscois McHardy, former head of publishing at Booktopia Publishing Services, selling books at Springbok Delights shop.

From: The Keeper of the Archive to
TRH The Prince of Wales and The Duchess of Cornwall

Private and Confidential

25th March 2014

Dear Mr Dearlove,

Thank you for your letter dated 18th January 2014, in which you asked whether The Prince of Wales would be willing to take on the Patronage of the Australian Rhino Project.

His Royal Highness has given careful consideration to your request, but has decided, with regret, that he cannot help on this occasion. He only takes on positions of this nature when he is able to give at least some time to the organisation concerned, and he is so heavily committed at the moment that he is having to turn down many interesting and worthwhile invitations, of which yours is sadly one.

I am sorry to have to send you a disappointing reply, but His Royal Highness was interested to hear about your proposals and much appreciated your thinking of him in this way. He has asked me to send you his best wishes.

yours sincerely

David Hutson

Mr Ray Dearlove

Above and following: Royal letters of support.

KENSINGTON PALACE

From: Mrs. Thea Coley,
        Assistant Private Secretary to HRH The Duke of Cambridge

Private and Confidential

17th February, 2014

Dear Mr. Dearlove,

The Duke of Cambridge has asked me to write and thank you for your letter of 18th January in which you ask His Royal Highness to become Patron of The Australian Rhino Project.

The Duke was most interested to hear about the project, and your plans to establish a secure breeding herd for rhinos in Australia. Having given careful consideration to the possibilities, however, I very much regret that The Duke reluctantly feels that he must decline.

The Duke has decided to focus his efforts on conservation through 'United for Wildlife', and initiative established by The Royal Foundation. His Royal Highness hopes that his continued commitment to conservation and combatting the illegal wildlife trade will mean that future generations are also able to experience these magnificent creatures in their natural habitat.

His Royal Highnesses was also extremely grateful to you for your kind invitation to visit The Rhino Project during their forthcoming visit to Australia. Unfortunately, the programme for The Duke and Duchess of Cambridge's upcoming visit has already been set and, sadly, I am afraid it will not be possible to schedule this engagement. I do hope you understand.

The Duke would have me send you his best wishes, and very much regrets having to send you this necessarily disappointing reply.

Yours sincerely,
Thea Coley

Mr. Ray Dearlove,
Founder, The Australian Rhino Project

Above: The author with Stephen McGown who spent six years as a captive of
Al Qaeda.

CHAPTER 19

RUGBY AND POLITICS

In April 2018, Margie and I received an invitation from Her Excellency Ms Beryl Rose Sisulu, High Commissioner for the Republic of South Africa, to a reception to celebrate South Africa's Freedom Day at South Africa House in Canberra.

We made the pleasant three-hour drive to Canberra on a gorgeous autumn day. Plenty of South African wine and beer was being served and I would have given anything for a bitterly cold Castle, but my pledge to myself of not drinking before 5 pm held strong. I had held to this 'vow' for thirty years or more although as one of my friends put it, 'You certainly make up for it after 5 pm'. Another smartarse suggested, 'It's 5 pm somewhere in the world, so why not just go for it?'

During a buffet lunch featuring traditional South African favourites such as boerewors, chakalaka, pap and bobotie, I saw a fellow whom I thought I recognised. I said to Margie, 'I think that's Anthony Abrahams, I wonder what he's doing here?' I had got to know Ant, a former Wallaby, during my time at the Sydney University Rugby Club. The only South African connection I could think of was through Ant's stance against apartheid in 1971. We wandered over and had a chat and as I suspected, that was the exact reason why he had been invited to the reception.

In 1971, Abrahams and six other Wallabies – Jim Boyce, Paul Darveniza, Terry Forman, Barry McDonald, Jim Roxburgh and Bruce Taafe – all stood down from possible selection to play against the all-white Springbok team touring Australia. Their protest against the apartheid system was probably another catalyst for the Australian government's decision to sever sporting ties with South Africa. The tour was plagued by protests though nothing matched the impact of the Wallabies 'Magnificent Seven'.

While South African skipper Hannes Marais insisted they were a rugby team and not political representatives of their homeland, protesters at the matches, including future Queensland premier Peter Beattie and NSW Legislative Council president Meredith Burgmann, chanted 'racists go home'. Meredith was also at the Canberra lunch as was former chair of the Australian ANC support group, Jane Singleton, who organised Nelson Mandela's visit to Australia in 1990. I attended the welcome event at the Sydney Opera House where Madiba addressed the crowd of about 40,000. As much as anything else, I wanted to see what he looked like since the South African government only published photos of him when he was sentenced to life imprisonment in 1963, twenty-seven long years before. Joining in the rapturous roars which greeted him when he appeared on the Opera House steps, I found myself wondering if we had made the right decision to emigrate. My heart was still very much in Africa but we had now weathered three extremely difficult years in settling in Sydney and I knew that for our children the move ensured a degree of certainty which was still very much a question mark in the Rainbow Nation.

While the troubled rugby tour of 1971 went ahead without Abrahams and the other six players on the Australian side, it would be the last time Australia would meet South Africa on the sporting field for more than two decades. The matches were interrupted by flour and smoke bombs; airlines refused to fly the players and hotels refused to serve them. The Queensland premier Joh Bjelke-Petersen declared a state of emergency and the Victorian premier Henry Bolte described the protests as a 'rebellion against constituted authority'.

In South Africa, when we had reports and saw photos of the protests, I remember one of my cousins much younger than me and like most of us a rugby fan asking his dad, 'Why do they hate us so much?'

In July 2021, exactly fifty years later, Meredith wrote in *The Australian* newspaper,

> 'The police must have been shocked when just after half-time we clambered over the picket fence and hared off into the scrum. We had no idea what to do when we arrived in the centre because it had never occurred to us that we would actually get over the fence. My sister Verity grabbed the ball and produced what *The Bulletin* called "the kick of the season"; while I just lay down in the middle of the ruck. We were soon arrested and I was dragged off the playing area and around the boundary. Spectators came down to the fence and spat on me. At my court case, the magistrate, who considered me the "leader" of the naughty foursome because I was a convener of the "Stop the Tours" campaign, gave me a two-month jail sentence. My lawyer was gobsmacked. I'm still the only protester to have been sent to jail for a simple demonstration offence.'

To this day, the South African government considers Abrahams and the other six Wallabies as well as Meredith Burgmann and Jane Singleton as true anti-apartheid warriors.

The following year, we were again invited to South Africa House when the current High Commissioner, His Excellency Marthinus van Wyk, warmly welcomed Jim Boyce, another of that same group of ANC heroes. As Marthinus wrote in a letter of condolence to the late Barry McDonald's family, 'I am well aware of the significant role he played in the fight against injustice in South Africa as part of the "Magnificent Seven" which later earned him a well-deserved Medal of Freedom from the then president of South Africa, Mr Nelson Mandela.'

CHAPTER 20

QUO VADIS AUSTRALIAN RUGBY

As I write, Australian Rugby is staggering from crisis to crisis. It seems it is always so. In 2012 once again the game in Australia seemed to struggle and I decided to write to friend Michael Hawker, the newly appointed chairman of the Australian Rugby Union, with some comments and suggestions. I started by saying I had just seen a TV panel program featuring the CEOs of the major sports in Australia, namely cricket, rugby league, AFL, soccer, tennis, netball and of course rugby. The facilitator's closing question to each participant was, 'What is your plan for your sport for the next three to five years?' Rugby CEO John O'Neill was the first to respond with, 'We want to be number one in the world.' The leaders of the other sports then outlined their vision, goals and strategy. I said to Mike I thought rugby's response was disappointing – there was no detailed plan or program how this goal was likely to be achieved. Unfortunately, within twenty-four hours of this particular TV program the Australian under-20 side failed to reach the playoff stage in the Junior World Cup adding to gloom around rugby in Australia.

I suggested to Mike that John's response seemed to summarise the situation in rugby in Australia. I said, 'The ARU seems to be solely focused on the Wallabies which is fine but surely it is also their mandate to develop a structure that addresses the rest of the rugby community? Many Sydney clubs are on their knees and are struggling to survive.'

I went on, 'The NSW Rugby Union has completely lost its way. The Waratahs, chock-a-block with Wallabies, will not make the finals. The structure whereby the Waratahs are split from the rest of the rugby community has been a complete disaster. The model is seriously flawed.'

I reminded Mike I had previously crafted an inter-provincial club competition model comprising clubs which included Sunshine Coast, Brothers, University of Queensland, Gold Coast, the Vikings in Canberra, Manly, Southern Districts, West Harbour, Sydney University (SUFC) as well as the Victorian state team. Every one of these clubs supported the concept of a national club competition.

David Mortimer, president of SUFC and one of Australia's top businessmen, joined me in presenting the paper to John O'Neill and his deputy Matt Carroll. David and I both thought the presentation had gone well and been positively received. John assured us it would be reviewed within the ARU. Nothing happened. A year or so later the ARU announced the National Rugby Competition. A completely different beast from what I had suggested. At the end of the season, it was generally agreed that it was an unmitigated disaster. I subsequently made the presentation to John's successors Bill Pulver and Raelene Castle, also to no avail. The dogs bark but the caravan moves on.

Not that Mike needed reminding but the Australian Sevens team had also been perennial under-achievers. I concluded by saying in my view, there was a huge disconnect between the people on the ARU and Waratah boards and what was happening at the grassroots of rugby. To get to the real, deep issues there needed to be a bridge between the people charged with running the game and the people who were involved at the grassroots. I offered to be a part of that bridging process and to 'do the work' since there is much opportunity and much to be done and I'm ready to help. My phone never rang.

At best I expected a one-line response from Mike but instead he suggested we get together for a chat. It was a serious and stimulating conversation. One of his concerns was the apparent lack of a clear pathway for talented young rugby players. By chance Margie and I had a trip planned to South Africa which coincided with a Wallabies vs Springboks match in Pretoria in a few months' time. I asked Mike if I could set it up, would he be interested in meeting Rassie Erasmus who at that time was general manager of high performance for South Africa Rugby. Rassie had responsibility for all the teams, male and female, 15s and sevens, under-16, under-20 through to the Springboks. That in itself was an eye-opener for Mike. Australian Rugby had no such centralised position or structure. Mike was keen to meet him saying he would fly from London for the match.

Over the years I had developed strong relationships with people in rugby in South Africa, one of whom was Hilton Houghton, owner of the Union Sports Group. Hilton's company acted as player agent for most of the Springboks as well as other players. He knew Rassie well and agreed to ask him. Within a day Hilton responded, 'I have spoken to Rassie, and he has confirmed he will attend the meeting.'

Mike booked flights from London and the venue for the meeting was set with Hilton adding, 'Due to the high profiles of Mike and Rassie, as well as the nature of discussion, this meeting will be confidential.' We suggested a lengthy agenda which could be described as 'wide-ranging' and included development of coaches, pathways, sevens and women's rugby.

As hard as we tried, Margie and I could only find accommodation at the Pretoria Sheraton Hotel where the Wallabies and entourage, including Mike, were staying. Since this meeting was supposedly 'secret', the risk of someone from the Wallabies seeing me might have raised some questions but we were where we were.

I picked Mike up at the hotel and we headed off to the Royal Elephant Hotel at Centurion between Pretoria and Johannesburg. I was like a cat on a hot tin roof but as always Mike was calm and focused. Hilton escorted us to the boardroom where he proceeded to lock the door. Seated at the table were Rassie Erasmus, Frikkie Erasmus, no relation but a lawyer and Rassie's business partner, Ruben Moggee, CEO of the Super Rugby Golden Lions team, and Gavin Jones from Hilton's company.

I had to pinch myself. Here we were, sitting in a locked hotel boardroom with the most powerful man in Australian Rugby and the second in command of rugby-mad South Africa who only a short seven years later would win the Rugby World Cup in Japan. And nobody knew about it. I felt like Henry Kissinger.

The meeting took almost three hours and went well. Mike and Rassie are both extremely courteous and polite men and the conversation ebbed and flowed. Neither the Springboks nor the Wallabies had made strong starts to the season and somewhat provocatively Rassie suggested John O'Neill must be under pressure to win later that afternoon. Mike just smiled.

Rassie briefed Mike about a proposed new competition which he had named the 20/20 contest. Unbeknown to anyone, the South Africans had already signed up 160 players from all the tier one rugby countries to participate in a three-week competition in January 2012. Players included All Black superstars Richie McCaw and Dan Carter who were as positive about the format of the competition as they were about the potential financial rewards. Rassie quoted Richie, 'This is exactly what rugby needs.' The January window was chosen because it was the only period when players from both the northern and southern hemispheres would be available.

All agreed that something needed to be done about rugby to maintain interest and to attract crowds. Rassie's concept was a series of matches played over three weeks in Cape Town and Durban while other venues in other countries could be used in the future. The matches would be twenty minutes each way with some slight modification to the rules but the key component was it would be 15-man rugby not sevens, nines or 10s. Some of the proposed rule innovations included:

- Two referees on the field.
- A specialised scrum ref who would adjudicate all scrums to ensure consistency and some simplification around the breakdown. (I knew Wayne Erickson would love that.)
- The ability to take a mark anywhere on the field.
- Reduction in the value of penalties.

Mike was clearly engaged and suggested the clock should also stop whenever there was a stoppage. I think all rugby fans would support such a rule.

The plan was to play three back-to-back matches which would be broadcast live internationally on a Friday or Saturday. The teams would feature the best players in the world and as part of the launch there would be a live auction in London where each player would be 'sold', much like the IPL cricket competition in India. In a clever touch, players would be paid half of their auction value. To ensure some balance the best players in any one position, say fly-halves Dan Carter, Morne Steyn and Jonnie Sexton, would be in different teams. An interesting innovation was that coaches would also be auctioned. Planning was well advanced and the South Africans had secured private or corporate ownership for all eight of the proposed teams.

While the planned 2012 tournament was shelved, according to Rassie because of the ARU's reluctance to participate, it was the intention of all involved to proceed in January 2013 and the competition had the blessing of SA Rugby. If Mike knew about this, he didn't let on. A very good poker player is he.

Like the so-called 'Dan Carter clause', the South Africans saw this tournament as an ideal way to handsomely reward players in a managed fashion which would reduce the exodus of their top players for purely financial reasons. This exodus was a major problem for SA Rugby and is still an issue today as it is in Australia which similarly does not have the funding to compete with what is on offer in Japan and Europe and inevitably, in the US.

One of Mike's hot buttons was a pathway for young players. With Rassie's all-encompassing responsibility for elite players, he explained how they hold a centralised national under-16 Craven Week in the July holidays, where teams from all fourteen provinces compete. From this tournament a squad of fifty players is identified and each member of the squad is provided with a personalised development plan which includes their weight, strength and skills. Each player is constantly monitored and they come together as a squad twice a year where the top coaches in the country put them through their paces. This squad is then reviewed and renewed at the under-18 annual Craven Week and a new squad goes through the same process thereafter. The national under-20 coach has responsibility for the under-20, -18 and -16 teams and squads and has visibility of all the players by the time they get to the under-20 level. This is not a closed system where the same players are identified and then given the inside running through the age groups. The South African system recognises that players' bodies change, as does their attitude and motivation, and new players are welcomed into the system.

At all Super Rugby matches involving only South African teams there are two curtain raisers, one featuring the provincial under-19 teams and the other featuring the provincial under-20 teams. As a result, coaches and selectors have plenty of opportunity to see emerging talent.

Rassie bemoaned the lack of quality back line coaches in South Africa and was implementing a ranking system for coaches who were 'in the system' from schoolboy level upwards. He would write to each coach and ask them to list whatever they felt were their strengths and weaknesses. For example, lineouts, scrums, back line, defence, etc. Where practical, Rassie would then invite a selected group to present on their coaching philosophy and rank each one and prepare development plans. He also insisted that the national coaches should be involved in actual coaching when they were not on duty with the Springboks. They were accordingly drafted into the under-16 and under-18 programs. Refreshingly novel, but equally simple to implement.

A few years before, Rugby World Cup winning captain Francois Pienaar had come up with the Varsity Cup concept which has grown into a highly successful tournament. There are two divisions where inter-varsities are played on Monday nights and draw very large live crowds from the students and public at large. The games are televised live, the prize money is significant and the events are as much about entertainment as they are about the competition itself. I had proposed a Universities World Cup to the ARU a few months before. Again, no response. Things seem to move at glacial pace with Australian Rugby and innovation is certainly not encouraged.

It was noted by Rassie that Australia had only one representative on the SANZAR referee panel and he happened to be a New Zealander, Steve Walsh. The South Africans take referee development seriously and have a comprehensive program which was run by Australia's favourite referee, Andre Watson. Rassie used the example of Jaco Peypers who did his apprenticeship as a referee through schools, club and then provincial matches. He is now one of the top refs in the world.

Despite their two national sides clashing in a few hours, the farewells were genuinely warm as Hilton gave me an 'I hope you're happy' wink. I certainly was but what was far more important, was Mike? He was very quiet on the return trip to the Sheraton. He was obviously impressed with Rassie's knowledge, commitment, creativity and passion and was excited about the 20/20 concept, but as a member of the International Rugby Board he was only too aware that group of highly conservative former players would probably push back. He was smart enough to realise though if the players decided to support it, it would proceed. To quote Mike, 'Something different just has to happen to change rugby in its current form', and his challenge was how best to introduce that change into Australian Rugby. I wondered how the next few hours would go with Mike sitting next to John O'Neill who perhaps was not aware of the meeting that had taken place just hours earlier.

Thanks to Hilton and Mike, Margie and I were given great seats at a packed Loftus Versfeld Stadium. Margie cut a lonely figure with her gold Wallaby jersey in a sea of myrtle green Springbok jumpers. She was seated next to an Amazon-sized South African supporter who, every time the Boks scored, which was often, would gently pat Margie on the head with a, 'There, there, my dear, it's only a game'. As if she meant it.

After the Springbok victory, Margie and I walked back to the Sheraton. Not our smartest move. As soon as we left behind the Bok fans enjoying their braais from their bakkies (utes) with plenty of brandy and cokes and the rugby anthem 'Shosholoza' ringing out, the roads became dark and frighteningly deserted. We made it safely to the hotel but not without a few scary encounters with some undesirables along the way. We reflected if the perceived danger was actually real or not.

I had my back to the entrance and we were enjoying a very much needed drink in the lounge when Margie said, 'Here come Mike and John O'Neill.' Oh God, I thought, how are Mike and I going to handle this? Independently we both feigned surprise at seeing each other. I invited them to join us but Mike declined saying he and John had some matters to discuss. I later glanced at the pair in earnest conversation. A month later, John resigned. He was replaced by Bill Pulver who in turn was replaced by Raelene Castle in 2017. Raelene was then replaced by Rob Clarke in 2020 and Rob by Andy Marinos in 2021 and Phil Waugh in 2023. For the average rugby supporter it is very difficult to remain passionate and loyal with such turmoil at the top of an organisation. Perhaps these constant changes in leadership contribute to the ongoing turmoil in Australian Rugby and hopefully the Hamish McLennan/Waugh combination will provide some sorely needed stability. The code desperately needs it.

CHAPTER 21

FUNDRAISING

Iseem to have spent my entire life arranging events and raising funds for different organisations, charities and causes.

When our sons were at King's, cricket was under threat from basketball as a preferred sport. It was the Michael Jordan era and his extraordinary athleticism was converting young cricketers to basketball at a rapid rate. Why would you spend hour after hour on a cricket field subject to the vagaries of the weather when you could play a high-energy, high-pitch game of basketball that's over in an hour and then you head to the beach? To provide some funding and to stimulate interest in cricket at the school the late Rick Symons and I started the Captains' Lunch. Over time it became extremely popular and raised significant funds for the King's School Cricket Club which Rick and I also started and continues to thrive.

Later, when both Kevin and Paul were playing rugby with the University of Sydney, I was asked to assist with fundraising for the club and so the Finals Lunch was born. This annual event has now become a permanent fixture within the Sydney business community and over the ten years I organised the event, it is estimated that approximately $1.8 million was raised. Not bad for an amateur rugby club. I also arranged fundraisers for the Rhino Project, the Australian Rugby Union, the South Sydney Rugby League Club, the Pennant Hills Golf Club and the Lifestart and Black Dog charities.

I created my own events management company and have my own simple formula that I work to in organising successful fundraising events.

Select a date that is relevant.

Select a venue which is convenient and suits the style of the event. I chose the Westin Hotel (now the Fullerton) in Sydney for most of the events I organised and general manager Mark Burns and Karyn Primmer and their teams provided consistently outstanding service.

Engage the best speakers you can find. It is these individuals who are the attraction and make the event that much easier to sell. People who attend such events want to laugh or learn or ideally both. A successful combination.

Sell the tables. This is often the most difficult task of all but if the first three points are sorted, it does become easier.

During the event, raise as much money as you possibly can from the attendees.

Andrew Coorey and Vince Sorrenti are my favourite MCs. These men have the skill to manage, calm and entertain a room of 1000 people or more. Vince is the funniest man I know. He does a wicked imitation of the South African accent and uses Saffa expressions such as, 'I'm telling you, man,' and, '... So where do you live, what car do you drive, which school are the kids at, etc, etc,' and, 'Let's do lunch ... your shout, I'll get my people to talk to your people.'

The choice of keynote speakers is vital since it must entice people to spend the money to attend the event. Over the years

I managed to secure speakers of the calibre of Sir Anthony O'Reilly, Sir Graham Henry, Sir Peter Cosgrove, Sir Richard Hadlee, David Campese AM, John Bertrand AO, Eddie Jones, Rear Admiral Lee Goddard CSC RAN, Jake White, Robbie Deans, John Eales AM, Tony Squires and any number of well-known sports icons.

I first met the now Chief of Army, Lieutenant General Richard 'Rick' Burr AO DSC MVO, after he had been recommended by John Bertrand as an ideal speaker for one of the University of Sydney lunches. Rick is a quiet, unassuming man, and you would never know he led Australian and international special forces task groups to Afghanistan and Iraq. It is difficult to reconcile Rick's demeanour with the special forces nickname, the 'chicken stranglers'. During his speech you could have heard a pin drop. At the conclusion of his talk, he received a standing ovation.

I subsequently invited Rick onto a panel for a parents and sons dinner at the university and he was joined by the late Dan Vickerman. Once the discussion was over, I invited questions from the floor. One of the parents, Bill Hovey, stood up and told Rick his son was being deployed to the war zone in the Middle East the following Monday. He asked what advice Rick could give him. Rick was silent for just a moment. As the room fell quiet, he said, 'I want you to know that your son will have the best training in the world before seeing any action and he will be better prepared for any situation than any other force in the world.' Bill had a tear in his eye. After I closed the event, Rick immediately made his way to have a quiet, reassuring word to Bill. Rick Burr is a remarkable leader of men. Australia is in good hands with him at the wheel.

Long-time friend Bruce Corlett AM founded and subsequently chaired Lifestart, a not-for-profit supporting children and young people living with disability or developmental delay, their families and carers. Until recently Lifestart's main fundraiser was Kayak for Kids, an inspirational paddling challenge on Sydney Harbour. The funds raised went to early childhood intervention and school-aged services providing individualised support to give the children the best possible start in life. When Bruce's CEO was struck down with illness he asked if I would take on the organisation of the race. I was keen to assist since Bruce was a really good friend and he did wonderful work for many charitable organisations never seeking any glory.

I got cracking and working from a strong base of previous attendees, I suggested we build on the existing program by introducing a competitive component. This would not only increase interest but also attract some of Australia's best kayakers such as Guy Leech, a previous World Ironman Champion who was already a Lifestart ambassador. To join Guy, I invited Jess Fox, Olympian and winner of seven gold medals in individual canoeing, making her the most successful paddler, male or female, in world championship history. Next on my ambassador list was Murray Stewart, the kayaker of South African descent and gold medallist in the London Olympics. Jess and Murray keenly accepted their invitations to be Lifestart ambassadors.

The race took place on a beautiful Sydney morning. Around 800 competitors dotted the Harbour and paddled their way over the 17.5-kilometre course from McMahons Point to Clontarf Beach. There were three categories, singles or doubles in their own boats, teams of three people paddling the full course and then the relay team challenge where teams of four divide the course into four stages. Lots of noise and lots of fun but highly competitive in this category!

In the second year of the race, I introduced a further layer of competition by offering two tickets for the winner to participate in the famous Molokai Class in Hawaii, acknowledged as the toughest paddling race in the world. Despite the predictions of the naysayers, I managed to secure two return airfares to Maui for

241

the winner courtesy of Hawaiian Airlines. This added spice to the event with the serious paddlers now keen to be involved.

We raised almost $180,000 that year. A lot of money, but never enough to meet the demand for Lifestart's services.

CHAPTER 22

THIS AND THAT

The great Roger Federer's mother is South African-born and in 2014 I decided to reach out to him to enlist his support for the Australian Rhino Project. Craig Tiley, who was born in Durban, had an illustrious tennis career as both a player and a coach before being appointed as CEO of Tennis Australia and director of the Australian Open, one of the four Grand Slam majors. Craig has supported me with 'money can't buy' auction prizes for every event that I organised and is a good friend. After briefing him on the latest bout of rhino poaching, I asked him if he could put me in touch with Roger. He kindly gave me the contact details of Janine Handel, CEO of the Roger Federer Foundation.

I called Janine in Zurich only to be told that she was actually in Australia with Roger preparing for the Australian Open. I called her mobile number which she immediately answered, speaking very quietly. It turned out that she was on centre court in Brisbane waiting for Roger to play a charity exhibition match against his good friend, Jo-Wilfried Tsonga. She was happy to talk as long as

I understood that as soon as Roger appeared on court, she would have to hang up. I launched into my pitch and Janine listened intently, saying that Roger was very much aware of the rhino poaching crisis since he tried to visit South Africa every year. Unfortunately, though, he wouldn't be able to help. His foundation is very specific in its fundraising goals and also the beneficiaries specifically focused on the education of South African children between three and twelve years old. To date, the Roger Federer Foundation has helped more than 800,000 children.

To quote Roger, 'I've been quite shy about making the foundation a massive deal. I'm not seeking attention. I came to it after travelling a lot to Africa with my mum. I saw poverty and children with no chance of going to school. I realised that I could make a difference, an impact.'

The public often only sees one side of those deemed famous or celebrities and it is only when one probes does one begin to understand and applaud the generosity of people like Roger Federer.

*

I met Sir Ian Botham at a fundraiser a few years ago and told him a story about his son Liam which he thoroughly enjoyed. Liam's English Rossall School toured Australia and played a game of cricket against King's in Sydney. Both Paul and Kevin were in the King's team. The match was played in late December and King's had a useful leg-spinner named Will Christmas. Liam was an aggressive batsman and after having a look at a few of Will's deliveries, he marched down the pitch and dispatched the ball over the clubhouse into the swimming pool. This was a huge six by any measure. Liam then strolled down the pitch towards Will and greeted him, 'Merry Christmas.' Even the staid and emotionless umpires laughed. As did Ian with more than a hint of pride.

*

In 1993 I had responsibility for marketing to and supporting the Australian education and health sectors for IBM. I loved the role because of the diversity of people and organisations I worked with. IBM had developed several software packages and systems that enhanced learning and saved lives.

One day, Alex, one of my team, briefed me about a teenager who lived in Baulkham Hills not far from IBM's head office. His name was Jonathan Wilson-Fuller and he came to be known as the 'boy in the bubble'. We arranged to meet him in what was one of many subsequent visits to his home. Every time, I had to take a deep breath and control my emotions. Here was a lad of fifteen, the same age as my son Paul, but that was where the similarity ended. Jonathan was home bound, in fact, he was limited to just two rooms.

As I got to know him it was obvious he was intellectually gifted but at the same time he suffered from wide-ranging physical disabilities including a severe intolerance to minute levels of ingested and inhaled chemicals which could kill him. It was a level of intolerance seldom found anywhere in the world. He had not been able to leave his house since he was ten. A year before we met him at the age of fourteen, he had commenced university studies by correspondence in maths, science and philosophy.

His parents Yvonne and Kevin sacrificed their professional careers because of the love and dedication they have for their son. Every time I met Yvonne, she looked absolutely exhausted.

I am proud to say that at our request, IBM donated a state-of-the-art personal computer to Jonathan with a commitment to upgrade the equipment, as required. Jonathan subsequently wrote me a lovely letter. Today, he's a published poet and writer. Now that is courage, while his parents Yvonne and Kevin are real heroes.

*

A few years ago, our niece Sharron's husband Brennan also known as BJ had an horrific motorcycle accent. He had served on a number of missions to Afghanistan and Iraq with the Australian armed forces and was on his way to a Post-Traumatic Stress Disorder counselling session in Brisbane when the accident happened. The surgeons did everything possible to save his leg which had been crushed by the motorbike. BJ spent three weeks in ICU in a coma and eventually there was a choice – amputate his leg or die from the infection. In reality there was no choice for his wife Sharron who has two young children. She confirmed that they should remove his leg.

At the time, BJ was a fit forty-four year old and he approached his rehabilitation with a strong positive attitude. He was eventually fitted with a prosthesis just above the knee. This artificial limb gave him endless grief and with limited funds he could not afford a more expensive fitting. BJ had tried, without success, to claim some of the expenses from both the federal departments of defence and administration. There is no question his mental health was suffering. He was seeing a psychiatrist and was also getting valuable support from the military vets organisation, Mates4Mates.

During the Rhino Project, I had met several federal ministers of parliament so I offered to try to help. My first call was to Defence Minister Marise Payne, whom I had met when I was running the Rhino Project. I sent her an email with a full brief at 6.50 am one morning and fifteen minutes later I had a response. *'Good morning, Ray. Thanks for your email, I will follow up with Minister Tehan's office this morning [Veterans Affairs] and see what I can find out. I agree it seems a very frustrating and difficult position for Brennan to be put in. Let me see what I can do.'* Astonishing responsiveness.

True to Marise's word, she and her staff tried everything they possibly could do to convince both departments of the merits of BJ's claim but to no avail. Sadly, the bureaucracy won. As BJ wrote to me, 'The policy states I must have lost 65 per cent of my femur bone and I've lost 62 per cent which is 2.8 mm too short, so the claim failed.' To me this suggested that bureaucracy had gone completely mad.

Around the same time, I had read about Dr Munjed Al Muderis, an Australian orthopaedic surgeon. It was an extraordinary story. Munjed was born under the Saddam Hussein regime in Iraq and studied medicine at various Iraqi universities, graduating with a bachelor of medicine, bachelor of surgery in 1997.

In 1999, he was forced to flee Iraq while working as a junior surgeon at Saddam Hussein Medical Centre in Baghdad. A busload of army draft evaders was brought to the hospital for the top of their ears to be amputated under Saddam Hussein's orders. The senior surgeon in the operating theatre refused and was immediately shot in front of several medical staff. Munjed decided to flee. He escaped the operating theatre and hid in the female toilets for five hours. Shortly after, he made his way to Jordan where local authorities moved him on to Kuala Lumpur. From there he took a people-smuggling route to Christmas Island in the Indian Ocean, 1500 kilometres north-west of the Australian mainland. He was eventually sent to Curtin Detention Centre in Western Australia and detained there until his identity was verified. After ten months he was granted refugee status but could only land a job at Mildura Base Hospital in rural Victoria as an emergency unit and orthopaedic resident. This was after sending out more than a hundred résumés to hospitals, health services and the like. Fast forward and Munjed became a fully accredited orthopaedic surgeon practising in Sydney.

Munjed developed the new generation of implant termed the 'osseointegration prosthetic limb' (OPL), which addresses several major issues previously faced by patients. For this invention he's received plaudits and awards from all over the world. Thanks to Munjed, traditional and rigid socket-based technology is now replaced with surgery that inserts a titanium implant into the bone. Fitting and taking off the artificial limb can be done in less than ten seconds. Osseointegration surgery provides amputees with greater mobility and reduced discomfort which exactly described BJ's situation. Given the issues BJ was having, including depression on top of PTSD and the effect it was having on his marriage and young family, I reached out to Dr Al Muderis.

I had low expectations but was delighted when his clinical coordinator Claudia Roberts called to say Munjed would be very happy to see BJ. At the time I discussed the fees involved and my conclusion was the cost of this surgery was going to be well out of reach. Nonetheless, BJ met with Munjed in Brisbane and in one word was inspired. The fee was several tens of thousands of dollars and BJ reluctantly told Claudia it was way out of reach. There were additional costs such as flights to Sydney which was the only city in which Munjed would operate and a lengthy stay in hospital for rehab.

I then took matters into my own hands and tried everything to persuade Munjed this was a special case while knowing full well he must receive many such appeals. It took time but Munjed finally agreed to dramatically reduce his fees and BJ was booked in. According to Munjed's team, it was a highly complex procedure but it had a great result and I am pleased to say BJ is a changed man with exceptional mobility given his disability. Each year Munjed travels to Iraq and works pro bono with soldiers and civilians who have lost limbs in the seemingly endless conflicts in that part of the world. A compassionate but often misunderstood man. Claudia must also take a bow; she helped and advised me all through these discussions.

*

In 2015, I was invited by Kyia Clayton to speak at the inaugural Tasmanian eco Film Fest (TeFF). TeFF is an initiative of the Tasmanian Conservation Trust, Tasmania's oldest environmental protection organisation. I was privileged to be part of an auspicious panel along with Dr Richard Kirby, plankton scientist from the UK; Todd Houstein, director of Sustainable Living in Tasmania; Chris Darwin, conservationist (and great-great-grandson of Charles Darwin); Ginger Mauney, international wildlife filmmaker and board member of Save the Rhino in Namibia; Peter McGlone, director, Tasmanian Conservation; and David Ritter, CEO of Greenpeace Australia. It was a fascinating discussion around the topic, 'All roads lead to the environment'. I have never seen myself as an activist but there were certainly a few of those on this particular panel.

The brief was, 'As there are eco experts on the panel that represent a wide range of focuses, we wanted to let each person have a moment to speak about their connection to environment and their concerns and campaigns and then the panel will discuss how all business, daily life choices, etc, lead to destruction or protection of environment'.

The discussion certainly got my brain cells moving.

After the panel concluded, Kyia said that the Rachel Ward wanted to meet and have a chat about rhinos. My heart skipped a beat. I had always thought Rachel was marvellous actress. She had also previously been voted one of the ten most beautiful women in the world. She was at the festival supporting her and her husband Bryan Brown's daughter Matilda, an actress, writer and filmmaker. Rachel was keen to know more about the rhino issue and wanted to get involved. We met in Sydney a few weeks later and she graciously agreed to become an ambassador for the Australian Rhino Project. Rachel was a wonderful ally, she knows a vast number of people and was always willing to introduce me to potential donors, sponsors or influencers. She and Bryan also attended an intimate fundraiser at JBWere in Sydney. This is a prime example of 'famous' people generously giving so much of their time.

*

And finally, apropos of nothing, a man walks into a zoo. The zoo has only one animal. It's a shitzu.

CHAPTER 23

THE SYDNEY OLYMPICS

After twenty-seven years with IBM in South Africa, Europe and Australia I felt I was ready for a change. IBM itself was going through a period of transformation from a hardware company to a software and services provider. I felt this was not my strong suit so I jumped at the offer from Peter Luffman to join his company, Balsam Pacific.

Peter and I had been friends for several years and he regularly turned out for my Kingfishers cricket team. He was a very good cricketer. He had started and built Balsam Pacific into the leading supplier and installer of artificial sporting surfaces in Australia and in Southeast Asia. His company manufactured and installed basketball courts, tennis courts, athletics tracks and increasingly popular multi-purpose courts, both indoor and outdoor. The company also sold a wide range of sporting equipment, which was a highly successful line of business. Peter was the first to admit he was not a sales guy but he was an extremely effective and successful chief executive. Needing a sales director, he asked if I would be interested. Bearing in mind my love of sport and the fact the Olympic Games was due to take place in Sydney in 2000, it seemed like a golden opportunity. I was quick to accept the job before Peter changed his mind.

Within weeks of joining, Peter gave me my first challenge – win the International Olympic Committee (IOC) tender for the supply and installation of the two field hockey pitches to be used at the games. Peter emphasised the critical importance of winning the tender since the winner would be entitled to use the five Olympic rings in all communications which would send an extremely powerful message to customers, suppliers and competitors. As they say, no pressure.

Knowing we were up against competitors from across the world, we threw everything into our proposal. We built a beautiful scale model of the hockey precinct in a presentation case made of the finest Australian wood to emphasise we were an Australian company. We made the point forcibly that our installation crews were all Australian and finally, we gave them a price they could not refuse and nobody could match. The price was absurdly cheap. Peter and I believed the Olympic rings would bring us more than enough business to cover the cost of the material and installation. We were right.

After a nervous wait we were finally advised we had won the tender. Peter and I were ecstatic and got cracking with the construction. Among his other skills, Peter was an outstanding project director. Paul and Kevin were studying at the University of Sydney and during their vacation they were part of the labour force which built the pitches so I could claim it was a family effort, topped by our daughter Hayley who danced at the opening ceremony.

Building the two pitches was a lot of fun. There was excitement in the air and, as passionate Australians, everyone was busting to make these fields a showpiece. We also wanted to give our men's and women's hockey teams any legal edge to increase their chances of success.

By 2000, the Hockeyroos' Alyson Annan OAM was the best player in the world while coach Ric Charlesworth had taken the team to the number one ranking. I decided to meet with Ric and Alyson through her agent Russell Feilen to see if within the laws of the game, we could prepare a 'home ground advantage' pitch. Both were excited to be approached and Ric confided that he coached his team to flick the ball over the stick of the defender and then run around and re-gather the ball. For this to be successful the artificial grass had to be a little longer and thicker so the ball could 'grip' the grass and enable the player to 'catch up' with the ball and keep attacking. I took this request back to our in-house manufacturing team who built the grass exactly to these specifications, completely within the law. The Hockeyroos won the gold medal.

The athletics track was a whole different thing. The tender was let and we felt we were perfectly positioned to win the business since we were the primary installer of athletic tracks in Southeast Asia. Peter cautioned me about getting ahead of myself. Then president of the International Amateur Athletics Federation (IAAF), Italian Primo Nebiolo, was very closely aligned to the Italian Mondo Company which also built athletics tracks. Peter was right. Despite us using similar sales and pricing strategies and tactics to our hockey tender, we lost to Mondo. Go figure.

The Balsam stable of products was world class and I spent a lot of time in Asia where the demand was strong. A good example was in Indonesia where President Suharto pushed to implement what was referred to as the 'Eastern European' model, where success in sport was believed to be a passport to recognition on the world stage. Today I believe it would be described as sports washing. With more than 250 million citizens, Indonesia is split into thirty-four regions and the vision was for each major city or region to have a sporting hub with athletic tracks, multi-purpose facilities, both indoor and outdoor to boost participation and, over time, excellence. The political reasoning apart, I supported this vision 100 per cent and Balsam benefitted strongly by building such facilities.

On another occasion, I paid a visit to Saigon to sell some Balsam equipment. Vietnam is a country of contrasts and it was a trip I'll never forget. As an African I have seen wealth and I've seen poverty, both of which were very evident in Vietnam. After one particularly robust negotiation I was invited to dinner at a restaurant supposedly popular with American troops in days gone by. I can usually hold my own when it comes to beer drinking but these guys were in a completely different league. After a lovely seafood dinner and lots of beer I was told we were going to another 'venue'. I was more than ready for bed but being so close to sealing the deal I thought I needed to take one for the team.

We hopped into the Mercedes-Benz, thankfully with a (sober) driver, and off we went. I had no idea where we were going but my translator, a Vietnamese university student whose parents were among the first boat people to Australia, assured me with a thumbs up that everything was cool.

The sealed road soon turned to gravel and the bumps had a serious effect on my bladder. I just had to go. No worries, I was told, not far now. Eventually we stopped at a furniture store shopfront where I was directed down a side passage. It was stiflingly hot as I made my way cross-legged towards the last room of the house. There I found two buckets. To this day, I don't know whether I used the right one but I was beyond caring. The relief was eye-watering and as I looked up taking a deep breath, I saw this huge bloody rat scurrying along the wall. I got a helluva fright and I stopped midstream choking back a yell. The rat left, I continued, and then unsteadily made my way along the side passage back to the car noting the whole family sleeping peacefully on the floor.

We eventually reached our destination which was a beautiful lodge deep in a forest complete with beautifully dressed dancing girls, karaoke, fresh fruit and you guessed it, more beer. I don't remember much about the trip home but the next day, I signed the contract.

CHAPTER 24

THE TED TALK

In late 2015 Siobhan Moylan approached me and asked if I'd be interested in doing a TED talk about the Australian Rhino Project at the Sydney Opera House. Would I ever? Siobhan sat on the panel which decided who appear on the following year's TED Sydney program.

TED is an international non-profit organisation devoted to spreading ideas, usually in the form of short, powerful talks. It began in 1984 as a conference where Technology, Entertainment and Design (TED) converged. Today it covers almost all topics from science to business to global issues, in more than one hundred languages, and has a massive global following.

I am a huge fan of the TED talks but never, ever did I think I would have such an opportunity. It would be a real coup for the Rhino Project giving us a reach we would never have normally achieved. Siobhan was measured in our discussions. To lower my expectations, she regularly pointed out the final decision had not been made about the speakers but that I had a chance. Well, I threw in everything I had to ensure I was selected. Outside of my family, I did not mention this to anyone, just in case it all fell in a heap. Siobhan was my official coach and mentor and she did an amazing job. She asked me to send through a draft of the talk, which I did, not realising this was going to be the first of many drafts.

Finally, Siobhan called and said, 'You're in.' I was at once elated and terrified. Siobhan was a rock in terms of guiding me as the intensity of the 'editing' of my talk increased. 'Rehearse, rehearse, rehearse,' she said over and over again.

I did a practice run with some senior executives at JBWere in Sydney. Donna Gulbin and her colleagues were brutally honest in their critique of the talk. It was uncomfortable, but invaluable. When the day of the final dress rehearsal arrived, I gave my talk in front of a small group of TED staff, all experts in their fields. It was tough. One was responsible for commenting and advising on content and another on presentation style, mannerisms, etc. I was told to speak more slowly, take deep breaths and use pauses for effect. All extremely useful advice which may seem mundane to the reader, but for me it was gold. It was a very positive, motivating and encouraging session. And direct. No room for egos.

I was mortified to learn there would be no teleprompter. All I would see in front of me on the stage were two screens, one showing what was being projected behind me and the other a clock timing the talk which I thought would be really distracting. When I asked how long I had I was told twelve minutes was the standard but that I could go to fifteen. I was also told I was last on the program. Another shock. I had hoped I would be speaking early in the day rather than having to wait all day with my nervousness increasing and blood pressure rising. Siobhan said the last two presentations were really important, and the organisers wanted to end on a high note. Gulp.

I was offered a 'good seat' in the Opera House with the sold-out audience to watch the other speakers, but I declined. I really did not want to see or hear other presentations and then be thinking, 'Oh God, why didn't I think of that?' or 'What a great line – I should have used that' or that my talk would be dry. Or boring. Or not at all enjoyable. As a result, Margie and I drove into the city in time for her to watch the afternoon session while I tried to read a book and for the umpteenth time, rehearse my speech. What scared me most was that I would forget the opening line, 'I want you to imagine that you are a rhino – a grandma rhino'. I was confident that, once I got past the opening line, I would be okay. And so, I sat waiting, nervous, taking deep breaths in the green room.

This event is superbly organised. The TED team thought of everything; drinks, food, quiet rooms, the lot. What was really special was how well each member of the TED team, most of whom are volunteers, cared for the speakers. I don't care how many speeches or presentations you've made, this one is special.

Eventually I was called to the make-up room. Again, the atmosphere was calm with some light-hearted banter all of which (sort of) settled the nerves. Then, in a flash, I was standing on the edge of the stage watching the speaker before me finish. In some ways I wanted him to hurry up but in another, I was happy for him to take as long as he liked. Then it was, 'Ray, you're on, good luck, wow them!' Out I walked to the designated spot. I looked up and all I could see was the first few rows and then just the outline of people. A *lot* of people. Five thousand in a packed Opera House. In addition, the whole day's event was streamed live on the internet and was being piped into a number of offices of major firms.

'I want you to imagine that you are a rhino – a grandma rhino.' I had barely started my talk when I noticed a woman in the front row sobbing. That was all I needed. I'm a pretty emotional guy at the best of times and I knew when I came to the line, 'And I want to say to all of the people in Africa who are fighting this undeclared war – you do not walk alone', I would probably choke up. For the rest of the talk, I avoided looking at the lady in the front row. I do hope she enjoyed it. As one wag put it, at least she wasn't sleeping.

While referring to Australia's strict biosecurity laws, my line about the actor Johnny Depp, who had recently been in Australia making a movie, was very well received. I am delighted to say I was given a standing ovation. A proud moment for me and my family and old friends Tom and Helen Lawless, all of whom were present.

Judging by the emails and SMSs received from all over the world, I am certain we significantly increased awareness of the rhino crisis that day. The TED talk was unquestionably one of the highlights of my life and resulted in significant publicity and a sharp spike in donations to the project.

To provide some context about the Johnny Depp comment, his troubles began when his then wife Amber arrived to visit him with their two Yorkshire terriers, Pistol and Boo. Amber had disembarked from their private jet without declaring the dogs which were supposed to be placed in quarantine upon arrival, as is standard practice in Australia. The Australian authorities were not happy and set down the conditions for the couple to rectify matters.

Australia's Agriculture Minister, Barnaby Joyce, had strong words for Depp, 'It looks like he sneaked them in. He either has to take his dogs back to California or we're going to have to euthanise them.'

That struck Johnny and Amber as a tad extreme. Sympathetic observers started a hashtag, #WarOnTerrier and created a petition asking for canine leniency. 'Celebrities aren't above the law,' Mr Joyce continued. 'If you start letting movie stars – even though they've been the "sexiest man alive" twice – to sneak dogs into our country, then why don't we just break the laws for everybody?' Eventually the couple agreed to send the pups back home. They were still charged and in court they acknowledged and apologised for their transgressions.

Mr Joyce was unimpressed, mocking their apology by saying it looked as if Mr Depp was 'auditioning for *The Godfather*'. Never one to mince his words, Barnaby added, 'It's time that Pistol and Boo buggered off back to the United States.'

Later, in an interview in the United States, Johnny got his own back by saying, 'Mr Joyce looks somehow inbred with a tomato. It's not a criticism, I was a little worried that he might explode.' And then everybody lived happily ever after. Sort of.

CHAPTER 25

SUPPORTING
THE TROOPS

Late in 2011 I saw a program on television about the Scottish golfer Colin Montgomerie visiting British troops in Afghanistan. One of the clips showed him conducting a clinic and demonstrating his golf prowess in the desert and finishing with tips to the attentive soldiers. Plenty of bunkers there! It was extremely well received by the armed forces and I thought, 'I can do that'.

I was well connected in sports circles and my idea was to ask some sporting greats if they would do a similar trip to support the Australian troops in Afghanistan or Iraq. I put the idea to Lieutenant General Rick Burr, now Chief of the Australian Army. He really liked it saying, 'Thanks again for your interest in looking out for our troops. You are a good man.'

Rick put me in touch with Lieutenant Colonel Ian 'Robbo' Robinson who was responsible for the entertainment for the offshore-based troops. When we met, although he loved the idea,

Robbo said it wasn't a good time as the future of Australian troops being deployed to the Middle East was uncertain. He did mention however that he was focusing on a new project to try to brighten up the recreation rooms of the troops in Afghanistan and could I possibly help?

People say I am like a dog with a bone. Once I start something, I give it a full go. Within a few days I had contacted Jason Allen, CEO of the Waratahs; Andrew Demetriou, CEO of the AFL; Mike Hawker, president, and Matt Carroll, CEO, of the Australian Rugby Union; Joseph Healy, board member, and Ben Buckley, CEO, of the Football Federation of Australia; Shane Richardson, CEO of the Rabbitohs; Pat Howard, high performance manager of Cricket Australia; and David Garnsey, CEO of the Rugby League Players Union.

The response was immediate and overwhelming. Every organisation I approached donated something. Within three weeks my garage was overflowing with gifts and I was able to deliver two carloads of donations to Robbo.

I wrote to General David Hurley, Chief of the Army at the time, naming all the donors, 'I am sure that you will be heartened by this support from Australian sport for the men and women serving in Afghanistan and I've been privileged to deal with these people on behalf of the Australian Defence Force.'

I happened to mention this effort to friend Peter FitzSimons from the *Sydney Morning Herald*. He was intrigued and asked if there was any possibility of him doing a show for the troops in the Middle East. Peter is a former Wallaby, a bestselling author and an excellent raconteur.

I spoke to Robbo who turned out to be a fan of Peter's weekly column the 'Fitz Files', and suggested we all have a chat. We duly turned up at Peter and Lisa's beautiful home in Cremorne. As always, Peter was dressed in his trademark red bandanna, barefoot and wearing a pair of rugby shorts that had definitely seen better days. A gruff but kind man, he invited us in as we clambered over the books he was using to research his latest bestseller.

As always straight to the point, Peter said he was very keen to do a show for the Diggers and asked Robbo what he thought might work. Robbo floored him with his response, 'Mate, what works best for the troops is a loud rock band, a comedian, and a singer – ideally a good looker with big tits.' In response, Peter stammered, 'Well, I don't think I meet any of those criteria.'

He must have done something right because a few weeks later Robbo gave me a call saying that Peter was on his way to the war zone. I wrote to him saying, *'Travel safe and keep your head down – that red bandanna is a dead giveaway!'*

Two months later the 'Fitz Files' featured this article,

'TFF writes from Afghanistan, where, believe it or not – I am more than a tad amazed myself – I am part of a travelling troupe of rock bands, etc, entertaining the troops before Chrissie. (My stuff is mostly between sets, telling sports yarns and stuff from some of the war books I've penned.) One touching thing is that at each Australian base in Kabul, Kandahar and Tarin Kowt, there are a myriad of sporting posters, paraphernalia and equipment to remind the troops of home. At the initiative of rugby identity Ray Dearlove, they have been gathered from all the main sporting codes, and include AFL flags from all of the clubs as well as balls, many Tennis Australia posters, as well as posters from eight of the sixteen NRL clubs, the Waratahs, Cricket Australia, and posters and Socceroo shirts from Football Federation Australia. The Australian Rugby Union was particularly generous in donating posters, balls as well as 500 scarves and 500 caps! Not one sporting organisation approached declined. Bravo to all and particularly to Mike Hawker, Matt Carroll of the ARU and Ben Buckley of the FFA, who went above and beyond the call of duty.'

I subsequently received a lovely thank you letter from Major

General Crane, Commander of the Australian Defence Joint Task Force in the Middle East who wrote, 'We have been overwhelmed by the positive reaction to our request and I am very pleased to advise that the scarves, caps, kit and printed material are on the way to Kandahar and Kabul. My thanks on behalf of all of the troops deployed in the Middle East.'

I framed that letter.

CHAPTER 26

HUNTING

I cannot abide the hunting of wildlife.

Many years ago, Margie and I travelled from Johannesburg to a friend's property in what was then Rhodesia. Our visit coincided with the annual culling of wild animals on the predominantly livestock farm. One evening, we were invited to join the professional hunter – known universally as the PH – for the culling. Not quite knowing what to expect we hopped on the Land Rover. The PH drove with his three lethal rifles lined up on the windscreen while the fellow with the spotlight was on the back of the vehicle with us. The first animal we saw was a magnificent kudu bull standing atop an ant heap. As Margie and I admired it, blinded by the spotlight this beautiful beast froze. A second later the PH shot it. Only one bullet was required and this regal animal became a lump of meat. As tears welled in my eyes, Margie was sick on the spot.

A more recent experience took place on one of my trips to South Africa to source rhinos, when I met Philip Mostert who owns the Hunting Legends group of lodges. We met him at his palatial Valley of the Kings Lodge at Thabazimbi a few hours north of Johannesburg. I have been fortunate enough to travel extensively and I can confidently say this six-star lodge is one of the finest I have ever seen. It caters for the extremely wealthy from all over the world who come to kill animals. A permit system allows legal hunting in South Africa and there is a strong body of opinion that says the income from hunting sustains the conservation of endangered species. What is absolutely clear is that if you have sufficiently deep pockets and the licence to kill you can hunt pretty much any animal including the 'Big Five' at Hunting Legends. Mostert's well-heeled clients include former US president Trump's sons Eric and Don as well as actor Tom Selleck. All macho men.

Philip Mostert is a charming man and a gracious host and knowing my interest was anti-poaching, not hunting, he related an interesting story. At another of his lodges most of the hunting was for so-called 'plains game', mainly antelope or zebra. Almost without exception the hunters, be they from America, the Middle East or elsewhere, only wanted the 'trophies' – the head, the horns and occasionally the hide of the animals. The hunters were always asked if they wanted the meat and the answer was almost always no.

There are four primary schools on the boundaries of the property and the pupils are from the lowest socio-economic groups where there is high unemployment and significant poverty. Mostert had established a small meat processing plant at the lodge and his staff vacuum packed the meat from the animals into 2-kilogram packs. Once a week they delivered the packs to the schools gratis. The principal of each school had two options: he could either sell the packs to the parents for a nominal R20 ($AUD2) so the proceeds flowed back to the school, or the school would conduct a weekly braai so the children got at least one substantial meal a week. Said Mostert, 'And you know, Ray, as a result of giving them the meat we have not had one poaching incident at the game farm for three years. As soon as a stranger, who could be a poacher, appears in town the locals inform the authorities.' Simple but effective. Engage the surrounding communities and give them an interest in the enterprise, and suddenly everything changes.

One final thought. The amount of annual tax revenue generated by hunting across Africa in 2016 was $US341 million. This is an industry which is not going away in a hurry.

CHAPTER 27

SOME RHINO STORIES

At the start of the 21st century, news started to emerge about the threat of poaching in Southern Africa. Until this time the region had been spared the onslaught affecting the rest of the continent's rhinos and elephants.

As I thought about the perils of endangered species and how the whole poaching issue was spiralling out of control, I reached out to Pfizer Corporation, the manufacturers of Viagra, with what I thought was an absolute cracker of an idea to curb the usage of rhino horn in Asian countries. Throughout my career I had come to realise if you want a result you start at the top of the tree, so I wrote to Ian Read, CEO of Pfizer International in New York, and requested his support for what might be called a 'left-field' proposition. I explained who I was and briefed him about the three rhinos being killed every day for their horns which are believed to have magical powers including curing cancer and improving sexual performance. I stressed there was no clinical evidence to support any such claims, but despite this the demand for horn was on the increase strongly influenced by the Vietnamese and Chinese, the latter being the biggest users of rhino horn. I wrote, 'I passionately believe that rhinos must be available to the world in the wild, not only in zoos.'

I then outlined my proposal that we could work with his team at Pfizer on a campaign which basically said, 'Viagra works. Rhino horn doesn't'. As I wrote to Ian, 'This may seem simplistic but the message is crystal clear.' I concluded, 'This is not a frivolous exercise, we cannot allow the oldest mammal on our planet to become extinct on our watch.'

Soon after, I received a response from Ms Oonagh Puglisi, director of corporate responsibility at the Pfizer Foundation, who was asked by Ian Read to respond. She said that unfortunately Pfizer were not in a position to extend support. Their strategy was 'to improve access to quality health care for underserved populations and their current focus was directing support towards non-communicable diseases, healthy aging and cardiovascular disease prevention'. She had shared my proposed campaign slogan with their Viagra commercial team but they were unable to provide endorsement to the idea, saying, 'Viagra is a prescription-only medicine indicated for the treatment of erectile dysfunction in men'.

Not surprisingly, I didn't think that was a particularly helpful response. They had entirely missed the point; I wasn't requesting support. I wrote back asking if we could have a telephone conversation to discuss the proposal. Her response took quite a while but eventually Ms Puglisi wrote back saying the idea was not a fit for funding from Pfizer and they focus on the areas where they believe they can make the greatest difference: health care. I hate being patronised and, in this instance, I really felt I was being patted away to extra cover. I was not asking for funding, but I am strongly of the view that wildlife trade is a global issue and would only be solved when the world realised that. So back I went. I had spent most of my life working for global American companies and was very familiar with the bureaucracy these organisations seem to breed. I wrote that while the decision was disappointing and I did understand their position, the world had to do something about educating the users of rhino horn, and a powerful message from a global leader in pharmaceuticals such as Pfizer was not only a positive message but a critical one. I concluded by reminding Ms Puglisi that solving this crisis was a global responsibility. No response. (On a completely separate note, I have nothing but huge admiration for Pfizer's work in bringing the COVID-19 vaccine to market in 2021. It has saved millions of lives.)

By this time, I was pretty fired up but unperturbed, I decided to approach Eli Lilly, the makers of Cialis and the competitor to Viagra. I wrote a similar letter to Ms Becky Morison, the general manager of Eli Lilly Australia, and received a response basically saying they could not participate. I figured I had nothing to lose and phoned Ms Morison. She turned out to be a wonderfully sympathetic and passionate person who really wanted to help but whose hands were tied by the constraints of her firm. She was kind enough to drop me a line after our conversation, 'Gosh Ray … as much as I love your initiative, I need to be transparent that submitting a request might not be a good use of time. I would not want you to take the time to complete and submit the application, when you likely have options with a closer fit.'

So here we are, several years later and more than 10,000 rhinos dead since our exchange. I still think it is a really good idea. Good friend Julie Furlong owner of the Design+Marketing Agency pointed out I should have included some potent imagery of a limp and droopy rhino horn; this may have made more of an impact.

Onward and upward.

*

Very early in my rhino journey, Barbara Buttery, one of our most enthusiastic supporters, introduced me to John Rendall. Initially, the name meant nothing to me until I realised that it was John who, together with fellow Australian Anthony 'Ace' Bourke, in 1969 had walked into Harrods in London where they had heard one could buy exotic pets. An hour later he and Ace exited Harrods with a lion cub which they named Christian. Thereafter they were a familiar sight walking Christian down the King's Road in Chelsea. In 1970 they handed the lion over to George Adamson of *Born Free* fame in Kenya in the hope that he would be successfully reintroduced to the wild. And so he was, and when Ace and John returned two years later, they tracked Christian down and he bounded up to them hugging them with his paws on their shoulders. That reunion has been watched by almost 20 million viewers on YouTube. But I digress. Since 2013, John and I corresponded and regularly spoke on the phone wherever he was in the world. He was always so positive and ready with real advice such as offering to give 'Malcolm' (former prime minister Turnbull) a nudge to encourage him to help me get the necessary approvals to import the rhinos. When I left the Rhino Project board, John sent me a kind note saying, *'Sorry to hear about your forced "retirement" but always remember, YOU got the project off the ground.'* Sadly, John passed away in February 2022, but the beautiful story about Christian the lion lives on.

In my ongoing quest to source rhinos for the Australian Rhino Project, fellow director, the late Godfrey Abraham, introduced me to Allan and Myra Salkinder. They owned a private game reserve in the north-west of South Africa. Allan ran a creative agency in Johannesburg with the somewhat provocative name the Ballz'n'Brainz Partnership, while Myra is a senior executive in the Kirsch Group.

I met up with Allan and Myra at their home in Johannesburg. Their story really moved me. They had owned twelve black rhinos but after successive poaching incidents they were left with just four, one of which had been relocated to Johannesburg Zoo. This particular rhino is named Phila and she had become something of a celebrity. An article by CJ Carrington takes up the story,

'Although I've always loved and respected all animals, the first time I was emotionally affected by a rhino, was when I met Phila, the poster child for rhino survivors everywhere. Phila is a black rhino who had been shot nine times in two different poaching attempts. I met her while she was still at her temporary home at the Johannesburg Zoo, when I brought some special food for her. Despite the brave girl's horrendous injuries and poor health, she still trusted us vile humans, and came running up to me when I called her name. I hand-fed her, and through my own tears, I could see the ancient pain and loss in her sad, dark eyes. A child's balloon popped, and Phila bolted to go and cower in her sleeping enclosure.

'I cannot call Phila a survivor in the true sense of the word, because to me survival needs an element of a fighting spirit. And that flame was gone from her wise old eyes.

'Phila is as happy as possible now, at a very special, highly guarded, secret sanctuary – where other severely traumatized rhinos quietly share their tragic tales of horror with her in a calm, defeated way of silent despair.'

I met Phila about a year later at the sanctuary and I can vouch for every one of CJ's words. I weep every time I read this story and am reminded of Martin Buber's words, 'An animal's eyes have the power to speak a great language.'

Allan told me that in 2010 in a poaching incident he lost three black rhino cows and Phila was wounded. Ten were left. Fast forward and now only four remained, one bull, one calf and two cows, of which one was Phila. The rest had been slaughtered by poachers. Allan pleaded with me, 'Ray, there is no alternative, these remaining rhinos must be removed and placed in a protected environment.'

I tried everything to help Myra and Allan get those four rhinos into Australia. I was advised I should refer this dreadful situation to the International Rhino Foundation (IRF) for assistance. The IRF's mission statement claims, 'For 25 years, the IRF has championed the survival of the world's rhinos through conservation and research. We do what it takes to ensure that rhinos survive for future generations. Based in the USA, we operate on-the-ground programs in all areas of the world where rhinos live in the wild. In five countries across two continents, we support viable populations of the five remaining rhino species and the communities that coexist with them.' With those words, 'We do what it takes to ensure that rhinos survive for future generations', it seemed to me Allan and Myra's situation was a perfect fit and I confidently reached out to the IRF.

I followed up a month later. No progress. I followed up again after another month. No progress. Finally, three months after asking for assistance I received a response, 'Although the IRF expressed some initial interest, they have landed on establishing a need to carry out some considered background work on the existing program within the USA. They are hoping to complete this in the next couple of months, following which, they will have a better handle on the overall opportunities and requirements of new founder animals to ensure success in the long term. So, at this point, timing is not aligning to enable them to consider the request from Allan Salkinder.' Seldom in my life had I heard such bloody mumbo jumbo and bureaucratic rubbish. My blood pressure rose but I bit my tongue.

A month later the Salkinders lost yet another rhino to poaching. Noting that black rhinos are classified as critically endangered I advised the IRF and their comment was, 'A great shame, and unfortunately even with all the intent in the world we won't prevent these examples.' In all the years of working on this

273

project, I found the IRF completely and totally ineffectual.

In 2015, the last of Allan's and Myra's rhinos was slaughtered. In an ironic twist, the poacher went hunting the black rhino on his own. Black rhinos have the reputation of being very aggressive. In fact, hunters are on record as saying the most dangerous animals to hunt are buffalo and black rhinos. In this case, the poacher shot the rhino who subsequently died, but not before the rhino killed the poacher.

In his note to me, Allan said, 'I am sick to the bottom of my soul. To say I am devastated is an understatement especially since we saw middens on the weekend and I was assured that all was well with the bull.'

I referred to Allan's and Myra's terrible experience in my speech at a Sydney fundraising dinner in September 2015. I said, 'In the audience tonight there is a family who contacted me two years ago. They told me they had owned sixteen black rhinos on their property in the northern part of South Africa. At that point, twelve had been poached and all that remained from the herd was a bull, a cow with a calf and another female. They were very emotional when they told me the story and almost begged me for their remaining four rhinos to be among the first batch to come to Australia. People, I promise you I tried everything I possibly could to get those rhinos into Australia and I failed. I had an email from Allan last week which had some harrowing photos in it outlining how the last of these sixteen rhinos had been slaughtered. Myra and Allan, I'm really sorry, I did my best.'

You could have heard a pin drop.

The first chapter of my previous book, *The Crash of Rhinos*, is titled, 'You can see rhinos around every corner', quoting the then South African Minister for the Environment, the late Ms Edna Molewa. That was in 2013, one year before the total number of rhinos killed in one year peaked at 1215. Since then, there has been a gradual reduction but it is generally acknowledged that the reasons for this is there are fewer rhinos in South Africa to be poached as well as vast improvements in protecting the sanctuaries, largely thanks to General Johan Jooste's efforts.

As the late Kenyan conservationist, Richard Leakey, said in 1997, *'Nature, like liberty, has no price tag, species are priceless, as are human dignity and freedom.'*

And it's not only the Big Five, here's what *The Economist* magazine said about pangolins in May 2020.

> 'Pangolins are the most trafficked animals in the world. Most end up in China. Practitioners of traditional Chinese medicine claim the scales have properties that can help breastfeeding and poor circulation. Some Chinese consider the flesh a delicacy. Live specimens occasionally appear in China's wildlife "wet" markets. Scientists speculate that a pangolin may have spread the COVID-19 virus to humans. The United Nations estimates that the equivalent of 142,000 whole pangolins entered various countries in 2018, more than ten times more than in 2014. While eating pangolins is illegal in China, putting their scales into medical concoctions is not. More than 700 hospitals in China are allowed to prescribe pangolin scales.'

Two studies in mid-2022 point to a 'wet market' in Wuhan, China, as the place where COVID-19 began, with progenitors of SARS-CoV-2 likely jumping from animals to human in two separate events. 'It's clear the viruses were circulating in the market and then exploded out of it,' epidemiologist Dominic Dwyer told *National Geographic*.

*

When I met Lennox Mathebula of the African Shangaan tribe, he was employed at the Sabi Sands Game Reserve as its community liaison officer. He had responsibility for educating locals about how important it is to protect the rhino. There are 650,000 people who live in very basic conditions on the borders of Sabi

Sands. When we met, Lennox proudly said, 'For the first time, we recently had a call from villagers giving up a poacher.' He then related a less encouraging story. He spent much of his time with the local Indunas, the tribal chiefs who still wield significant influence and authority over the communities. He described how he was making slow but gradual progress with these Indunas until a twenty-three-year-old young man drove into the village in his sparkling late-model BMW. The source of his windfall? Poaching. 'We had to start all over again,' said Lennox. 'The other youngsters see the fruits of poaching, ignore the risks and sign up for the next foray into the Kruger Park.'

As JR Tolkien said in *The Return of the King*, 'Oft hope is born when all is forlorn.'

We must never give up this fight.

CHAPTER 28

MY SON

Bestselling author David Jones wrote, 'It is both a blessing and a curse to feel everything so very deeply' and there have been times over the past decade that these words have really resonated with me. I am not into heavy self-analysis but I know myself well enough to accept I am an emotional person. To the surprise of many I am also fairly sensitive, belying the seemingly tough exterior of this big South African. In my youth, I was often inclined to use my fists in resolving perceived 'issues' when a robust conversation would have sufficed. Thankfully those days are gone and hopefully I have gained some of the wisdom that comes with age.

I have always written poems and found it to be a calming experience. Almost without exception the poems have told a story rather than writing on matters esoteric, and I suppose in that sense I am a storyteller. In recent years, my poems have almost exclusively been about rhinos, for example, 'For the Rhino'; about poachers, 'Is it need or is it greed'; about wildlife veterinarians, 'I am a Vet'; and about the world of game rangers, 'The Game

Ranger'. I have also written about heroes and people whom I admire who live in the wildlife protection eco-system such as the sadly missed Dr Ian Player, Major General Johan Jooste, Adrian Gardiner, Andrew Muir and the one and only Dr Jane Goodall.

In 2018, I published a book of poems entitled *A collection of poems – for the rhino*. General Jooste kindly wrote the foreword saying,

> 'Ray's passion for the African bush in all its facets and splendour combined with his dedication to the cause of the rhino, has made him a sort of "rhino whisperer" as he relates the realities of the rhino poaching scourge in a very authentic and genuinely emotional way. He has also unwittingly assumed the role of "rhino ambassador" who has committed personal time and resources to the overall rhino campaign. This will never be taken for granted. Using his rare talent of writing up his experience of and exposure to the brutal so called "rhino war", he has a unique appeal to us Africans and specifically those of us in the front line of combating those who plunder our natural resources and slaughter our rhino in a barbaric way. These unique creatures of pre-historic origin which could be saved from near extinction in South Africa in the previous century are relying on us and we, in turn, rely on the genuine and demonstrated support of friends like Ray.
>
> 'I salute him with gratitude on behalf of all those who would forever get a lump in the throat when we read the valued poems.'

General Jooste's words mean a great deal to me.

My children and now my grandchildren often ask why everything I write is so sad. It is not strictly true, but as I try to explain to them, while the world is a beautiful place and we are blessed to be permitted to share in the earth's beauty and bounty, the world also has a dark side which just cannot be ignored.

I hope my poetry can make just a wee bit of difference in shining a light on and spreading the awareness of the cruelty and greed that is associated with the wildlife trade. Bearing in mind these are the self-same people who trade in drug trafficking, weapons smuggling and the curse that is the trading in human lives.

In 2019, I wrote what everyone seems to think was my best poem ever. If ever I wrote a poem from the heart, this was it. I gave it the title, 'My Son'.

As we wander through the glade
I watch my first born, searching for shade
Soon it will be night
With the full moon burning bright

No natural enemies on the plains
Certainly confident, perhaps even a little vain
So little but already has the strut
Superior to all animals no ifs, no buts

The moon is high, it could be daytime
I am blessed with my little man, approaching his prime
I feel the pain before I hear the shot
A deep burning pain in my side, burning hot

My son runs towards me, terrified
I breathe hard, running for the forest, must hide
We crash through the bushes, through the trees
More shots, so close, when will it cease

Deep in the bush we stop, searching for a thicket of thorns
All these people want is my horns
Why must they kill me to win their gory prize
I wish that mine were not such a great size

I lay down to rest, my boy by my side

We must be deathly quiet and hide
How long can I withstand this terrible pain?
I must rise, I stand, but then I fall again

We stumble a few steps, him nuzzling my neck
Sobbing, crying, am I ok, he wants to check
My world goes dark and black
Someone, anyone, please save my son from this cruel attack

I was stunned by the reaction to the poem, both far and wide. Good friend Adrian Gardiner, patron of the Wilderness Foundation, read the poem at several South African wildlife conferences with always with the same reaction, complete silence interspersed with sniffling and quiet weeping. The well-known South African husband and wife band of Lourens and Esté Rabé, with the somewhat unusual name of The Bottomless Coffee Band, attended one of these events and upon hearing the poem were moved to write a song about 'My Son', called 'Wilderness', which became a hit single in South Africa.

The words to the song are:

'My father once told me when I was young. That man and beast once roamed along. The expanse of beauty, reflecting perfection. The earth was good, and all was well

'He said, son, we are born from this wilderness.

'The sunrise was clear and the moonlight was dear as we lived in harmony, no enemies known. But then came the man that so desperately haunts me. To take what I have, naturally grown. Without his condolences, stripped me of pride as I fell to the ground, he trampled my soul.

'I thought Man, are we not born from this wilderness? We are born from this wilderness We're more than this. We are born from this wilderness … We are the voice of the wilderness

'A beast in the valley of the shadow of the trees, isolated

unimportant to the ignorant eye, but out of its treading, out of its stride grows another piece of life. Another piece of life.

'But the game of money, the feeding of the greed puts oil on the fire of the underlying need to be king to be sire so quickly ranked higher than the giver of life. Another piece of life We are born from the same wilderness ... We are the voice of the wilderness ... We are born from this wilderness.'

Very powerful indeed.

Around the same time, I had a request from Tony White's creative director, Judy Roman, of US digital transformations solutions company enChoice, asking if she and her colleague JP Palhinhas could build some video footage around the poem. Tony and I worked together at IBM in Johannesburg and we have been friends for more than fifty years. Now based in San Francisco, Tony founded enChoice, which has enjoyed significant success and growth in the highly competitive US market.

After several weeks of dedication Judy and JP produced a remarkable and chilling visual of the poem which has been widely viewed on YouTube.

Then, in early March 2021, out of the blue, I received a request from teNeues Publishing, one of the leading publishing houses in Germany, requesting my permission to use the poem 'My Son' in author Joachim Schmeisser's upcoming book *The Last of Their Kind*.

My research told me Joachim had been photographing elephants and other endangered African species at close range for years, creating exceptionally intimate portraits of species threatened with extinction. In *The Last of Their Kind*, he focuses on the beauty of creation and its fragile transience with the quote,

'These striking images are timeless works that can be interpreted on different levels: as depictions of a distant past or as iconic memories in a not too distant future in which we can only admire these majestic creatures in zoos. They are both an

281

homage and a final warning – visual revelations that sharpen our clouded view of nature in all its infinite complexity as well as recognizing what treasures we might irretrievably lose.'

Needless to say, I wrote back saying I would be honoured if my poem was included and I received a note from Joachim (Jogi) saying, 'I found your poem on the internet and it touched me deeply. Almost every time I read it now and see the picture, I have a tear in my eye. I hope that with my book I can contribute something so that we humans take better care of our environment and biodiversity and protect it. Best wishes from Germany and thank you again for your contribution.'

Whether it is great days such as when I received Jogi's note or bad days, I am always comforted and strengthened by the note I received from the legendary Sir David Attenborough, 'Your plan to create breeding herds of rhino in Australia sounds very exciting and I am flattered that you should invite me to support them. I most certainly welcome anything that safeguards the future of African rhinos which are now so desperately endangered … I most certainly wish you every success.'

CHAPTER 29

RHINOS AND RUGBY

My first interaction with Mervyn Key was in 2013 when Margie and I were travelling through the Kruger National Park and discussing where we could locate the rhinos once they arrived in Australia. My intention was never ever for them to end up in a zoo. Margie said why not ask Jake and Lindy White about their property in Western Australia? Lindy's husband, Tony Taberer, who had passed away a few years before, had bought a large property in Western Australia.

I called the Taberer-owned Avontuur vineyard and stud farm outside Stellenbosch and was told that the family was actually in the process of selling the Western Australia property – the Yeeda Cattle Station – and suggested that I call Mervyn Key who was buying the property. I called Mervyn as soon as I returned to Australia and told him what I was planning. He was keenly interested and we agreed to meet when he was next in Sydney. Mervyn is a former South African who lives in Perth. A lawyer by profession he is a fascinating man. When we finished chatting about rhinos as is often the case when South Africans meet, the conversation turned to rugby.

In the early 1980s, Mervyn was legal counsel for one of South Africa's leading banks, the Volkskas Bank. The country was in the middle of the sporting boycott and one of the casualties was the famous Ellis Park Stadium in Johannesburg. While Ellis Park continued to host domestic rugby, it had been many years since the stadium was anywhere nearly full and, as a result, the company which owned the stadium went into liquidation owing millions to their banker, Volkskas. Enter Mervyn Key who was instructed to do whatever was necessary to fill the stadium and generate some revenue. He came up with the idea of recruiting the all-powerful New Zealand All Blacks to undertake a tour of South Africa. With the international boycott of any sporting contact with South Africa being rigidly enforced this was a very big call and Mervyn's first stop was to meet the legendary Dr Danie Craven, president of the South African Rugby Board. Craven's response was along the lines of, 'see no evil, hear no evil, speak no evil'. Go for your life. Mervyn then briefed the occasionally bombastic Louis Luyt, president of the Transvaal Rugby Union, who enthusiastically supported the plan. He sent Mervyn with his cheque book on his way to start recruiting the New Zealand players.

Mervyn reached out first to the late Andy Haden who was at the time one of the senior All Blacks, who agreed to be the 'point man' for the recruitment. During this period rugby was a totally amateur sport and it would be ten years before the game turned professional. Many of the All Blacks had full-time jobs and several were men of the land who worked hard to be able to play rugby in their 'spare time'. So, when Mervyn came knocking the players were receptive.

Volkskas had authorised Mervyn to offer each player $US200,000. This equates to almost $US700,000 or approximately $NZ1.1 million in today's money. The offer was life-changing;

these players were not earning a cent representing the best rugby team in the world. Mervyn spent three months in New Zealand securing the signatures of all but two of the All Blacks team. An often-asked trivia question is, 'Who were the only two All Blacks who refused to sign up for the Cavaliers tour?' The answer, Sir John Kirwan and David Kirk MBE.

Everything was going according to Mervyn's plan. Astonishingly, there were no media leaks until six of the most senior and capped All Blacks were selected in a Barbarians team to compete in the Centenary match in London just weeks before the South African tour. Mervyn was acutely aware that as soon as the news broke, all hell would break loose and enormous pressure would be placed on the six who included Andy Haden, Murray Mexted and captain Andy Dalton to return to New Zealand. A genius plan was then hatched by Mervyn's wife, Michelle. While they awaited the arrival of the players, the wives and families of the six who were in New Zealand were invited to spend two weeks in South Africa at the spectacular private game reserve Tanda Tula in the Timbavati, located in the Greater Kruger National Park. As expected, the London All Blacks were encouraged, cajoled and finally threatened to return to New Zealand but they were able to say they couldn't because their families were in South Africa.

And so it was on 23 April 1986, the New Zealand Cavaliers played their first of twelve matches in South Africa. They won eight but lost the series against the Springboks by three to one. From a spectator point of view, it was an unrivalled success with the Cavaliers playing in front of packed stadiums. The Volkskas Bank was delighted. Mervyn, a quiet and humble man, proudly attended all the matches. As an extra, he also persuaded Volkskas to share the gate takings from the final test with the touring side, a gesture deeply appreciated by the Cavaliers who faced an uncertain rugby future when they returned to New Zealand.

Legendary All Black Murray Mexted is a good friend and I asked him about his recollections of the tour. He expressed mixed emotions saying they were treated like royalty in South Africa and not surprisingly wherever they went everyone wanted to talk rugby. Exactly as it is in New Zealand. The rugby was hard just as they had expected but always at the back of their minds was the question of what would happen when they returned to New Zealand. They were right to worry since all players were suspended for two matches and some, like Mex, never played for the All Blacks again.

I recently had an interesting conversation with David Kirk MBE, captain of the winning All Blacks in the 1987 Rugby World Cup, and asked him about his recollections of the Cavaliers tour. As mentioned above, David was one of only two current All Blacks who did not participate in the tour. I asked him the reasons why he hadn't toured. He was firm in his belief that there were two moral issues at stake. The first was the breaking of the ban on sporting contacts with South Africa which in his correct view was working, and the second was his absolute reluctance to accept money to play the game of rugby in what was strictly an amateur era. Interestingly, he mentioned that, in his recollection, none of the members of the thirty-strong Cavaliers team has ever acknowledged that they were paid to play.

Given the long history of competition between the All Blacks and the Springboks, the two best sides in the world, he was pretty certain that the members of the Cavaliers team were under the mistaken impression that the New Zealand public would support them. They completely misread the situation and the New Zealand government-owned television station refused to televise any of the matches from South Africa. As a result, it was very difficult to engender any form of support for the team in the absence of details of the matches.

David certainly agreed that there were concerns among

the touring party about how they would be treated when they returned to New Zealand shores. A number of the players were approaching the end of their careers and they were not selected to play for the All Blacks thereafter. There was one exception, Andy Dalton, who captained the Cavaliers side. This was seen by many as an attempt for Dalton to be the peacemaker between those who toured and those who did not since there was definitely ill feeling and suspicion between the two groups. Dalton was subsequently injured and David Kirk was appointed captain for the World Cup campaign. The rest, as they say, is history. David's All Blacks won the inaugural Rugby World Cup in 1987.

David has absolutely no regrets about rejecting the offer to join the Cavaliers in South Africa and today he runs a highly successful growth management fund in Sydney.

CHAPTER 30

THE GAME THEY PLAY IN HEAVEN

In 1991, the second Rugby World Cup was held in the United Kingdom and France. With South Africa still banned from international competition, I had become a keen Wallabies fan. I was working at IBM at the time with Andrew Poidevin, brother of the legendary Wallaby, Simon Poidevin. One day while we were chatting, I suggested a fax blitz to support the Wallabies. I wrote to the then president of the Australian Rugby Union, Joe French, who loved the idea. Soon enough, with the cooperation of the media, the Wallabies were flooded with faxes from Australia in support of their quest for what is undoubtedly the holy grail of rugby. Simon Poidevin was kind enough to write me a lovely letter saying how much the gesture had been appreciated. The faxes were apparently posted all over the Wallabies' changeroom reminding them exactly who they represented. The Wallabies won the World Cup.

Eight years later, the fourth World Cup took place again in

the United Kingdom. New Zealand had won in 1987, Australia in 1991, South Africa in 1995 and by 1999 the World Cup had become a major event on the global sporting calendar. It was an interesting time in that rugby had only recently become professional and the northern hemisphere nations felt it was their time. I wrote this poem a few months before tournament.

'The Wallabies – 1999'

Three World Cups, three different winners
Who will it be this time? The only subject at dinners
In '87 it was David Kirk and the All Blacks
In '91 Australia, Farr-Jones, the forwards, the backs
In '95 South Africa reached the levels stellar
With a little help from Nelson Mandela

So here we are in '99, this time in Wales
Only three teams can win it, so say the fairy tales
Must be Wallabies, Springboks or the All Blacks
Do not be deceived, there's always the Mac's
Or the Poms, or even the French
Or Wales, with Jones-Hughes warming the bench

Samoa looks hot with all their All Blacks
What a game, if they met – not a step taken back
It won't be Italy, they've gone back to Rome
And most of the Tongans are already back home

As the rugby world is about to learn
There is only one team, even without Phil Kearns
From Matt Burke at the back with his searching raids
To the front row of Paul, Harry and Blades

If it's height you want, start with John Eales
Throw in Giffin, Cockbain and even Wilson on his heels
If it's speed you want, give me Tim Horan
Over the 100 he'll come home stormin'
The skills of Larkham, Gregan's tackling style
Tell me Jeff Wilson isn't still tasting the bile

In the centres with Herbert, they don't come tougher
And Burkie's kicking – he'll make them suffer
They can talk about Locket but there's only one Tune
He'll mark Lomu – bring it on soon!

That leaves big Joe Roff – he's due for a big one
And if not him, Little would kill for a run
We've got the best coach, our own Rod McQueen
He's honed the team, so strong so hungry, so mean

So, can the Wallabies do it you ask?
Only they know how big is the task
All Blacks are favourites, but remember the Stadium
Go back to July when the Wallabies flayed 'em

GO YOU WALLABIES!

Recently we invited John Eales AM, the captain of that team, to be guest speaker at the Pennant Hills Golf Club Sportsmen's Dinner. I gave him a copy of the poem and his response was, 'I just love your poem, it brings back so many good memories'. Unbeknown to me John also enjoys writing poetry and he shared one about his dad which was deeply moving.

Since I was born in South Africa, Margie in Australia, Paul in France and Kevin and Hayley in South Africa, I have often been conflicted in terms of my rugby loyalties. Especially since Paul and Kevin represented Australia at rugby at a junior level; Kevin for the Australian Schoolboys and Paul for the Junior Wallabies side. Over time I quietly (or not so quietly according to Margie) 'reverted' to being a Springbok supporter.

I have often wondered why it is that New Zealanders who have lived in Australia for decades are never asked if they support the Wallabies. And yet it is almost the first question a rugby person will ask a South African irrespective how long that person has lived in Australia. Having said that, South African expatriates in Australia are often split in terms of which country they support. More often than not this will depend on the circumstances in which they left South Africa. As an example, one of our friends was a senior executive in the South African human rights organisation, the Black Sash movement, and she does not have good memories of the country and now enthusiastically supports the Wallabies. Either way the passion for rugby persists.

After school, our son Paul enrolled at the University of Sydney and took the fairly natural decision to play rugby for the university. A few years later Kevin did the same. Established in 1863, the Sydney University Rugby Club (SUFC) is the oldest rugby club in Australia and the fifth oldest in the world. It is a wonderful institution with a deep and proud history of producing Wallabies and representative players for other countries.

I became involved in the club in 1998 and to this day Margie and I have retained strong ties. I was general manager for several years on a part-time basis and I have been a fundraiser and an enthusiastic supporter. During my tenure, I applied for the role of CEO of SANZAR, the controlling body of the three-way tournament featuring Australia, New Zealand and South Africa. I didn't get the job but one of my referees, Steve Surridge, former All Black and SUFC coach, commented, 'I wouldn't be too concerned, Ray, you've got the best rugby job in the world'.

Steve was quite right. My time with SUFC spanned the golden

years with the club winning multiple trophies and producing what seemed to be an endless line of Wallabies including Phil Waugh, the late Dan Vickerman, Nick Phipps, Berrick Barnes, David Lyons and even Israel Folau. It was a fun job being paid for being involved in a sport I love and with club president David Mortimer AO encouraging innovation. The club was perennially accused of not developing our own juniors but rather poaching the talented players from other clubs. So Andrew Wennerbom and I worked hard to establish our own junior club which continues to thrive. Current Wallabies Jake Gordon and Tola Latu have graduated from the ranks of the SUFC junior program. Another innovation was the weekly presentation of jerseys to first and other grade players before the match. Former prime minister Tony Abbott won a premiership with a SUFC side and is a highly popular presenter of jerseys to teams competing in a grand final.

I was not the only one at the University of Sydney who took the duty of care of our players seriously, but sometimes it was difficult as all Sydney clubs struggled to make ends meet financially. One of the casualties of the Australian Rugby and New South Wales Rugby hierarchies' decision to cut the annual grants to clubs was medical care at club games and, as a result, a number of clubs then dramatically limited the medical care provided at matches. At the university, we took a completely different view. I stood alone and introduced an enhanced level of care. I reached out to Professor Michael Tonkin, a former SUFC player and one of Australia's leading hand surgeons, and together we built the SUFC Specialist Medical Panel. The panel comprised specialists from head to toe – neurologists, orthopaedic surgeons, radiologists, the lot. Most but not all had trained at the university and had played rugby for the club. Michael invited/ encouraged these men and women to see the players as a priority if they were injured in a match. They would prepare the way for the player at the hospital and, within reason, see them or arrange for them to be seen by the appropriate specialist doctor. It was an extraordinary group of medicos under Michael's direction and he never, ever let us down, even when he took my call while he was on the bus in New Zealand heading to Carisbrook to watch a Bledisloe Cup test match! The parents of players were unanimous in their praise for the initiative and everyone benefitted. In my eyes, these doctors were unsung heroes.

In days gone by, the Australian Broadcasting Corporation (ABC) would televise matches from the Sydney First Grade competition known as the Shute Shield. Jim Maxwell and Brett Papworth would call the game from a rickety tower on the edge of the university field which visibly shook in a strong wind. Although Jim is internationally known as 'the voice of cricket', he loves his rugby and Pappy represented the Wallabies on fifteen occasions. One particularly cold and blustery winter afternoon I decided to warm them up and walked across the pitch with a good bottle of red and two glasses. They loved it and this became something of a tradition with other clubs joining in the fun. As Jim wrote in his excellent autobiography, *The Sound of Summer*, 'The pleasure of calling club rugby was sometimes improved by refreshments. Ray Dearlove from Sydney University produced a fine bottle of red at University Oval and the habit kicked in with other clubs.'

The role of general manager of a rugby club with a high-performing aspirational group of testosterone-fuelled young men was not without its challenges. Some, had they not been so serious, were quite amusing. There were a few sets of brothers who played for the club at the same time and occasionally twins, and of those very occasionally, identical twins. Let's call them Jed and Bono. Both were terrific rugby players and they were difficult to tell apart. At one memorable Finals Lunch the global airline Etihad was one of the main club sponsors. As part of their marketing promotion, they suggested placing a model Etihad airplane in the foyer of the Westin Hotel. This was no Dinky toy model. The wingspan was easily one metre on each side and it was in a prominent position at the lunch. As had become customary, many of the attendees repaired to the bar upstairs afterwards to continue the celebrations and reminiscing. As usual I left pretty much as soon as the lunch was over and was having a quiet beer at home with Margie when the phone rang. It was the Etihad marketing manager informing me they could not find their highly prized model airplane. I went into a slight panic and promised I would call him back. I called the Westin only to learn the security employee who managed the closed-circuit television system had left for the day. Early the next day I drove to the Westin more than a little apprehensively. Through CEO Cramer Ball, Etihad were an excellent and generous sponsor. In fact, they were more of a partner than a sponsor. Losing them would have left a very large hole in our budget. I arrived at the hotel and went through the recordings of the previous afternoon's events with the security manager.

As you would expect, the Westin had excellent CCTV coverage and we soon picked up someone carrying the model airplane to the elevator to the ground floor. Alas, the airplane would not fit in the lift so he and his mates carried it up the escalator and headed for the exit. One then turned around and seemed to gesture towards the bar. Without being able to read his lips it was obvious he thought a cleansing ale might go down quite well and believe it or not he then casually checked the model airplane in with the concierge while he and his mates headed for the pub.

Having viewed the footage, I could clearly identify who it was. It was either Jed or Bono. Both had been at the lunch, but which one of the identical twins should I phone first? I called a sleepy Jed who denied knowing anything about the missing aircraft and suggested I phone Bono. Not surprisingly, Bono denied any knowledge of this saga. 'It must have been Jed.' By this time my patience was wearing thin and with a few choice expletives I told him to phone his brother and let me know where the hell the missing airplane was.

Half an hour later I had a sheepish call from one of the twins who said the good news was he had the airplane. The bad news was it was missing a wing. 'I am not quite sure where the wing is.' We had a fairly pointed and robust conversation and I told him to take what was left of the airplane and return it to the Westin. I then had the uncomfortable task of phoning the Etihad marketing manager but fortunately for the twins and the club, I had a very good relationship with him and he saw the humorous side despite the damage running to thousands of dollars. It was never mentioned again. The twins avoided me for several weeks. Several other incidents fall into the category of 'what happens on tour stays on tour'.

*

The year 2003 was special for Australian rugby, having been selected to host the fifth Rugby World Cup. With some foresight and some luck, I had booked the Westin Hotel in Sydney for a function the day before the final.

At the lunch, we put on a celebration of rugby that was truly one for the ages. One thousand rugby fans packed into the Westin ballroom to enjoy John Williamson singing the national anthem while actor Rhys Muldoon, alias the bloodthirsty Hottie van der Straaten, painted a satirically colourful picture of the inside of a Springbok rugby training camp. Former Irish and Lions legend Sir Anthony O'Reilly regaled the crowd with any number of rollicking yarns in his soft Irish brogue. For years I had tried to secure Tony as a speaker and we had many conversations. He was so natural in our discussions and on one occasion he said that he had recently been in Paris and had met with 'Nelson' and asked if I knew Mr Mandela at all. Different spheres. Once he got to

Sydney, he called me a number of times about his speech – he didn't want to offend anybody. Very flattering for a simple Saffa. Tony now lives out his retirement in a chateau in Bonneville in France.

Back to the lunch. There was also a nod to the multiple nationalities at the event. In something of a coup, I arranged for the singers from Ireland, Scotland, France, Wales and New Zealand who had been engaged by the RWC organising committee to sing the national anthems before the matches, to perform at our lunch. They were spine-tingling moments.

During the tournament the United States Eagles team was drawn to play against Japan's Cherry Blossoms in Gosford on the New South Wales Central Coast. One enterprising young man had designed a T-shirt which read:

1941 – PEARL HARBOR
1945 – HIROSHIMA
2003 – GOSFORD – THE DECIDER

Classic Aussie humour. He managed to sell his entire stock before the authorities moved him on.

Since 1899, the University of Sydney has produced 127 Wallabies – almost 15 per cent of the total number of men who have represented Australia at rugby union, an extraordinary record. In 2019, I floated a proposal that the club should recognise these men and hence the Sydney University Football Club Legends Lunch was born. Skipping 2019 when COVID-19 prevented the lunch being held, there have now been three where the oldest living SUFC Wallabies were honoured. To date we have recognised twenty-two of these giants of the game since 1946 and each one displayed the humility and modesty of men who played the game for the love of it, certainly not for money; men like Dr Dick Tooth, Dr John Solomon, the Boyce twins, Jim and Dr Stewart, Dr Geoff Chapman, Rupert Rosenblum and the incomparable Jim Roxburgh. The club is blessed to have Andrew Coorey as a facilitator of the panels who treats each of these men with utmost respect and empathy and gently prises the highlights and lowlights of the careers on and off the playing fields. There are always misty eyes during and after the lunch. These men, their stories and their contributions will not be forgotten at the University of Sydney.

All but one of the major rugby countries has a rugby museum. In New Zealand there are two, in England at Twickenham, in Wales in Cardiff, in South Africa in Cape Town and in Limerick in Ireland. However in Australia there is no such museum. With the men's and women's Rugby World Cups due to take place in Australia in the next decade, it seemed to me to be a golden opportunity for the University of Sydney to take the lead in establishing such a museum on the campus.

Arguably, the Sydney University Rugby Club has the most complete and comprehensive records and memorabilia of rugby in Australia. With the strong support of SUFC historian, Dr Tom Hickie, I put forward a detailed proposal to the SUFC Foundation board and the concept has rapidly grown legs.

I suggested the opportunity existed to cherry-pick the state-of-the-art contents from the existing rugby museums around the world and build a modern, futuristic facility that will house all of the University of Sydney's and Australian rugby's memorabilia in one place. All of these could be captured in a digital fashion so that through the use of innovation and technology it will provide a full sensory, interactive, and immersive experience.

I do believe that it will be built and then named for some bigwig. Success has many fathers; failure is an orphan.

One of the SUFC's stalwarts and his wife were invited by the late David Clarke to attend the launch of a new wine named Cockfighter's Ghost at his Poole's Rock winery in the Hunter

Valley. It was a special occasion enjoyed by all and on the way home, the stalwart's wife was waxing lyrical about the superb food, the delightful people and that new wine Cocksucker's Ghost was 'simply the best'. For just a moment, there was a stunned silence. The car then rocked with laughter. Fortunately, the correct name stuck.

CHAPTER 31

COVID-19

In 1953 at the age of six I contracted scarlet fever and was placed in an isolation ward in Pietersburg Hospital. Scarlet fever is a disease resulting from a streptococcus infection. The signs and symptoms include a sore throat, fever, headaches, swollen lymph nodes and a characteristic rash. It most commonly affects children between five and fifteen years of age.

As of 2023 there is no vaccine for scarlet fever which is very contagious and can be caught by breathing in bacteria in airborne droplets from an infected person's coughs and sneezes, touching the skin of a person with a streptococcal skin infection and sharing contaminated towels, baths, clothes or bed linen. The disease is treatable with antibiotics which prevent most complications. Outcomes with scarlet fever are typically positive if treated but long-term complications include kidney disease, rheumatic heart disease and arthritis. In the early 20th century before antibiotics were available, it was a leading cause of death in children. An antitoxin was produced before antibiotics however it was never made in sufficient quantities and could not be used to treat any other disease, as antibiotics can.

Does all this sound familiar? Welcome to COVID-19. As with the terrorist attack on the World Trade Towers on 11 September 2001, the COVID-19 outbreak in January 2020 dramatically changed the world. International travel ceased and cities around the world went into lockdown. At the time of writing, almost 7 million people have died and the situation in India, Brazil and parts of Africa remains dire.

In March 2020, right at the start of the pandemic in Australia I wrote this poem never thinking that, more than two years later, the world would still be fighting this dreadful disease and stuck in lockdown.

'COVID-19 – SYDNEY 2020'

As we sit in not so splendid isolation
Our days and nights subsumed by the dreaded virus
Confined to our homes and fear across the nation
Learning some harsh lessons, it's not all about us

We yearn for the peace of the bush and all
We dream of the freedom of travel
We long for the fish eagle's call
When will this situation unravel?

Then we pause for a while and consider our circumstance
We have a home, a freezer, power and light
What of those less fortunate, do they have any chance?
Each day is about survival, now stop and consider their plight

Our healthcare is world class, our doctors and nurses the best
The speed and intensity of this virus puts all to the test
Consider the poor, the homeless and the lonely

No power, no doctors, no clean water, death may come slowly

So as this terrible disease takes its awful toll
Nobody is spared, but mostly the frail and the old
There is no other place in the world that I would rather be
But on this special island that is girt by sea

Within weeks of the announcement of the pandemic, the gravity of the COVID-19 situation hit home. My sister Yvonne had suffered from dementia for a few years and was in an aged care facility in Dorset, England. To all intents and purposes, she was physically healthy. In a cruel blow, one of the women in the home was admitted to hospital with an infection unrelated to COVID-19 and seemingly contracted the virus in that hospital. For whatever reason she was returned to the home and within days we had a call from Yvonne's daughter Hazel, herself a highly trained ICU sister, telling us Yvonne had contracted COVID-19 and the future looked grim. Forty-eight hours later, my sister was gone. Needless to say, we were devastated and we were equally stunned by the speed with which the virus took her life.

Like so many other countries at the time, England had tough restrictions on the number of people who could attend funerals. Because of border closures, it was impossible for us or for Yvonne's son Chris who lives in New Zealand to attend, so the funeral was made available to us via Zoom. It felt so impersonal as I dressed in a suit and tie to 'participate' in the service. While better than nothing this became more and more distracting and disturbing since the camera was focused on the coffin for the duration of the service and there I was watching my only sibling in a box on the other side of the world. An emotional ending to a sad death. Hopefully one day we will be able to visit Yvonne's final resting place in Dorset and properly say our farewells.

During my time with the Australian Rhino Project, I became

friends with His Excellency Adam McCarthy, the Australian High Commissioner to South Africa. He was an active supporter of what I was trying to achieve and when his tour of duty came to an end, he made a point of introducing me to his successor Gita Kamath. In early 2019, I met with Gita in Sydney before she took up her posting in Pretoria and found her to be both engaging and engaged.

In early November 2020, I sent Gita an email, 'I am blessed to live in Australia and even more since I live in Sydney where it is generally acknowledged the NSW government has implemented the gold standard in terms of managing COVID-19 and protecting the 7.5M residents of the state.' (How rapidly things change, this was before the COVID-19 Delta variant almost overwhelmed New South Wales and Australia in August 2021.)

'Without claiming to be anything other than an ordinary citizen, the systems and processes and tracking and tracing regimes of New South Wales seem to be world class and I wondered if the appropriate executive South African authorities had been offered or could be offered access to these systems and processes? My understanding is that New South Wales has an army of more than 1000 people dedicated to tracking and tracing and it is obviously working through applications such as the QR scanning system.

'We are all members of the global village and in my humble view, we have a responsibility to look after each other and being South African-born, I have a keen interest in helping those who are less fortunate in the country of my birth. Gita, is there any way that the New South Wales experience and expertise could be shared with the appropriate people fighting the pandemic in South Africa? It may be that all this is already in place and if so, well done to all involved. I stand ready to help in any small way that I can.'

I copied in Wendy Black, chief of staff to the then Australian Health Minister Greg Hunt, who had provided great support to me with the Rhino Project when he was Minister for the Environment.

This may seem presumptuous and possibly even arrogant, but I take the view we are put on this planet to help each other and in this case, Australia had so much to offer. What was vital was that the South Africans didn't see this offer as patronising. They (we) can be a sensitive lot.

Gita's response was quick saying,

'South Africa's private health system is world class. Compared to other African countries and many developing countries outside the continent, it also has a relatively sophisticated public health system and processes for dealing with communicable diseases. This has been built up over many years as a result of its experience in dealing with HIV and TB epidemics and strengthened this year as a result of COVID-19.

'Thank you for your continuing interest in supporting and assisting South Africa during this challenging pandemic.'

Almost simultaneously I had a note from Wendy Black, saying the Department of Health would like to help. Wendy was pretty sure she could arrange for 'someone senior' from the Department to have a chat to the South Africans. This was a real coup. The next question was where to start? South Africa's population is 58 million living in an area of 1.22 million square kilometres. I called Gita who suggested we should make the focus the city of Tshwane, formerly Pretoria, which had a similar population to Brisbane although Greater Brisbane is twice the area. A further advantage of Tshwane was that Mayor Randall Williams of the Democratic Alliance party was seen to be a mover and shaker. The next challenge was for Gita to secure a meeting with Mayor Williams to present our proposal. This was not a straightforward exercise.

The following week Wendy advised she had approached Professor Michael Kidd and he had agreed to reach out to the South Africans. I cannot describe how excited I was. Professor

303

Kidd AM is the Principal Medical Advisor and Deputy Chief Medical Officer with the Department of Health. In other words, the number two man.

I sensed Gita was as excited as I was. The following week, she confirmed she had secured a meeting with Mayor Williams. The adrenalin was pumping and I wrote a brief note thanking Professor Kidd. He responded, 'I am looking forward to the discussion. I was based in South Africa about 15 years ago, supporting the development of HIV testing and treatment programs in the northern part of the Limpopo province of South Africa. I thank you for initiating this contact.' Gold.

My next move was to alert the South African High Commissioner to Australia to this dialogue and the plan. As I said to Marthinus van Schalkwyk, 'If this initiative saves just one life, all the effort would have been worth it.' His response was to confirm the plan was now included in the regular government to government meetings. More gold.

All that was now required was to lock down a meeting with the appropriate level of authorities in South Africa. Professor Kidd could then pass on the knowledge, systems, processes and lessons learned to a country which like so many others was dealing with a vicious third wave of coronavirus. This proved to be much more difficult than any of us had anticipated. It took all of my diplomatic, no pun intended, skills to maintain the interest of the Australian health professionals as the South Africans pondered and deliberated as to their next step.

Finally, a few months later, I heard from Sonya Koppe, the Deputy High Commissioner at the Australian High Commission, 'We have finally heard back from the mayor's office in the City of Tshwane regarding the proposed virtual discussion with Professor Kidd. Regrettably, health officials in the City of Tshwane are not in a position to proceed with the virtual discussion at this time, due to their preoccupation with the current rise in COVID cases and the impending third wave. The mayor's office has asked that we regroup on planning for the virtual discussion at a later date. They have also conveyed their apologies for not being in a position to hold the discussion at the present time.'

This was crushing news. Not because of any ego trips but because I sincerely believed dialogue between the two countries would be a positive step forward in managing and controlling any further damage that COVID-19 was doing to people's lives and their mental wellbeing, let alone the economies of all countries. I received this note in early May and sat on it for a while. I then thought, what the hell, I know how governments work and often their best decision in their own minds was no decision. So, in early June through LinkedIn, I reached out to Jordan Griffiths, the chief of staff to Mayor Williams. I briefed him on the actions and activity to date. I was completely open about my role about being an ordinary citizen without any standing or power but asked again if we could engage with the responsible Tshwane executives. To this day I don't know if Jordan was aware of the previous discussions between Randall and Gita Kamath but he responded almost immediately, 'Thank you for reaching out. I have copied in my colleagues Koena (Head of Health) and Member of the Mayoral Committee (MMC) Sakkie Du Plooy for Health. You are welcome to engage them directly should you wish to connect further and possibly set up an engagement between some of our health officials and the Australian teams.'

I thought this was massive progress and phoned Sakkie who was gracious and polite but only mildly interested in my proposal. I had encountered a similar reaction from the South African bureaucracy when I was building the case to export rhinos. There was this suspicion somehow that there was an ulterior motive to the plan. There wasn't.

Just like before there was no hidden agenda or sinister reason for my COVID-19 dialogue initiative. My view was why not share the best practice experiences in another country? Yes, I get it, it is infinitely easier to control a pandemic in Australia because it is an island whereas South Africa has porous borders. Also, Australia is a first-world country whereas South Africa is an amalgam of first- and third-world economies. But at the end of the day, we are talking about saving people's lives and surely that goal ought to transcend borders and ideologies.

I waited a few weeks and heard nothing from South Africa. Quite frankly, I was losing my nerve. Was I wasting everybody's time? I wrote to Sakkie saying I felt I had this gold in my hand that I could not even give away. Perhaps this struck a chord with him and also that we spoke Afrikaans on the phone, and he eventually agreed a time for a Zoom conversation with Professor Kidd who immediately cleared his diary. I was privileged to sit in on the conversation which took place in early July 2021. Sakkie did not pull any punches about the situation in South Africa but was hopeful the country was close to the peak of the third wave with new cases currently running at about 25,000 per day. Deaths were averaging 500 a day.

Years of ANC neglect and corruption had scorched the province's health systems and other essential services. The opposition Democratic Alliance (DA) was slowly rebuilding the economy and critical infrastructure in Tshwane. The ANC's legacy to the 3 million residents of Tshwane was debt of $US200 million. (I recently discovered a new word, *kakistocracy*. It's amusing to South Africans because of the first three letters, *kak* [turd]. The word is actually a few hundred years old, being traceable to at least the 17th century and meaning a government that is ruled by the least suitable, able or experienced people in a state or country.) A sad reflection on many governments and equally sadly how little has changed over four centuries.

Much of the conversation was around vaccinations and the critical need to up the pace of inoculation. Sakkie and Michael agreed the media had a strong role to play and both expressed disappointment most mainstream media were promoting negativity and seemed to be shirking their social responsibility. After the call, I did a self-critique on how it went. The men got on very well and to my delight Sakkie was completely open-minded and made no attempt to sugar-coat the crisis engulfing the country. Was there a silver bullet? Absolutely not. I sensed Sakkie didn't have many people he could confide in. Leadership can be lonely and Michael was happy to listen and comment with thoughtful and considered observations to the degree that further discussions were agreed. Sakkie and I had a brief chat after the call and he asked how on earth I had managed to get Australia's second most senior health bureaucrat to assist the City of Tshwane.

From a personal point of view, I was proud I had been able to initiate the dialogue. From small beginnings.

After that breakthrough discussion there were monthly Zoom discussions and the profile of the team members was lifted by the inclusion of additional executives in the Tshwane health system. These discussions were much more focused and included tracking and tracing systems and quarantine controls.

The number of illegal immigrants in South Africa, estimated to be up to 5 million, was of deep concern since they avoided any contact with authorities. Most are from Zimbabwe, considered by many to be a failed state.

At that time, I was in the 'Dearlove Wing' of the Sydney Adventist Hospital in Wahroonga, also known as the SAN, and I was feeling pretty fragile and vulnerable. I had just had the fifth replacement of my right shoulder and the surgical team had discovered an infection in the joint and were trying to get rid of it. In addition, Sydney was in COVID-19 lockdown and no visitors were permitted. No big deal for some but I hadn't seen my wife for two weeks or my children and grandchildren for three months.

Yet, as I participated in the Zoom call with the South Africans from ward 839, I could not help but feel this overwhelming sense of sorrow for the millions of people who had COVID-19 or would get COVID-19. Most would survive but many would die leaving loved ones saddened and stunned by this virus that seemed to come out of nowhere and attack everyone, young or old, rich or poor. As it did with my sister Yvonne.

It strengthened my resolve to do whatever I could however small, to play my part.

As the discussions with Tshwane continued, I sensed that we had reached what the consultants call an inflection point. There was lots of talk but no action or even a plan of action on the South African side. All participants were engaged but there was no evident power or authority to implement some of the radical systems and processes being applied in Australia. I expressed my concerns to Michael and he agreed so I spoke to Sakkie and since his term of contract with Tshwane was coming to an end, we agreed that we would terminate the discussions.

That was all fine but I had unfinished business. The South Africans were not gaining the benefit of Michael Kidd's experience and knowledge and it was painfully obvious to me that we were operating at too low a level with the South African authorities. After quite some research, I learned that the South African Medical Research Council (SAMRC) was charged with the responsibility of rolling out the COVID-19 vaccines. The internet is a wonderful tool and it soon led me to the chief executive, Professor Glenda Gray. To her surprise, her cell phone rang while she was watching animals in a game reserve in Namibia where she was enjoying some very welcome R and R. She listened intently to what I was offering and undertook to respond when she got back to Cape Town. True to her word, she put me in touch with Jane Simmonds who was to become the glue in this venture. We had another Zoom teleconference with much higher executive representation on the South African side and it was agreed to continue the dialogue. On 24 November disaster struck as South African scientists discovered a new COVID-19 variant named Omicron and which was exponentially more contagious than the existing Delta variant which had already claimed millions of lives around the globe.

Michael Kidd moved fast and asked me to convene another call with the South Africans and within one week of the discovery of Omicron, an emergency teleconference took place. There were Australian scientists and health executives participating including Dr Brendan Murphy, Secretary of the Department of Health, Professor Paul Kelly, Chief Medical Officer and his deputy, Professor Michael Kidd, as well as representatives of all Australian states and territories. On the South African side, one of the scientists who discovered the new variant gave an outstanding presentation and all kimonos were opened. There were over a hundred people on the call. Margie sat with me through the two-hour discussions and I was moved to tears at what we had started.

Because the dialogue was already in train and relationships had been established, there was full and open exchange of ideas. Another major plenary session took place in March, again attended by almost a hundred people involved in fighting Omicron, and Professor Sharon Lewin, director of the Doherty Institute in Australia which advises state and federal government on best practice including COVID-19 was moved to say that this dialogue with the South Africans had shaped Australia's response to Omicron. Dr Murphy chipped in saying that he was having a cup of Rooibos tea in solidarity. In a recent article written by Alice Park in *Time* magazine, she says, 'Collaboration quickly put lots of different eyes on the same urgent problem'. My family and I were very proud.

I have mentioned Professor Michael Kidd on several occasions and I cannot speak highly enough of him. He is gracious, patient but firm, gentle and, and, and. He is the antithesis of what is described or perceived as a typical public servant. Michael has an extremely deep CV and vast experience and knowledge. I was privileged to work in his shadow during the Australian and South African dialogue and hopefully we saved lives.

I suppose I am a chatty person. It keeps me sane. When I was in hospital, I was surprised to hear from one of the nurses she was not vaccinated because, 'she did not want anyone or anything messing with her DNA', and '... it's a government plot, why else would they be giving the vaccines away for free rather than charging for them'. I could not believe what I was hearing. This was an educated, articulate mother of three and the comments were not made in jest. She was deadly serious. It troubled me that as an unvaccinated person she was permitted to be in contact with people in an orthopaedic ward who were often elderly and vulnerable. I would also have thought that she was putting other staff at risk. When I was discharged, I wrote to the CEO of the hospital expressing my concern. I received an immediate response saying that, at that point, the hospital was not permitted to make vaccinations mandatory but it was his highest priority to rectify the situation.

On 24 April 2021 just days after the COVID-19 pandemic exploded in India, the award-winning Australian journalist Gideon Haigh wrote an article in the *Weekend Australian* newspaper. It questioned, 'Why the Indian Cricket Premier League (IPL) goes on amid India's COVID-19 chaos', with the sub-title, 'The IPL show goes on for Pat Cummins and the Kolkata Knight Riders', and described the chaos in India and compared it to the IPL where the players are paid staggering, some might say obscene, amounts of money to play cricket for six weeks. It read,

'In the Indian city of Nashik on Wednesday, twenty-two COVID-19 patients in a hospital ward perished when the oxygen tanker on which their ventilators depended sprung a leak. Meanwhile, at Mumbai's Wankhede Stadium, twenty-two extravagantly rewarded cricketers, including Australian fast bowler Pat Cummins, were playing in an IPL game of cricket.

Haigh went on, 'But don't worry. Our Pat is fine. So are the 200 players in the IPL, including thirteen other Aussies. They are cocooned in impermeable bio-bubbles, ferried from place to place by charter flights through special terminals, tended by minions in masks, shields and hazmat suits. But some victories are pyrrhic, and I wonder if this is one. When more than 300,000 people a day are coming down with COVID-19, how much satisfaction is obtainable from your own comfort and safety? For sure, no country does extremes of private wealth and public squalor like India. Crematoriums are operating round the clock.

'Should the IPL continue? It's arguable that the damage is done. Cancelling it would do little to stop COVID-19. There would still be a pandemic; just a pandemic without cricket. The hotels would be empty; the 700 staff involved in putting the broadcast to air would be unoccupied. But let's at least be frank about it. The show must go on mainly because for it not to would cost the Board of Control for Cricket in India, the IPL franchises and the players hundreds of millions of dollars. So now there's the question of seemliness. At what point does cricket's posture of normality become too difficult to reconcile with the general abnormality? 400,000 cases a day? Or 500,000? A quarter of a million deaths? Or half a million? This time around, cricket has done nothing, just gone on raking its millions while its fans die, having earlier contributed to the incipient crisis. The time is ripe for, at the very least, a substantial charitable gesture towards the suffering millions, and an end to the sickening pretence that all cricket need do is keep itself safe and profitable, because nothing must impinge on the annual celebration of corporate power. Cricket's credibility in India is leaking.'

It was a hard-hitting article which made me think. I sent Gideon a note, 'Congratulations on your incisive article today – it absolutely sums up the situation in sport in general and in this case with cricket, where the players are in their own often selfish bubbles – completely oblivious of the realities of life and in India's case, the desperate situation of so many of their citizens. Wouldn't it be great if the top ten IPL earners each donated $100,000 to the Indian COVID effort? You and I both know that such a donation would need to be targeted otherwise those in most need wouldn't see any of it. Maybe buying oxygen tanks – something tangible.

'If you think it is worth a try, Gideon, I'd happily start the ball rolling by writing to the BCC, alternatively Pat Cummins could lead the way and challenge the rest to join him.'

This clearly struck a chord with Gideon so I got to work. I tracked down Pat Cummins' manager, Neil Maxwell, and suggested exactly what I had written to Gideon that Pat should lead the way with a donation and challenge other IPL cricketers to the same. I should mention Pat Cummins is probably the most respected and liked cricketer in Australia. He is also the highest paid, earning approximately $3.1 million from his six-week IPL contract.

Within twenty-four hours of my call to Neil Maxwell there was a major press announcement saying Pat Cummins had donated $50,000 for the purchase of oxygen tanks to assist in saving the lives of Indians struck down by the coronavirus. Pat also challenged other IPL players and franchises to do the same which they did to the tune of more than $5 million.

I wrote to Pat and thanked him saying, 'Firstly, huge congratulations on your very generous donation in support of the Indian COVID-19 catastrophe. I thought I'd give you a little background. I read Gideon Haigh's article and I contacted Neil asking that perhaps you could make a donation to assist the effort to contain the COVID-19 virus and reduce the soaring number of deaths. Why you, you may ask? Well, in my humble opinion you represent everything that is good about the game of cricket and you are, again in my opinion, a natural leader. Where you lead, others will follow. As you may know, your generosity and thoughtfulness has been widely lauded and rightfully so.'

I finished the note by saying I was proud to have played a small part in this very worthwhile donation and hopefully many other IPL players would follow his example. I did not expect any response so I was pleasantly surprised when the following morning there was an email from Pat saying, 'Thanks for your very kind note, Ray, and for the foresight to reach out and make a difference. It's quite hard for us to grasp the situation around us and we feel in an incredibly privileged position. We have a couple of things in the works to try to widen our efforts over the next couple of weeks too. Thanks Ray, really appreciate your idea and the message.'

I'll treasure that one. (As of November 2021, Pat was appointed the captain of the Australian cricket team – an excellent and popular choice – the position is often described as the most important in the country after the prime minister.)

While I was in hospital, I wrote a note to my three adult children. I was feeling particularly fragile and vulnerable and, in hindsight, this reflects in the tone and content of the note.

'The world is entering uncharted territory with this Delta variant and the situation with lockdowns, police powers and the resulting fear and uncertainty has not been seen since 1939–1945. Obviously, I wasn't around in those days, and the closest to those times in my lifetime were periods in South Africa, 11 September 2001 and the GFC.

'At the best of times nobody likes to give or receive bad news so the measures, including a three month lockdown, announced yesterday by the NSW premier, Gladys Berejiklian, will shake the confidence of the general population even more. You are all smart people and will make your own way through the next three months but I offer you only one piece of advice and

313

that is to communicate even more over-communicate at every opportunity.

'Communicate within your family, some of the young ones will think that home-schooling, Zoom, Facetime, masks, social distancing, not seeing other members of the family and so on are the norm. Communicate with your extended families. They will be feeling the same way. Communicate with your staff – they will be scared of losing their jobs. Be honest (and generous where you can).

'Listen, really listen to what people are saying (or not saying) to you – they want assurance and reassurance. At work communicate up, down and across. Communicate with your clients on a regular and added-value basis. Nobody else will do so and people will remember you for it. Communication is the key to relationships. Apply it and lead.'

I hope it helped them through these difficult times.

In summary, this has not been an easy chapter to write since I did not want the stories that I have related to have an aura of personal trumpet-blowing or big-noting. For me, the important thread through the chapter is that we can all make a difference by seeing an opportunity and seizing it and acting as a catalyst, rather than sitting back and waiting for something to happen. This can be achieved through being creative, being persistent and being proactive.

I hope you agree.

CHAPTER 32

THE TRAGEDY OF AFRICA

'I dream of an Africa which is in peace with itself. I dream of the realization of the unity of Africa, whereby its leaders combine in their efforts to solve the problems of this continent. I dream of our vast deserts, of our forests, of all our great wildernesses. We must never forget that it is our duty to protect this environment.'

Nelson Mandela

Wise words from Madiba but who was listening in 2011 when he uttered these words of hope?

By contrast, when British Prime Minister Harold Macmillan made his 'Wind of Change' speech to the South African parliament on 3 February 1960 in Cape Town, it made a lot of people and governments stand up and pay attention. The speech clearly signalled that the British government had no intention of blocking the independence of what had previously been British colonies. Macmillan's exact words were, 'The wind of change is blowing through this continent. Whether we like it or not, this growth of national consciousness is a political fact.'

And so it was. In the 1960s, Britain and France between them granted independence to thirty-three countries, including Ghana, Senegal, Somalia, Uganda, the Congo, Somalia, Botswana, Kenya, Zambia, Tanzania and Swaziland.

When the Belgian Congo gained independence in 1960 after fifty-two years of Belgian rule, I can vividly remember the cars with their blue number plates streaming into South Africa, fleeing the violence that accompanied independence. There were many nuns who had been targeted in the violence in the convoy. My mother was an active member of the Catholic church in Messina on the Rhodesian–South African border and she and her committee arranged accommodation, food and blankets in the church hall. Even way back then the writing was on the wall for the rest of Africa. The significance of this exodus was pretty much lost on this thirteen year old, but I recall Dad saying to Mum that one day this could be us, except 'we have nowhere to go'.

Watching the flood of refugees from Ukraine trying to escape the murderous bombardment inflicted by Putin's Russia is a sad reminder that the world has learned very little and that tyranny is always lurking in the shadows.

In 2021, the nine poorest countries in the world were in Africa and every single one was previously a colony of Britain, France or Portugal. The tenth is Afghanistan. (Go figure why the major powers fight over that country.)

According to the World Bank, the population of sub-Saharan Africa in 1960 was just 227 million,. In 2020 it was 1.1 billion. An increase of 900 million in sixty years, just two generations.

According to the National Bureau of Economic Research,

'While the rest of the world's economy grew at an annual rate of close to 2 per cent from 1960 to 2002, growth performance in Africa has been dismal. From 1974 through the mid-1990s growth was negative reaching minus 1.5 per cent in 1990–1994. As a consequence, hundreds of millions of Africans have become poor – one half of the African continent's citizens lives below the poverty line. In sub-Saharan Africa per capita GDP is now less than it was in 1974, having declined over 11 per cent. In 1970, one in ten poor citizens in the world lived in Africa, by 2000, the number was closer to one in two. That trend translates into 360 million poor Africans in 2000, compared to 140 million in 1975.'

Why is it so? I am not a political commentator, but I have seen the corruption in certain African countries with my own eyes. It's rife. Greed and self-aggrandisement seem to be the order of the day. Positive leadership is extremely rare.

One of the many casualties of the COVID-19 pandemic was the South African flagship, South African Airways (SAA). The airline wasn't alone. With international borders being sealed and airplanes sitting in deserts in Arizona, Alice Springs and elsewhere, it was a disaster for the industry. As the airline world tip-toed out of the bans, I reached out to the SAA CEO Thomas Kgokolo and his chief commercial officer, Simon Newton-Smith, and offered to be their very informal eyes and ears in Australia. Both were most appreciative for the snippets I sent them. When Margie and I were recently in South Africa, we had a delightful meeting with Simon who is a renowned aviation expert and respected throughout the industry, having an extensive international airline background. He is described as a veteran in the media, a title I'm not sure he would enjoy! Simon let on that, at its peak, SAA employed 10,000 people but that number is now 600 and only six SAA aircraft are in service. (Qantas has 124.)

The tragedy of Africa has so many dimensions but none more so than the brain drain from which many countries, including Australia, have benefitted greatly. This in itself has torn families apart where offspring have left the fold to escape crime and corruption and seek opportunities and certainty elsewhere.

Another example of such a tragedy of Africa is the decimation of wildlife, which I have addressed elsewhere in this book. The conservation of rhinos in Botswana is a case in point. In 2014, I met with the then Botswana Minister for the Environment, the Honourable Tshekedi Khama, in his office in Gaborone. Tshekedi, who insists on being called TK, is one of three sons of Sir Seretse and Lady Ruth Khama. Sir Seretse was the first president of Botswana and is still revered by Botswanans. TK's brother Ian was then president of Botswana.

At that time rhinos were extinct in the wild in Botswana but the Khama government had recently taken the brave decision to reintroduce the species to the landlocked country knowing full well controlling the 4500-kilometre border with four countries was a serious challenge. It was a chilling thought that at that time, as pointed out by TK, Australia had more rhinos than Botswana. On the subject of poaching, TK showed his lighter side as he said, 'Ray, my job is not to judge the poachers … that is God's job. My job is to arrange the meeting.' Touché.

It is worth noting the Botswana Defence Force (BDF) which had the responsibility for protecting the rhinos had a 'shoot to kill' policy. To further ensure the safety of the animals, the BDF had a one-to-one ratio of soldier per rhino.

To speed up the reintroduction of rhinos into Botswana, the South Africa-based travel company &Beyond under the leadership of Les Carlisle, and Dereck and Beverley Joubert's Great Plains Conservation, had joined forces to create an organisation named Rhinos Without Borders. The goal was to move rhinos from poaching hotspots to a safer environment – exactly what my vision was for the Australian Rhino Project. Rhinos Without Borders aimed to translocate one hundred rhinos from high-risk poaching areas in South Africa to the comparative safety of Botswana with a budget of $US4.5 million. Les and

Dereck had undertaken extensive research and concluded that Chief's Island in the Okavango Delta was an ideal destination for the rhinos. Ideal indeed.

When I mentioned the Botswana initiative to Ian Player shortly before he died, he said, 'Ray, Botswana has allowed their rhinos to become extinct in the wild twice in the past, what makes this one different?'

I had a far deeper concern. Africa's politics are volatile at the best of times. Botswana has maintained a strong tradition of stable representative democracy with a consistent record of uninterrupted democratic elections and the best perceived corruption ranking in Africa. Since independence the party system had been dominated by the Khama-led Botswana Democratic Party. At the time, and pointed out in my book *The Crash of Rhinos*, I asked the question of what would happen if there was a change of government or even a change of president? President Khama is a passionate conservationist but there was no guarantee his successors would feel as strongly about endangered species such as rhino.

Sadly, this is exactly what happened in 2018. The Khama dynasty lost power and today more than eighty of those hundred relocated rhinos have been poached while the rest allegedly moved to another 'safe' haven in Botswana. My prediction has been proven correct, we can but pray that Ian Player's doesn't.

What lessons can be learned from Africa's steady decline? Here we are in 2023 with the world recovering from the effects of the COVID-19 pandemic and the apparent intentions and actions of some powerful nations to extend their spheres of influence. The callous President Putin has invaded Russia's neighbour, Ukraine, with early indications that the war could spill over to NATO members and start a third world war with the ever-present threat of the use of nuclear weapons. Hong Kong will never be the same again and the residents of Taiwan do not rest easily with the aggression of their all-powerful neighbour China.

There is a vacuum of World War II 'Churchillian' leadership in the western world. The actions taken by governments in trying to contain COVID-19 disturb many in terms of citizens regaining their freedom of living, of expression and of basic human rights. The United Nations is no longer united and seems to be increasingly ineffective, while critical global bodies such as the World Health Organization seem to have lost their way and are subject to outside influences. We need to be aware and vigilant, particularly as we head into what is looking like a pretty turbulent few years.

As Lord Acton said, 'Power corrupts, absolute power corrupts absolutely.'

CHAPTER 33

ON WRITING A BOOK

I published my first book, *The Crash of Rhinos*, in 2020. The title is a play on words, a 'crash' being the collective noun for rhinos. It also describes the carnage wrought by poachers in Africa who have slaughtered more than 10,000 rhinos – three a day – in the past decade to feed the seemingly insatiable demand for rhino horn in some Asian countries. The book tells the story of the creation and the progress of the Australian Rhino Project. One reviewer described the book as, 'An insightful, frustrating, humorous and humbling story that will make you laugh, cry and tear your hair out in exasperation'.

Celebrated educationalist John Haigh, a friend from way back and originally from Zimbabwe, now living in Sydney, is a man I greatly respect. He wrote me a long note after reading the book.

'I read it with such mixed emotions having to "live" through the agony and ecstasy with you. I shared your experiences, not only because I know you as a friend but also because I'm Southern African at heart and in my psyche. Ray, we have to face the fact that there is something different about those of our age or similar who were brought up in Zambia, Zim and South Africa. We have a tap root to Africa and for better or worse we are deeply passionate people. We are also very direct and call it as it is! This can get us into a certain amount of trouble in Australia. We are sometimes judged as arrogant because of this trait.

'I loved your book but it had a tragic dimension. Tragedy as in *Othello* who wore his "heart upon his sleeve" and his passionate nature was both his strength and downfall. As admirable as it is to be passionate it also makes one vulnerable: it can be used against us. In Aristotle's definition of tragedy, the prerequisites are that the protagonist must be noble, honourable and admired for his inspiration but he has a tragic flaw or "stamp of one defect". This latter characteristic coupled with the workings of fate, bring about a tragic fall. This is not in any way a criticism, rather the opposite. We are so used to just getting on with things for the greater good and in the name of common sense. Unnecessary bureaucracy can drive us mad and bring about our downfall.

'I've known few people with your drive to get things done. You have a rare gift of knowing how to cut to the chase, to focus on the essentials. You are also remarkable in the way you can inspire and engage the rich, the famous and the influential and the sensitivity to also relate with the humble. All this is manifest in your book and I followed your thoughts and feelings as you chronicled them. Your passion for saving the rhinos can only be described as the most noble of ambitions. You inspired so many with this passion but you were "brought down" by the ignoble. You have blazed a trail. Your groundwork has achieved so much for the future of the rhino. It will happen.

'There is a postscript to Aristotle's definition of tragedy. He states that ultimately tragedy is redemptive and that a great learning takes place. Your noble efforts will not have been in vain. Good will out. Think of all the wonderful people you have met in your endeavours. You have so many fascinating tales to relate. I salute you, my friend. I don't know where you find the energy for the fight. Your dreams are inspirational.'

Friends Dame Jane Goodall and George Gregan AM kindly wrote forewords for the book increasing my and the book's credibility. Proceeds of sale of the book are donated to the all-female, anti-poaching group, the Black Mambas. They are an extraordinary group of women who form the first line of defence and are responsible for the early detection of poaching insurgents through monitoring and surveillance. This allows for armed anti-poaching units to remain within the reserve with the rhinos. The Black Mambas' strategy includes visual policing through daily boundary patrols conducted on foot at first light and by vehicle at last light. Observation and listening posts are stationed in critical areas such as known entry and exit points for poachers, as well as popular rhino waterholes to monitor for signs of poisoning. Disruptive patrols are performed within areas of high rhino density. Roadblocks involve searching vehicles for any illegal or suspicious items and regular sweeps are conducted throughout the game reserve in search of snares; a crude and cruel method of catching game. The snares are wire or cable traps which are set by so-called 'bush meat poachers'. The intention is to catch antelope for their meat to eat or sell but these traps are non-selective and catch anything that moves, thereby causing a slow excruciating death primarily due to dehydration. Larger animals can usually break the traps but are then left with the wire cutting into the body causing infections, amputations or, in severe cases, an extremely painful death.

The Black Mambas' founder Craig Spencer also established the 'Bush Baby Program', whereby local youngsters are taught the benefits of conservation and why animals like the rhino are worth more alive than dead. The long-term goal is to create an environmentally literate community.

Our family sponsors the Bush Baby mini-bus for the young and elderly to visit Kruger, most of whom have never seen a lion, a rhino, or even a giraffe. Why protect an animal you have never seen?

I wish I could say writing the book was either a labour of love or cathartic as some suggested it would be. I had been forced to resign from the Australian Rhino Project and while many of my friends suggested that it was an opportunity to ignite the adage of revenge being a dish best served cold, as tempting as it was, I resisted doing so. After all I was the one who came up with the idea of bringing rhinos to Australia. Moreover, I had founded the Project and still passionately believe it is a very good concept. The publication of the book gave it a substantial boost both financially and in terms of general awareness of the potential threat of extinction. In the words of Frank Sinatra, 'They can't take that away from me'.

Having said that, there were dark times during the writing as I laboured through some of the setbacks, challenges and failures of that journey. Some of these were deeply personal. They hurt then and they hurt now.

In the words of Stephen McGown, who attended the same school as I did in Johannesburg, and wrote the extremely powerful, *Six Years with Al Qaeda*, 'Being able to truly feel, deeply, is an absolute blessing ... I learned that one should never shy away from emotion. To be able to be emotional makes every part of being alive that much more special.'

It's been several years now since I left the Project but the tightness in my stomach will not go away when I think about bringing rhinos to Australia, and that is often. Recently visiting Hans Kooy's property Thaba Manzi in South Africa where 'our' rhinos are being housed before being sent to New Zealand re-opened all the old wounds. While I am still angry at the way I was treated, my overwhelming emotion is one of deep sadness. I passionately believe that the concept of taking the rhinos out of the danger zone in South Africa is absolutely feasible and practical. Rhinos are still being killed, on average, at one a day and this will not change; it will only get worse.

I also believe that any project requiring significant change or decisive action needs a leader who has passion and time. You may have the passion but if you don't have the time, the project will likely fail, and likewise if you have time, but not the passion, it will also fail. I was fortunate that I had (and have) both and yet to be excluded from any information, discussion and communication about the current status and future movement of the rhinos hurts. It hurts deeply and I expect that hurt will not go away. I have not heard one word from the directors since leaving in 2016.

Once I had completed the book, I searched for a literary agent. Thanks to good friend Peter Malouf, he put me on to Selwa Anthony without whom the book would have taken much longer to be published, or not at all. Selwa is an absolute gem and dispassionately informed me the book was far too long and that the majority of published books had between 80,000 and 95,000 words. Selwa then arranged for the manuscript to be edited by Glenda Downing, who sliced it from 150,000 words to approximately 120,000. Once Glenda had finished, Selwa engaged Drew Keys, who happens to be a lawyer, to proofread the slimmed-down manuscript. Drew told me he really enjoyed it but strongly suggested that I get it 'legalled'. While I had never heard the expression, I had knew what he meant. Good friend and lawyer Andrew Wennerbom then put me on to Richard Potter, generally acknowledged as the best defamation barrister in New South Wales and, arguably, Australia. I knew this was going to cost me financially and more than one of my close friends suggested I pull the plug and cut my losses, but I was determined to proceed to publication. Jane Goodall's advice was ringing in my ears, 'Ray, this is a story that must be told'.

Richard was great to work with. He read the manuscript and then got to work with his red pen or whatever the digital equivalent is. He pulled no punches. He was firm in terms of what needed to be softened, rephrased or deleted. It was painful. There were incidents and conversations for which I had emails and people prepared to confirm these. There was one particular conversation with the board, which was not very pleasant and brought my usually strong-willed wife to tears, that I really wanted to retain. I pointed out to Richard it was true and someone very close to me had overheard the conversation. Richard's response was firm and also instructive. 'In a court of law, there are many versions of the truth.' Personally, I prefer 'the truth will set you free'. Ultimately, that particular conversation ended up on the cutting-room floor.

The actual writing of a manuscript requires discipline and obviously, time. Of course, you could engage a ghostwriter but few people can express the passion, be it joy or be it sadness, or anything between, nearly as well as the person who actually experiences it.

I can't speak for writing fiction but the method that worked for me was to start with a series of headings which may or may not become chapters. I then put bullet points under each heading and soon enough the memories come flooding back and suddenly you have the contents of a chapter or a new chapter.

One thing of which I am certain is that there is no cookie-cutter approach to writing a book. You need discipline, patience, perseverance and resilience. Once the manuscript is ready, finding a publisher is the next challenge. Successful authors are able to sign contracts with publishers and be paid an 'advance' before the manuscript is ready. This is definitely the ideal scenario, but competition is intense and first-time authors are often seen as high risk. The good news, perhaps the only good news, is that during COVID-19 book sales soared. It also became clear most readers prefer a printed book over electronic versions.

Publishers can be and are highly selective and, generally speaking, drive a hard bargain. Selwa Anthony approached several and their responses were pretty much all the same: *The Crash of Rhinos* was too niche for them to take on. However disappointing this was, I could understand their view despite the fact the world had 'rhino fever' and the rhino was the 'poster child' for endangered species. Despite these setbacks I was determined to proceed and sought advice from Selwa what my alternatives might be. I think she quietly admired my doggedness and suggested I go down the self-publishing route. She put me in touch with Franscois McHardy, former head of publishing at Booktopia, the largest book distributor in Australia.

All of this was pretty daunting for me but Franscois, who just so happened to also be South African-born, was a tower of strength and a fount of knowledge. Fortunately, he enjoyed reading the book which helped, and he guided me through the process, introducing me to other Booktopia executives such as Jonathan Seifman and Scott Whitfield. Together they made a formidable team. Franscois then introduced me to David Henley, co-founder of Brio Books. Brio is a boutique Australian trade publishing company which was recently been acquired by Booktopia. David is a creative genius and is responsible for the beautiful covers of *The Crash of Rhinos* (and *Tales of Two Countries*).

These gentlemen didn't waste any time and within months my book was published. I'm obviously biased but I love the cover, the finish, the lot.

So, the message here is to work really hard to secure a contract with a publisher as early as you can. This is not easy and if you can't it's not terminal since you can always go the self-publishing route. There are many websites which will assist and guide you through this process. Be aware it can be tedious, and it can be expensive. If you are self-publishing you should engage a reputable organisation to market and distribute your book. They will push it through other online bookshops and also on their own website. This is another reason to have as beautiful and enticing book cover as possible. People will notice your book if the cover is appealing and if they notice it, they will pick it up and probably read the back cover. We spent as much time designing the back cover of *The Crash of Rhinos* as the front and there is no question seeing the messages from Dame Jane Goodall and George Gregan helped since, in my target market, both Jane and George are household names.

One hard lesson that I learned early on is that most bookshops don't 'sell' books; they have books 'for sale' and there is a major difference. Unless you are a popular author you are unlikely to get any push from the bookshop staff. This is understandable since they don't get paid unless they sell books, but it's tough for new authors. I tried hard to build relationships with bookshops, particularly those near where ex-pat Southern Africans reside. I also spent hours signing books outside Dymocks, one of the leading bookshop chains in Castle Hill. I dressed in a pith helmet and my safari gear and that was often enough to get people's attention. In Sydney, Jonty Gill of Stanley Street Butchers and Reon Wilsenach of Springbok Delights, the two shops which sell all the good stuff – biltong, boerewors, Ma Ball's chutney and so on – kindly allowed me to set up at the entrance to their shops and through social media encouraged people to visit.

While selling the books, there were times I felt completely frustrated and helpless. On one occasion a Chinese family stopped by. The mother went into Dymocks to buy a book, leaving Grandma and two young boys, aged approximately twelve and seven, outside. The older one approached me and was quite keen to have a look at the beaded rhino that I displayed on the table. He said he knew the horns were being cut off and used by 'some people'. I asked him if he knew where and why. He mumbled 'Africa', and as I started to explain to him it was actually in China and other Asian countries, Grandma grabbed his arm and dragged him away. I gently tried to suggest to her he really should know the truth and that it was his generation that could fix the problem. She wasn't in the least bit interested. So sad. Nothing will change until the Chinese and others stop buying the horn. When the buying stops, the poaching stops.

I sold a lot of books sitting outside bookstores and Saffa shops. It was labour intensive but I like meeting and talking to people so it was not a hardship. I also wrote personal emails to more than 1200 of what Margie termed 'my closest friends', encouraging them to buy the book. David Henley assisted me in getting Amazon to sell the book, although this was not particularly lucrative. They certainly take their pound of flesh. I also engaged Blue Weaver Media in Cape Town to distribute the book in Southern Africa. CEO Mark Hackney and client executive Muneebah Osman have been a tower of strength and sales have been better than I hoped. More than anyone else I concede that *The Crash of Rhinos* is a niche book with a fairly narrow audience, so I was determined to get as many copies sold as possible. This was not driven by money since my family agreed all profits would be directed to the Black Mambas, but I wanted as many people as possible to know about the carnage being wrought by poachers in Africa.

I received a note from the SANParks communications executive, Katlego Morulane, which I will always treasure. 'We express our heartfelt appreciation for the notable contribution which you make towards conservation in our country and the world at large.'

I was flattered that Ralph Koczwara, founder and CEO at Hemmersbach, a large German conglomerate which sponsors the Rhino Force, an anti-poaching organisation dedicated to saving the rhinos from extinction with night vision, stealth boats, drones, and, if necessary, armed force, wrote to me saying, 'Your Australian rhino project was an inspiration for us when we started. We always said, why didn't we have this idea?'

I sent about forty complimentary books to 'people of

influence', including journalists, radio and TV personalities, and conservationists. I even sent a copy to Prince William who kindly acknowledged the book with a congratulatory note. As did Prince (now King) Charles.

I also arranged three targeted book launches which were by invitation only. Sydney is a big city with each area having its own population and nuances. Each launch followed a similar pattern with me showing the audience some footage of rhinos in their natural habitat and then those that had been slaughtered. It was a powerful presentation and I included clips from my TED talk. Attendees were kind and generous and bought a lot of books. I also arranged several radio interviews with supportive people like Mick Molloy who has a huge following in Australia.

I hope this chapter is of use to you as a potential author. The late British–American author Christopher Hitchens famously said, 'Everyone has a book in them.' What is not as well-known is he added, '… but in most cases that's where it should stay.' A little unkind but that should not deter you.

I much prefer this quote from Vincent van Gogh: 'If you hear a voice within you say "you cannot paint" then by all means paint and that voice will be silenced.'

CHAPTER 34

MY CRYSTAL BALL

I am often asked how I see the future of rhinos and other African endangered species.

I am on the record as predicting that at the current rate of poaching, rhinos could become extinct in the wild by the mid-2020s. This prediction was made in 2015 and the graph below is self-explanatory given that the Kruger National Park is home to more than 95 per cent of the world's wild rhinos. The situation is even more bleak for black rhinos which are on the critically endangered list.

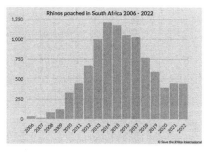

In a recent article by Peta Thorneycroft in the *Daily Maverick* newspaper, she cautioned that the rhino population in SANParks had fallen by almost 800 to 2809 in 2021. 'We're doing everything we can, but from a resource point of view we're overstretched,' said Dr Luthando Dziba, head of conservation services for SANParks. At that rate of depletion, Kruger could have no more rhinos – one of the big five animals that all African game reserves rely on – within three or four years.

'The consequences of that are chilling for the park's international reputation,' said wildlife writers Don Pinnock and Helen Kriel in a recent report on the issue. 'Kruger would no longer be a Big Five destination.'

Tip-offs for where to find rhinos and other animals often come from the 2 million or so locals who scrape together a living in the towns around Kruger which straddles two largely rural provinces, Mpumalanga and Limpopo, where astonishingly, most residents have never been inside the park.

In August 2022, it was reported that two men had entered the Khama Rhino Sanctuary in Botswana as tourists and located two rhinos, shot them and exited the sanctuary with the horns. How brazen can that be.

When discussing remaining rhino populations, it is important to specify in the wild, since up to 60 per cent of the continent's remaining rhinos are in private hands. One man, John Hume, owns almost 2000 of these. Sadly, but probably inevitably, given that Kruger's dwindling number of rhinos are that much harder to find, these private reserves are now in the poachers' direct line of fire. In the first two weeks of December 2021 alone, twenty-four carcasses were found nationwide on privately owned game reserves.

John Hume is a good friend and I admire him greatly for what he has done to create a sanctuary for rhinos. Many (most?) people range from being suspicious to vocally critical of John, questioning his motives. I describe him as a mix of conservationist and entrepreneur. He is a tireless proponent of legalising the trade in rhino horn.

Some who argue for legalisation suggest a De Beers Central Selling Organisation (CSO) type model. In the late 1800s after the massive diamond discovery in South Africa, a diamond rush was born and Cecil John Rhodes bought as many diamond mining claims as he could, including farmland owned by the De Beer family. By the turn of the century Rhodes had accumulated enough properties that his company accounted for the majority of the world's supply of rough diamonds. He called his company De Beers Consolidated Mines Limited. As De Beers maintained a hold on supply through the first quarter of the 20th century, rival financier Ernest Oppenheimer began accumulating shares of De Beers and reached a controlling stake of the company by the mid-1920s. Under Oppenheimer's control, De Beers further expanded into every facet of the diamond industry, intent on monopolising distribution. De Beers successfully convinced most of the world's suppliers to sell through their channel thus gaining control of the global supply not produced by De Beers mines. The cartel was born giving Oppenheimer the power to influence diamond supply and thus diamond prices. The De Beers CSO distribution channel had the power to sell diamonds when and where they wanted to. In order to maintain a stable but rising diamond price, De Beers had the power to stockpile inventory in a weak market. In an excessively strong price environment, they had the excess supply on hand to release to the market when needed, thereby repressing disorderly price increases.

It was a brilliant business model which served De Beers well, but could it work for rhino horn? The rhino 'industry' is so fragmented and, in truth, probably controlled by international crime syndicates. There would be immense suspicion if any private organisation started such a channel. Could the 'government' control such an organisation? Possibly, but there is no way that the South African government could do so – the corruption within flows deep and a 'Central Rhino Selling Organisation' would fail.

The South African government needs to first tackle the issue of corruption before any trade can be properly regulated, while cynics argue that the syndicates effectively run a CSO today.

Personally, my concern about John Hume's rhinos is far more critical and urgent. In June 2022 he announced plans to annually release a hundred farm-bred rhinos into the wild to help restock the population. The deal is to 'annually rewild approximately one hundred southern white rhinoceros to their natural habitat in Southern Africa'. Now hang on, while it is a really interesting development, my knowledge of John is that nothing is for nothing so I expect he would want payment. The other obvious question is, where will they go? As I understand it most private rhino breeders are getting rid of their rhinos, rather than acquiring more, because of the cost of keeping them safe. Furthermore, I met with veterinarian Dr William Fowlds in April 2022. Will is acknowledged as one of the foremost experts on rhinos in the world. In his experience third generation captive rhinos cannot be rewilded – they don't know how to survive, and don't.

Finally, releasing a hundred rhinos each year will take twenty years and that is not even taking into consideration the annual birth rate. The plan is fraught.

Either way, consider this: John Hume is not a young man and while he is/was very wealthy, one of two things will happen; either he will run out of capital or he will die. (When last Margie and I visited him and his wife, Albina, we estimated that, at current prices, he had up to $US100 million in rhino horns stored in bank vaults around Johannesburg and Pretoria.) Either way, the question remains, what will happen to those 2000 rhinos? The government won't buy them and individuals have neither the capital nor the available land to acquire them. John's children have not expressed any interest in taking over the sanctuary. I have raised the issue with the International Rhino Foundation (IRF) whose mantra is 'taking the approach of maximizing options and minimizing regrets, tackling the challenges facing rhinos using multi-faceted strategies' – but they ran a mile. I like veterinarian Dr Markus Hofmeyr's suggestion, but have zero confidence that it will come to pass, 'The quickest and best solution is to place all John's rhinos back into Kruger National Park as a public private joint venture and finally upend the corruption in Kruger.' It seems that everyone hopes that the matter will just blow away like a feather in the wind. For me it is an absolute time bomb.

In another innovation in May 2022, as reported by Elizabeth Moran, the World Bank issued a Wildlife Conservation Bond raising $US150 million for sustainable development projects with circa $US10 million in interest payments being given to rhino conservation projects in South Africa. As my old friend George Bell would say, 'I'm excited, but I'm suspicious.'

Under the terms of the rhino bond, investors will forgo an annual interest payment and will instead receive their original capital and an additional payout depending on how much the rhino population grows by over the next five years. The principal of the bond and the possible payout at maturity will be paid by the Global Environment Facility, which has received donations from more than forty countries and was formed before the Rio Earth Summit in 1992.

'The launch of the Wildlife Conservation Bond – the world's first financial instrument dedicated to protecting a species – is a watershed moment for wildlife conservation,' said Dr Andrew Terry at the Zoological Society of London (ZSL). 'ZSL has spent more than five years working with many outstanding organisations to lay the groundwork for this innovative new financing mechanism that will bring a much-needed injection of new and long-lasting capital into rhino conservation efforts in Africa and help put nature at the heart of financial decision making.'

Success will be determined by the rhino growth rate. From an environmental perspective, it is hoped that the bond will:

- Secure the current population of rhinos and encourage further population growth.

- Protect broader biodiversity and support improvements in planetary health through improved management effectiveness of the ecosystems that rhinos inhabit.
- Change conservation funding strategies, providing a model of investment for investors looking for a financial return while supporting biodiversity conservation.

In my humble opinion the concept is great but flawed. There will be many investors to whom this will appeal but I predict that it truly is a minefield in execution/implementation. Some of the issues that I see include:

- The starting numbers of black and white rhinos that are subject to this plan. For the past eight years I have been unable to get accurate numbers from anyone. Noting that both the chosen locations of Addo Elephant Park and the Great Fish River sanctuaries are state-run, I would be even more sceptical about the accuracy of the numbers. Have they been validated by anyone within the two reserves? In this instance it would be to their advantage if they low-balled the numbers to demonstrate growth and qualify for a dividend.
- Poaching remains rampant in South Africa and while the numbers may have 'stabilised' in the Kruger National Park, this is because there are fewer rhinos to find/kill and also because of improved anti-poaching methods. The poachers have now turned their attention to KZN where the slaughter continues unabated as it does in Botswana and Namibia – the so-called best practice examples of protecting rhinos. Could Addo and Fish be next? A matter of time perhaps.
- Who will monitor the grants to these reserves? The country is rife with corruption and greed, and if the states have proved one thing, they cannot protect their wildlife (and they are not really good at managing money either).

Another great idea with an uncertain future or outcome.

By contrast, as mentioned above, I sat on a panel with Ginger Mauney, international wildlife filmmaker and board member of the Save the Rhino in Namibia. She came up with an initiative that really worked. In her own words, 'A few years ago, I had lunch with the CEO of B2Gold Corp, which was founded in 2007 and has an operating gold mine in Namibia and proposed that they produce a Rhino Gold Bar, sell it at the cost price of gold plus a 15 per cent conservation premium, so the premium could be applied to conservation efforts immediately and the cost price be invested for long-term sustainable funding. I worked with Charles Loots of B2Gold in Windhoek, a great supporter of rhino conservation and lo and behold, they went for it and within ten months of the launch, all 1000 ounces had been sold. The conservation premium has kept seventeen tracking teams in the field after their funding was cut because of COVID's impact on conservation and tourism.'

I love that story.

An old adage it might be, but the truth is that when the buying stops the poaching will stop. As obvious as it may be, if there is no demand for rhino horn at any price, supply will dry up. While it is an established fact that international crime syndicates do hoard rhino horn in order to manage and manipulate pricing, this supply cannot last forever. In any event, in my opinion, this is all largely irrelevant since the demand shows no signs of abating. The only chance the rhinos have is if *all* governments involved in the sales of rhino horn agree to stop it. These include China, Vietnam, Laos and Cambodia on the demand side, and Southern Africa on the supply side. Good men such as Princes William and Harry, Sir David Attenborough and others have added their voices to the cause but sadly while each have influence, they have no power. It will take one or more of the leaders of South Africa, of Mozambique, of Laos, Vietnam, China and Cambodia who must take the lead and own the issue. Sadly, rhinos are extinct or nearly extinct in all countries north of the Zambezi River.

If you are an optimist as I am, you will have taken heart from China and Vietnam closing down wet markets – where you can obtain pretty much anything in animals and reptiles, alive or dead – during the COVID-19 pandemic. But I am also a realist; a 2017 report by the Chinese Academy of Engineering valued the wildlife-farming industry at 520 billion yuan (US$74 billion). The wet markets will reopen in China.

In June 2022, police in Vietnam arrested a man with 138.78 kilograms of rhino horn (that equates to about twenty-eight dead rhinos), 3108 kilograms of lion bones, 456.9 kilograms of ivory and 6232 kilograms of pangolin scales, with a total value of $US12.9 million. (It is worth noting that there are half as many African lions as there were just twenty years ago. Why? The answer is heartbreakingly simple: it's humankind. Whether it's habitat loss due to human population growth, poaching for pelts and bones, killing for sport, or climate change, people are the cause when it comes to the negative impacts decimating lion populations.)

A study published at the end of 2021 identified 345 rhino horn consumers in Vietnam, where the horn is used as a treatment for hangovers and fevers, and as a detoxifying agent. The researchers found that, on average, those surveyed were willing to pay more for horn from wild or semi-wild rhinos due to the belief that these have more potent medicinal properties. Notably, wealthy respondents with a high 'need' favoured wild rhino horn, while those with lower incomes and a lower 'need' preferred semi-wild horns.

Hold onto your hat.

CHAPTER 35

FUTURES

As I mentioned above, I have had a good life. I have met some wonderful people, many of whom are mentioned in this book, but there were others like Phil Liggett, the voice of cycling, and his Olympian wife, Trish, true conservationists and friends; Gillie and Marc Schattner of *Rabbitwoman* and *Dogman* fame, and the 'Muscles from Brussels', Jean-Claude van Damme, who said, 'I fully support Ray's efforts to take rhinos to Australia to keep them safe until this tsunami of poaching is brought under control.' Genuinely generous people like Gary Edstein and Ruffy Geminder. They all have one thing in common: they are good people.

I view my life as a number of interconnecting circles where each circle represents a time from childhood through adolescence to adulthood to where I now am in the twilight of my days on this planet. I also see the circles as representing the 'families or groups' that have strongly influenced me, such as my parents, my school years, my sporting associations, travelling and living in different countries and meeting different people, the volatile and turbulent world of conservation, leaning on the support of the medical fraternity, and my own family.

As I write, the COVID-19 pandemic has been declared over, however the world remains in turmoil with the risk of another world war lurking in the shadows as a result of Russia's invasion of Ukraine. Who expected such a conflict? With the fluid situations in China, North Korea and, as always, the Middle East, the future is unknown and uncertain. Children are still being home-schooled, depriving them of critical social skills. Teleconferencing has its place but is no substitute for building relationships, be they business or personal. Words and expressions hitherto unknown or rarely used are now commonplace such as COVID-19, social distancing, self-isolating, lockdown, Zoom, Pfizer and Astra Zeneca.

And yet there are green shoots. The world collaborated in developing a COVID-19 vaccine in record time; lockdowns have caused people to check on their neighbours' wellbeing and, generally speaking, families have become closer. In 2021 Sir Richard Branson flew to the edge of space in his Virgin Galactic rocket plane, which opens all sorts of opportunities for our children and grandchildren. As the American psychologist Abraham Maslow wrote almost eighty years ago, our three basic needs are physiological, safety and belonging, and love. Nothing has changed.

Personally, my priorities of my family, our health and assisting in the conservation of endangered species remain paramount.

As Sir David Attenborough so succinctly put it, 'We moved from being *a part* of nature to being *apart* from nature.' So sad but so true. Then again, in terms of what the future may hold, having been fortunate to have been on this planet for seventy-five summers, I really like Satchel Paige's comment, 'Sometimes I sits and thinks, and sometimes I just sits.'

Onward and upward. In the immortal words of Clint Eastwood, 'Don't let the old man in.'

APPENDIX 1

Special thanks to friends Peter Malouf, Selwa Anthony, David Henley, Franscois McHardy, Joan and Michael Eyles and Peter Walker. Also to Rod Morrison of Words and Pages who has been a tower of strength for me.

APPENDIX 2

A Short Anthology of Poems

'For those who have difficulty expressing themselves, reading poetry can have a similar positive effect as writing it. Reading poetry allows one to see into the soul of another person, see what is weighing on their minds and on their hearts, and can open doors to feelings that are sometimes suppressed until that door is opened. Reading can shine a light on all those dark and hidden crevices of the heart and mind once thought permanently closed off to the world.'

The Writers' Digest

'For the Rhino'

I wrote this poem in the middle of the night while flying from Perth to Johannesburg. It was the first poem that I wrote about rhinos and indicates the depth of my passion for these extraordinary and iconic animals. It is estimated that rhinos have been on the planet for approximately 10 million years and yet if current trends continue, they could become extinct in the wild within ten years. *Cry, the Beloved Country* was the title of Alan Paton's prescient novel of 1948.

See them stand
Side by side
Mum's super large horns. His just starting to grow
Both so proud

See them run
The oldest mammals on the planet
Majestic, powerful and free

See them stop
Sniffing, staring
Uncertain and nervous

Hear the shot
See her fall
Trembling, shuddering

Hear the saw. Feel the pain
Ruthless, cruel, greedy humans

Hear his cries
His mother's face a bloody mess
All alone

Mother and child. No reunion
Cry the Beloved Country

Ray Dearlove

'Dr Jane Goodall DBE'

Countless words have been written about Jane Goodall. She has won awards, received any number of accolades for her pioneering work with chimpanzees, and is considered to be the expert in her field. Jane travels the world spreading her messages of the need for action and education but also of hope for the future. I have been privileged to meet Jane on several occasions and every time I do, I am inspired by this one woman who has dedicated her life to making a real and meaningful difference to the world in which we live. The world needs more people like Jane Goodall.

Child of the depression, in London born
She lived through the blitz and Europe at war
At peace in the country with the birds, the bees and the trees
Her closest friend, the little chimp teddy named Jubilee

Love of animals led her to Africa, just twenty-three
Never backward in coming forward, she phoned Louis Leakey
His need was to research chimps in the wild
She accepted and, from above, the gods just smiled

Sixty years at Gombe and counting
Her chimp work revolutionary and lasting
Often challenged and as often proven
Chimps can be as wise, smart (and cruel) as humans

Slight in stature but strong of heart
She travels the world, year in, year out
Ever ready with a smile
Her deep concern for nature drives the extra mile

Our generation has made a complete mess
Our forests, streams and oceans in distress
Belief in youth, she founded Roots and Shoots
Bringing hope to issues so acute

In company she is often quiet
Listens carefully, assessing the conversation
Gently steers the chat in the right direction
Her steady gaze reinforcing her conviction

All goes quiet as she enters a room
The slight smile like a rose in bloom
Her calm manner always gracious
You are in the presence of greatness

Friend to kings and queens, princes and popes
Her message that education is our only hope
Put down the gun, pick up the shovel
It's the only way out of the planet's trouble

My burning passion is rhinos, three killed a day
Her wise words comfort and guide me in every way
She said, 'What will our grandchildren say or do
When the only rhinos they will see are in a zoo?'

Loved, admired and respected by all
There is only one Jane Goodall
Ready to help, never to complain
The world will never see her like again

The best kind of people are like sunshine – they are warm and brighten your soul with their light.

Ray Dearlove

'As Cowards Do'

I wrote 'As Cowards Do' after meeting Dave Powrie and hearing of his narrow escape from death. Dave is a good friend and was security warden for an internationally known large and popular private game park in South Africa. He had responsibility for protecting all animals and also people. He and his wife were asleep one night when suddenly the bedroom light went on and at the foot of the bed were five men, three of whom were armed with machetes and one with a gun. Dave and Loma were completely helpless and their dog – which slept in their room every night for protection – had been drugged. The poachers demanded that Dave hand over 'the rhino horn'. After a few minutes things got really ugly when one of the poachers grabbed Loma. Dave, in his own words, 'lost it' and exploded out of the bed. Despite the overwhelming odds he fought these five poachers out of his house. He then collapsed with sixteen knife wounds to his body as well as a punctured lung. His wife was also stabbed but fortunately their one-year-old baby in the next room slept through the whole nightmare. I'm pleased to say that Dave survived and he is back on the job. This demonstrates the lengths to which some people will go to get their hands on rhino horn. Life is cheap in Africa.

They came in the middle of the night
As cowards do
Armed to the teeth and driven by greed
The target a man, his wife and a child aged two
A hot, hot night, not a breath of air
Windows open, fast asleep
Faithful dog in his spot, on guard
Any scent of trouble, ready to leap

Suddenly, shockingly, on goes the light
What the hell they say, who can it be
Five poachers at the foot of the bed
Machetes and a gun are all they see

Where is the rhino horn, where is the horn
That is all they say, give us the sack
We have no horn, we have no horn
Why won't my dog attack?

Five to one, this is no contest
They will not go away, what to do
One jumps on his wife, intent very clear
To hell with that, it's me or it's you

The dog is drugged, no help there
His wife is stabbed, the fight is on
One on five, a man possessed
Inch by inch, this man won't quit, this man won't run

Out of the door he fights them, one by one
Then he drops
Sixteen stab wounds and a punctured lung
The pain, the shock and then it stops

Six months later, back on the job
Him and the poachers both
No arrests and the rhino slaughter continues
He does his work, he abides by his oath

'Each time a man stands up for an idea or acts to improve the lot of others or strikes out against injustice he sends forth a tiny ripple of hope and those ripples build a current which can sweep down the mightiest walls of oppression and resistance.'
Robert F Kennedy

'Is it Need or is it Greed?'

As has become more and more obvious throughout this book, my passion is rhinos. As George Orwell said in *Animal Farm*, 'All animals are equal, but some animals are more equal than others.' And as the philosopher Immanuel Kant said, 'We can judge the heart of a man by his treatment of animals.'

I wrote 'Is it Need or is it Greed?' after being told about little Sabi, the orphaned rhino.

Russel Mokoena who was on bail from a previous poaching charge was one of five men accused of poaching a baby rhino at the Care for Wild Rhino Sanctuary close to Nelspruit which was owned by Petronel Niewoudt. Mokoena was working at Care for Wild at the time of the incident.

In terms of background, Sabi's mother was poached in Sabi Sands Game Reserve. Sabi was brutally mutilated and his front legs had been chopped off by these callous men. He was gradually being rehabilitated by Petronel's team.

Apparently Mokoena boasted that little Sabi had not even tried to get away from him on the night that he shot him. The poor little creature had actually approached him having known him as someone who could be trusted. Sabi's little horns which Mokoena dug from his head were sold for $US3000 to a Chinese national.

The poem explores the different reasons why men poach animals. Certainly, there is the criminal factor and the desire for money and then doing it again for more money but there is also an element of food security. Most of the poachers enter the Kruger National Park from Mozambique which is the seventh poorest country on the planet.

Today a poacher died
Not of sickness nor disease
He was shot while yet another rhino horn he tried to seize

On bail he was. For what crime you ask?
He shot an orphan rhino. Sabi was his name
A little fellow whose front legs had been hacked
His Mum yet another helpless victim of the poaching
His courage and cheeky attitude had brought him a wee bit of fame

The poacher worked the farm where Sabi lived
Sabi knew him and ran to him – as littlies do

348

The poacher, callous and cruel, shot him dead
And dug his tiny horns from his head

For thirty pieces of silver

Tonight, another poacher will take his chances
They'll hit the rhinos at the nearby ranches
His family of seven all need food. He has no job.
A first for him, he'll join this killing mob

But first to the witchdoctor to be smeared with muthi
Nobody can see them, nobody can hear them
Now protected from all of the dangers
From lions and leopards and the guns of rangers

They walk and they run. It seems like hours
But they are fine, they have the muthi powers

Now they see it, the rhino's midden
It is a big one – see her horn
Very soon it will be sawn

Hear the shot, see her fall
His hands are shaking, he saws and saws
His hands are bloody, her face is raw

Back at home his young wife waits
Her caring man has met his fate
He did his best, but now he's gone
We need to eat, next time I'll send my son

'The General'

In 2012, South African National Parks approached Major General Johan Jooste to head a special projects group in an effort to implement mitigation measures to deal with the severe increase in rhino poaching. His brief was to put in place paramilitary strategies, structures and systems that would enable SANParks to respond to this increased threat.

It was clear from the outset that counter-poaching measures conducted within the boundaries of the national parks alone would not be sufficient, and the term 'clearing the park from the outside' was coined by the General.

At the time of his appointment Jooste said, 'I will do my best to bring acceptable results. This fight against poaching is not about an individual and success depends on the collective collaboration and commitment from the men and women tasked with the responsibility of conserving our heritage.'

In 2013 I met Major General Jooste who is, without doubt, one of the most impressive men I have ever had the pleasure of meeting. He is an extremely humble man who will always look out for his rangers and share any credit that may come his way. A true gentleman.

He'd done his duty. He'd served his country well
He'd hung up his boots and was preparing for the quiet life
The phone call came, now a different threat
Would he lead the team with people he'd never met?

The poachers come, well trained and armed
Our rhinos their targets, the stakes so high
They know the bush, they are well prepared
We are not prepared, our men are really quite scared

The clock is ticking, the time is short
Up steps the general, they must be caught
We need a leader, say the rangers
We'll take up the fight, we know the dangers

The general pauses, we need a plan
We must win this battle; I know we can
He starts afresh. He picks his team
He shares his vision, he shares his dream

The rhinos are dying, the poachers are winning
His steely eyes narrow, this is just the beginning
The country is supportive, but it will take time

This man is a leader, he will lead from the front
The rangers walk tall, we now have a plan
We have faith in the general, we know he's our man

Ray Dearlove

'For Killer'

I wrote this poem after hearing about the death of the anti-poaching hero Belgian Malinois dog named Killer. The breed originated from a small town in Belgium called Malines. Because of its energy and intelligence, the breed was enlisted in World War I.

Killer worked with the Kruger National Park's special operations team to prevent rhino poaching. In 2016, he was awarded a PDSA Gold Medal for his anti-poaching work.

Killer's lineage can be traced to the Iraq war and the Belgian police. His father had parents that served with the US in the Iraq War. His mother was bred from two Belgian police dogs and was entered into an exchange program and sent to South Africa.

Killer was put down in 2020 after a long illness.

A legend in the world of anti-poaching
Alert and aware as these cruel men were approaching
Killer wants to chase, Amos says slow
We must catch him before he finds our rhino
Quiet and obedient until Amos said 'Let's go'
Evading bullets and pangas, Killer would stun the foe

A fiercely loyal protector
Heaven help any intruder
Who tried anything in the dark
Killer would imitate the great black shark

His needs were simple, not a demanding dog
Two square meals a day
And the soft bed on which he lay
And always, always, ready for a jog

Killer has big, beautiful and trusting eyes
Which would light up when Amos, standing tall
Sounded the 5 am Kruger anti-poaching K9 call
When Killer would meet other dogs and their guides

He loved everyone in the K9 family
Other handlers could scratch him, quite happily
But Killer knew only too well
It was Amos to run to when he heard the dinner bell

Today we took him to the vet
One of the toughest days of our lives
Such a big brave dog and yet
The heart of a warrior and one that always forgives
But we all were comforted because we knew
That this very tough but gentle dog's spirit flew

At peace and at last pain-free
New forests, oceans and friends to see
Whereas you could hardly see Killer in the dark of night
There is now a new star in the galaxy, burning bright

'The Game Ranger'

I have always had enormous respect for game rangers. My cousin Trevor Dearlove started the first walking trails in the Kruger National Park in 1978.

As a youngster, I read all the books that I could lay my hands on about James Stevenson-Hamilton, Harry Wolhuter, Sir Percy Fitzpatrick and in later years Bruce Bryden and others. I fulfilled some of my boyhood dreams when many years later, I took a cricket team from my firm IBM and played against the Kruger National Park team, appropriately named the Game Rangers at the beautiful field within the staff village in Skukuza.

In 2014, I was invited by Major General Jooste, head of anti-poaching for SANParks, to attend the International Rangers Day as a guest of honour. I was unable to attend but this poem and 'For the Rhino' featured in the official program of the day and both were read out at the celebration of all South African game rangers at the Paul Kruger Gate.

I wrote this poem for the game rangers – all good, brave men.

I was born to be a game ranger
When I was young, Kruger was my second home
I loved animals and looked forward to seeing danger
The men in the green uniforms were my heroes
I read all about Wolhuter, Stevenson-Hamilton and all those ou's
I had a dog named Jock

I joined the team. I earned my stripes
I cared for animals, I cared for people, they cared for me
I loved my job

With a volley of shots, my world was changed
The innocent rhino in their sights
Why oh why, my children ask me?
How can I explain man's greed and cruelty?

Now I am a ranger with a gun
I am a target whilst the rhinos run
Is this what god intended, surely not
I mourn, I cry, while my rhinos rot

There must be something the world can do
We rangers were trained to nurture and protect
Now we are trained to survive
And try to keep all our rhinos alive

I curse the poachers; I curse those who buy the horn
I pray to God for a bright new dawn
I rejoice for every rhino born

'Am I a poacher?'

This whole poaching issue is so complex. The ranking of rhino poachers can be illustrated by a five-level pyramid. Number one is the hunter. Number two is the handler who provides the hunter with resources such as the weapon and ammunition. Number one hunts the rhino and saws off its horns and hands the horn to number two in exchange for payment.

From there the horns make their way to number three who would typically live in the town or the city. Number four then receives the horns and ensures that they are delivered to number five – the end buyer in countries such as Vietnam, Laos and China.

At level one there will be the men who carry the food, mobile phones or may have some knowledge of the area to be targeted. One of these is probably also the fellow who needs to feed his family who is literally picked up on a street corner on the day and made a hard-to-refuse offer to join the hunt.

Please note that a 'Sangoma' is a witchdoctor and 'Muthi' is the magical potion brewed by the Sangoma. Among all the supposed benefits, here is unshakable belief that if you are smeared by the appropriate Muthi, you become invisible.

My father is long gone, my mother is sick
One brother has Aids, another has left town
I have four little kids, but what can they eat
They cry from the hunger, Dad, please get us some meat

Now there's a stranger in town, flashy car and all
Throwing money around saying 'please call me Saul'
Buys food for the people and free drinks at the hall

Saul seems to like me and asks – how fast can you run?
I'm looking for helpers who are looking for money
More than ten grand, I'm not being funny

I speak to my wife; she says I should do it
I say to Saul, where are we going?
To shoot just one rhino and bring back his horn
If you are fast, we'll be back before dawn

But first to the Sangoma, to smear us with Muthi

Nobody can see us, nobody can hear us
We now have protection from all of the dangers
From lions, from leopards and the guns of the rangers

Tonight, is the night, be ready at sunset
We are lucky, there is a full moon
You carry the saw and also the food
Be not afraid, we will return very soon

We walk and we run. It seems like for hours
But we are ok, for we have the powers

Saul says stop, all of a sudden
Here I see it, the rhino's midden
It is a big one – eish, see his horn
Very soon it will be sawn

Hear the shot, see him fall
Be quick, cut it off, get it all
My hands are shaking, I saw and I saw
My hands are bloody, his face is raw

We are now back in town, safe and sound
Where's my money, I ask of Saul
He laughs at me and points his gun
No money for a fool, let's see you run

Ray Dearlove

'Do They Really Care?'

This poem is aimed fairly and squarely at the 'authorities'. I am convinced that the poaching menace will never go away unless governments stand up as one and say, 'Enough is enough, no more'.

This poem is also a cry for help. Good men such as Princes William and Harry, Sir David Attenborough and others have added their voices to the cause but where are the leaders of South Africa, of Mozambique, of Laos, Vietnam, China, Thailand and North Korea who must take the lead on firstly stopping the demand and then the poaching. Agencies such as the CIA, the FBI and Interpol are all involved. Why can't it be stopped? Unless all of these governments step up our wildlife will be gone in the next ten to twenty years. Then who will they blame?

I am an African, as was my dad, as was his father's father too
Our natural heritage is slowly dying, what can we do?

There are so many tragedies in this continent's long history
Drought, floods, coups, wars, genocide, the list goes on and on
Some disasters natural, but more, many more show man's hand
How much more pain can the occupants of this great land stand?

Not satisfied with making war on each other every day
Some people now turn their attention to yet another prey
All creatures great and small are God's gift
But when all is said and done how few will be left?

At the root of all of this slaughter is pure insatiable greed
Men risk their lives to fulfil this so-called need
Elephants, pangolins, lions and rhinos, none are spared
Misguided, ill-informed, pagan beliefs drive others to despair

Poaching is big business, the stakes are high
But the world has faced threats before, equally dire
So where is the will to stop it at this critical time?
There must be a leader who will fight fire with fire

One rhino is poached every three hours, that is true
While Governments chatter, saying... we know what to do
Our heritage is dying, under mortal threat
Much talk, no action, is all that we get

Where is our leader, our lighthouse of hope?
Think of your children and grandchildren, how will they cope?
Imagine a world, empty of wildlife
Where greed and corruption still are so rife

Now, more than ever, we need leaders with vision
Leave a true legacy, make that your mission
Stop this carnage, stop this slaughter
If only for the sake of your sons and your daughters
You have the resources, now please show the courage

'The only thing necessary for the triumph of evil is for good men to do nothing.'
Edmund Burke

Ray Dearlove

'Poachers' Moon'

Full moon in Africa seems to shine so much more brightly than anywhere else. Perhaps this is because, by and large, the continent is relatively sparsely populated and many residents do not have electricity. This is a gift to poachers, since they can see everything so much more clearly than on a dark night. So, in recent years a full moon has seen poaching incidents increase dramatically. In South Africa, full moon has become known as 'poachers' moon' when there are more than forty poaching incursions per day and night from Mozambique into the Kruger National Park.

I wrote this poem to try to describe how a once beautiful sight has become a time of danger. A time of danger for both man and animals. The words of John Fogarty's song 'Bad Moon Rising' for his band Creedence Clearwater Revival could easily have been written for the rhinos. Here is the first verse:

'I see the bad moon arising
I see trouble on the way
I see earthquakes and lightnin'
I see those bad times today
Don't go around tonight
Well it's bound to take your life
There's a bad moon on the rise'

My poem attempts to give the sense that the reader is on the killing team.

Blue moon, you saw me standing alone
Without a dream in my heart
Without a love of my own

In '69 man walked on the moon
Today the poachers kill by that self-same moon

They cross our borders, guns in hand
Darkness falls, they are ready
Trained to live off nature's land
Powered by Muthi, their hands are steady

This is no hunting trip, the target is known

The well-paid informer has been on the phone
North of Satara on a path well worn
You'll find the black rhino with the enormous horn

Full moon a real bonus, they can see so well
Not like the dark which can be such hell
Their progress is swift, the killing is done
This is so easy, this is such fun
Three hours to the border
No need to run

With the stakes so high, they need some stealth
Altho' with horn in hand, they can already taste the wealth

There was a time I loved full moon
Now, for our rhinos, it just spells doom

'The Big Five'

The 'Big Five' are synonymous with Africa. The lion, the elephant, the leopard, the buffalo and the rhino are so called because the early big game hunters considered them the most difficult to hunt on foot. Hunting in those days was far 'fairer' than it is today. Then the hunter actually had to work for his trophy.

From across the globe, they come for the Big Five
This is our heritage, this is our Africa

The magnificent lion – fearless and majestic – king of the jungle
The giant elephant – intelligent, intimidating but oh so caring
The powerful buffalo – he looks so sleepy, but feared by all
The stealthy leopard – now you see it, now you don't

So that makes four, but isn't there one more?

Yes, indeed there was
Today we lost our last rhino – we had named her 'hope'
She was shot by poachers
We have her body, they have her horn
Welcome to the Big Four

'I am a Vet'

In the four years of my journey with the Australian Rhino Project, I met many wonderful people. What they all have in common is the passion that burns for conservation.

At the sharp end of wildlife crime stands the veterinarian who often makes the difference between life and death. Unlike in human medicine veterinarians must rely primarily on clinical signs as animals are obviously unable to vocalise symptoms as a human would.

This poem draws on real-life experience with real-life veterinarians whom I know very well and who work with injured poached animals and also contribute towards the conviction of the perpetrators. Dr Will Fowlds travels all over the world sharing his personal testimony of the brutal reality of poaching from the coal face as well as efforts to bring back rhino from the brink of death with his pioneering veterinary care.

Dr Pete Rogers is a gruff on the outside, marshmallow on the inside kind of man. He vents his anger and frustration on the authorities who don't or won't act to stop the poaching.

Dr Markus Hofmeyr has spent much of his life in private game reserves and the famous Kruger National Park where he was head scientist and chief vet. Markus is effectively writing the book about veterinary care for rhinos.

Dave Powrie is the warden of the Sabi Sands Private Game Reserve who was attacked at his home by poachers.

This poem is a tribute to these men and also to all of the men and women who protect the world's animals. God bless you all.

Our generation was brought up on 'All creatures great and small'
James Herriott brought to life animals, large, little, short and tall
The local vet was a friend who you could always rely on
A smiling face ready to have a cuppa and all satisfied once he'd gone
A gentler time indeed

Fast forward to Africa today for one of the world's most admired professions
'Your choice students – cats and dogs or some very different lessons'
Saving a life or saving a species? That's your choice
Whatever you decide, you are the animals' voice

I am a Vet. My name is Will.
I took my oath, I love my animals, I always will
The call in the night, yet another poaching slaughter

Ray Dearlove

Will Thandi survive, will her daughter?

I am a Vet. My name is Pete.
Today, I notched my 227th rhino, quite some feat
Why so, you ask? I say – to save its life
It's the poaching, man, its cruel, it's rife

I am a Vet. My name is Markus.
The area I protect is vast, the animals rely on us
The enemy is armed, the rhinos are not and we are not
The horn regrows – why kill this mum and leave her to rot?

My name is Dave. I am not a Vet.
This is a war; the stakes are high and no rules are set
Mercy? Why should we show any at all?
Kill or be killed as our rhinos fall

My dress is now a bullet proof vest
My rangers are trained, they do their best
The vets are my friends, they are my heroes
They bear the brunt of man's greed and are the poacher's worst foes

'Dr Ian Player – the Father of Conservation'

Ian Player is a legend in rhino conservation. Ian was an internationally recognised environmentalist and conservationist. He served with the South African forces in Italy in World War II and returned to South Africa at age nineteen in 1946 with no idea of what he wanted to do with his life.

He joined the Natal Parks Board and pioneered Operation Rhino which succeeded in saving the white rhino from extinction. He also founded the Wilderness Leadership School during the troubled days of apartheid, a multi-racial and experiential program which was to spawn a global network of conservationists committed to saving wilderness and wildlife throughout the world.

I first met Ian Player in 1977 when he and Sir Laurens van der Post organised the first ever Wilderness Conference in Johannesburg at the suggestion of Player's friend and mentor game ranger Magqubu Ntombela. I wrote to Ian and briefed him on what I was trying to achieve and invited him to be a patron of the Australian Rhino Project which he kindly accepted. 'I would be very happy to become the patron of your project and will lend my full weight to help make it an outstanding success, which it deserves to be.'

I care not in which God you believe
Nor which religion you follow
What matters most to the planet upon which we sit
Is that you leave this place better than you found it

Look at what we have been given – and all for free
Day and night, sun and moon, plant and tree
Animals, both pets and wild
People black, white, mostly meek and mild

And yet today, there are those who ruthlessly steal and plunder
And do their greedy best to tear this world asunder
Their targets are the elephants and the rhinos
Their motives make me weep, make me wonder

But there is one man who will always take a stand
Having served his country well in a foreign land
He returned to the soil that he loved, his beloved animals to protect
He started Operation Rhino to save the few that were left

Ray Dearlove

Through thick and thin, they fought the odds
Less than a thousand rhinos left, they took on the sods
Moved the rhinos to safer places, no matter the cost
Without these actions, a species was lost

Magquba Ntombela and Ian Player – such men of honour are few
They did the business, the numbers grew
With courage, commitment and unfailing care
These two went to extremes where few men dare

Well pleased, but never satisfied that the job was done
Ian changed direction and formed the Foundation
A new challenge, the focus now on education
Another mountain to climb and perhaps a little more fun
Ian's passion a beacon, a path to the sun

He hung up his boots and life followed its course
Then twenty years later all hell broke loose
Again, his rhinos under threat
Hope turned to despair
Another tough challenge to be met

The fire burns within this lion-hearted man, but his hands are tied
His eyes became wistful as thousands more died
Man's greed is insatiable, his cruelty relentless
These ancient creatures completely defenceless

One senses the rage, the despair and the anger
For here is a man who has survived great danger
He will not give up, he will never surrender
On behalf of his rangers and his rhinos and his great rainbow nation
The baton must be passed to a new generation

'Age shall not weary them', we all wish it were so
Ian Player is a living legend and a true hero
Attenborough, Durrell, Fossey, Goodall, great names all
But for me, Ian Player is the one – he stands tall

'COVID 2021'

I wrote this poem after learning of my sister Yvonne's passing in May 2020 as a result of COVID-19.

The sun is shining
The birds are singing
But around the corner
Death is lurking

Four million dead and counting
The speed of the virus quite astounding
Dear and close ones seemingly healthy
Yet it strikes the old, the young, the poor and the wealthy

Lockdown takes its mental toll
Nobody exempt, it affects one and all
The impact unknown on those who are alone
Or on our children, irrespective of comfort shown

Fear stalks the streets, the future unknown
New rules every day greeted with a groan

The scientists have done their bit for mankind
Getting a vaccine to market in time redefined
I just cannot understand the hesitation
Go and get the bloody vaccination

Ray Dearlove

'Adrian Gardiner – Son of Africa'

Adrian Gardiner is a remarkable man who has led an extraordinary life. Among his many accomplishments he founded Shamwari Private Game Reserve, the first Big Five game reserve in South Africa's Eastern Cape. He restored degraded, drought-ravaged and abused land to its natural state with the introduction of all the wildlife that originally inhabited the land. Lives were changed by this creation. It went from land that employed fifteen people to a changed environment employing some 350 people – a critical flow-on contribution to the welfare of hundreds of people.

In my admittedly biased view, Adrian Gardiner's finest achievement was his work with Dr Ian Player on the Wilderness Foundation Africa.

Northern Rhodesian born, a child of the land
Running free with dad with the thrill of the hunt
At boarding school, the boy became a man
Showing early promise of leading from the front

Restless at Uni, broke records in getting his degree
Funds were short, time to earn some money
Working for the man is not for me
Cape Town offices stifling, set me free

With Shirleyanne, his mantra 'happy wife, happy life'
Each year a different venture, some ups, some downs
The eternal optimist, he dealt with trouble and strife
And helped PE become a city, no longer a town

Call of the land was deep and strong
He bought some acres, arid and bare
The soil was poor, but his vision long
Shamwari was built, stone by stone, on a wing and a prayer

This germ of an idea became the gem of the area
The animals, the birds, the environment pristine
A key factor, the absence of malaria
Decades since most of the animals had been seen

A tough decision, his pride and joy now in other hands
In a shrewd move he kept the jewel

With traversing rights over all the land
Must protect the environment, his golden rule

He spread his wings to join another giant
Ian Player and Adrian Gardiner – a formidable team
Saving our rhinos, every step defiant
Fought battles and took risks to fulfil their dream

In time, as his resolve grew stronger, Ian's body grew weaker
He cast his canoe on the river taking him to the other side

Said Adrian, 'One smile can start a friendship. One word can end a fight.
One look can save a relationship. One person can change your life.
For me, that man was Ian Player
A legend, my mentor, my brother and my hero.'

Who would take up the baton?
In his quiet way, Adrian stepped up
Out of the shadow emerged a new dawn
As he gently but decisively built a new line-up
His love of sport is widely known
Grimaces with every tackle and smiles at every try
Loves his Springboks and Proteas, never to complain, never to moan
Lives every moment, never say die

His country's challenges are complicated and deep
His passion for Africa drives him most
No path too rocky, no mountain too steep
He drives change from coast to coast

Community Conservation Fund Africa his creation
Yet another Everest to climb
His urgent determination to unite a nation
Calls for a man of faith and inspiration, there is little time

He's had his halftime oranges; he smiles that cheeky smile
Confident he will always go that extra mile
A strong man with a strong family, his energy legendary
A kind man, loyalty his creed in both word and deed
Our wild and wilderness owe a debt to Adrian Gardiner

Ray Dearlove

'2020 Vision'

I wrote this poem in August 2020 when the origins of COVID-19 were (and still are) unknown. It is an appeal to consider the plight of animals across the globe.

Across the vast plains of the African continent
The tapestry of wildlife is in the crosshairs of the poachers' gun
Man's greed and insatiable demand is never spent
For decades, animals landed up in the wet markets of Wuhan

For ever, man and beast have lived in harmony
Mostly killing, not for fun nor greed, but for the pot
Man then found a way to make some easy money
And rhinos and elephants in their thousands were shot

Some sympathy, for sure, but a crisis it was not
Then bats and pangolins combined and a virus was born
Spreading like wildfire, an unstoppable juggernaut
Misery and death aplenty, hopes of a cure forlorn

A million corona deaths and counting, no end in sight
No respite for animals, the killing continues, unabated
When will the supposed superior being see the light
And realise that all species are equal and need each other
Protect and respect. Before it is too late

'Trixie Dearlove'

I wrote this poem after our very special little doggie Trixie died.
Being able to truly feel, deeply, is an absolute blessing. I learned that
one should never shy away from emotion. To be able to be emotional
makes every part of being alive that much more special.

Buster had gone to doggie heaven, the family wanted a puppy
Decisions, decisions, what will it be?
Big dog, little dog, German Shepherd or labradoodle?
Mum's not sure, let's have a look at Google

Dad snuck off to the mountains, read the paper
Eventually found the farm, what a caper
Four little Jack Russell's, take your pick
All beautiful, but one little girl gave me a lick

Brought her back in the shoe box
Tiny little dog with a really scary bark
Dropped in to King's to show the boys
Suddenly this little dog had lots of toys

Back home to Mum and Hayley
Your job, must be fed lots and daily

Mum's job, give her a name
Trixie it is, quite appropriate for a dame
The house in uproar, can't move for piddle
Don't pick on Trixie, she's only little

As Trixie grew, she was really quite naughty
But as girls can be, she was also somewhat haughty
A year later, little Pugsley joined the house
But, like most men, he knew who was boss

The Cheltenham neighbours got to know little Trix
At every opportunity she took off to the sticks
Hi Margie, we've got Trixie, can you pick her up
We're on our way now to fetch our errant little pup

A close shave at Copa under a truck

Ray Dearlove

But with a shake and a sidestep
Our Trixie knew when to duck

So age shall not weary them?
Not sure about that, as time started to take its toll
As Trixie slowed up and the years began to roll
She lost her hearing and then her sight
The attitude was certainly still there, despite her plight
Every evening, bumping Mom, time to eat
Where's my food, my rice and my meat

Today was very, very hard, the vet came
It's time he said and we felt the same
So, Trixie lives on in our memories and in our hearts
A lovely natured, beautiful little dog of many parts
We'll miss her, have no doubt
But for seventeen great years, we've had her about
A part of our lives, a part of our family
But it'll be ok, we still have Pugsley
Man's best friend, that is so true and will always be

Sleep well, Trixie

'Pain'

This poem requires no introduction or explanation.

Pain is lonely
Pain is personal
Pain won't kill you but pain can kill you

Pain can make you weep
Pain won't let you sleep
Pain can make you angry
Pain can make you grumpy

'Describe your pain'
It's like a vice in my brain
'Oh, what's that like?'
Christ, please just take a hike

'What is the scale of your pain?'
Terrible, what's it on your scale?

'Where does it hurt?'
Where doesn't it hurt?

'Surely, it's mind over matter?'
'Would it help to have a natter?'

'Have a little rest, that might ease it'
Thanks, I think I'll leave it
I try very hard not to show it
But often just ten steps can blow it

Most people try to show they care about my pain
In reality, they think, can it really be that bad?
If it is, try fish oil or some other fad

Everyone has the answer
Try this and try that
Well fuck this and fuck that

(Try) and walk a mile, no not a mile, 100 yards, in my shoes

Pain is lonely

'Poetry surrounds us everywhere, but putting it on paper is, alas, not so easy as looking at it.'
Vincent van Gogh

Printed in Great Britain
by Amazon

42385486R00236